TEXT SETS
in Action

"*Text Sets in Action* unites pragmatism with philosophy and creativity to demonstrate how the most effective instruction is deeply grounded in quality children's literature, while also allowing for skills-based pedagogy. Replete with concrete examples, testimonials from teachers, and research-based literacy theory, Cappiello and Dawes's approach to building and using text sets is timeless. This book is ideal for preservice teachers, veteran teachers, and everyone in between."

— **Amina Chaudhri**, author of *Multiracial Identity in Children's Literature*

"We know that knowledge building is essential for student success in school and in life. We also know that the best way to make knowledge-driven learning memorable and joyful is through rich, authentic texts, especially when texts are bundled in text sets. But where do we begin? With a resource that is first of its kind, Mary Ann and Erika are here to help. Not only do they share text sets that will spark new energy and excitement for content learning in your classroom, they support you with innovative ways of how to use these texts to best suit your students' needs. Through their signature approach of scaffolds, immersion, extensions, and student-created texts, you will feel supported to add text sets to your teaching right now in language arts, social studies, science, and math. Whether you have a curriculum in place or are building your own, *Text Sets in Action* is essential reading to give all children greater knowledge of the natural world, our complex history, and how we can create a more sustainable, equitable world."

—**Katie Egan Cunningham**, author of *Start with Joy: Designing Literacy Learning for Student Happiness*

"Text sets present an unmatched opportunity to deepen our students' understandings of the complex world in which we live. Whether readers are seasoned veterans or new to text sets, they will never look at text sets as just a stack of books again. With invitations for text set design practice and crucial tools throughout, *Text Sets in Action* will help teachers create their own rich curricular text set journeys with and for their students."

—**Julie Waugh**, former committee member of NCTE's Orbis Pictus Award for Outstanding Nonfiction for Children

"Sometimes you don't know what you want until you see it. Such was the case when I first read *Text Sets in Action*. It is the perfect resource for preservice and practicing classroom teachers. Cappiello and Dawes are experienced educators who understand the nuances of using nonfiction children's literature across the content areas of the curriculum. Their pragmatic and insightful perspectives on selecting books, teaching with text sets, and engaging students in productive literature-based learning experiences merit our attention and appreciation. I will be sharing this book in all of my children's literature courses for educators."

—**Denise Davila**, Assistant Professor of Literacy and Children's Literature, University of Texas at Austin

"This book is *the* essential guide for teaching with text sets: informative, inspiring, and amazingly thorough and practical. Mary Ann Cappiello and Erika Thulin Dawes have made a groundbreaking contribution by showing educators how to use text sets to promote student inquiries that incorporate disciplinary literacy, outstanding literature, and a wide range of multimodal texts. Their use of supportive questions to use when planning, suggested models of instruction, and invitations to explore really got me thinking."

—**Myra Zarnowski**, Queens College,
City University of New York

"This book is a treasure trove of pedagogical possibilities and multimodal resources that offers a rich instructional portrait of how to help children comprehend, think critically about, and compose contemporary, multimodal texts within an interdisciplinary curriculum. Grounded in and guided by the classroom practices of teachers and students in elementary intermediate grades, Mary Ann Cappiello and Erika Thulin Dawes serve as instructional coaches for how to design and use text sets for interdisciplinary learning. Through detailed lesson plans, text set and graphic organizer possibilities, teacher reflections, and student artifacts, Cappiello and Dawes offer real-world instructional guideposts while also providing an optimum degree of autonomy and flexibility. They model what they are advocating: an empowering form of student-centered, inquiry-based learning using multimodal texts for interdisciplinary connections and creations."

—**Jennifer Graff**, Associate Professor, Literacies and
Children's Literature, University of Georgia

"In *Text Sets in Action*, Mary Ann Cappiello and Erika Thulin Dawes present a powerful teaching strategy for integrating language arts with science, social studies, and math to make every precious minute of instructional time count. After a lucid explanation of the rationale for building rich, innovative learning experiences around carefully curated groupings of fiction and nonfiction children's books, digital resources, primary source materials, and artifacts, the authors share a variety of real-world classroom experiences and then offer a range of easy-to-implement sample text sets designed to meet the standards *and* engage young minds."

—**Melissa Stewart**, author of more than 180 nonfiction books for children
and coauthor of *5 Kinds of Nonfiction: Enriching Reading and
Writing Instruction with Children's Books*

TEXT SETS
in Action

Pathways Through
Content Area Literacy

Mary Ann Cappiello
Erika Thulin Dawes

Stenhouse
PUBLISHERS
www.stenhouse.com
PORTSMOUTH, NEW HAMPSHIRE

Stenhouse
P U B L I S H E R S
w w w . s t e n h o u s e . c o m

Library of Congress Cataloging-in-Publication Data

Names: Cappiello, Mary Ann, author. | Dawes, Erika Thulin, author.
Title: Text sets in action: pathways through content area literacy / Mary
    Ann Cappiello and Erika Thulin Dawes.
Description: Portsmouth, New Hampshire: Stenhouse Publishers, 2020. |
    Includes bibliographical references and index. |
Identifiers: LCCN 2020009554 (print) | LCCN 2020009555 (ebook) | ISBN
    9781625312976 (paperback) | ISBN 9781625312983 (ebook)
Subjects: LCSH: Language arts--Correlation with content subjects. |
    Interdisciplinary approach in education.
Classification: LCC LB1576 .C3168 2021 (print) | LCC LB1576 (ebook) | DDC
    372.6--dc23
LC record available at https://lccn.loc.gov/2020009554
LC ebook record available at https://lccn.loc.gov/2020009555

Cover design, interior design, and typesetting by
Jill Shaffer for Eclipse Publishing Services

Manufactured in the United States of America

PRINTED ON 30% PCW
RECYCLED PAPER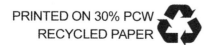

26 25 24 23 22 21   9 8 7 6 5 4 3 2 1

To our mothers,
Mary Thulin and Mary Ann Dowd Cappiello,
one an art teacher and school librarian,
one a preschool and elementary teacher,
both our North Stars.

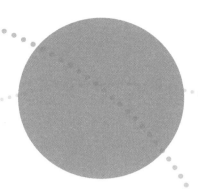

Contents

Acknowledgments

We are so grateful for the support we receive from our colleagues at Lesley University. During the years in which we were working in classrooms and writing this book, each of us was awarded course releases provided by Russell Scholarships within the Graduate School of Education and Faculty Development Grants from the Lesley University Faculty Life and Development Committee. It would have been impossible to cocreate and implement curriculum with our public school partners without the time these course releases afforded us. Our Language and Literacy colleagues Margery, Valerie, Stephanie, Grace, Barbara, Laura, Amanda, and Meg; Irene Fountas and our colleagues in the Center for Reading Recovery and Literacy Collaborative; Sue Cusack; and the Graduate School of Education leadership, including Jack Gilette, Amy Rutstein-Riley, and Patricia Crain de Galarce, all shape our work each and every day, formally and informally, through our programs, our meetings, and our conversations in the hallways.

We could not have written this book without our teacher partners. We owe them such a debt of gratitude, and it feels strange to be unable to name them due to the need to protect their privacy and that of their students. You know who you are, though! Thank you for the countless hours you invested in this work, for the stimulating curriculum discussions, for your thoughtful observations about student work, for your tireless efforts collecting permission forms and student work samples, for your willingness to take risks, and most of all for opening your classrooms and sharing your wonderful students with us. In addition to the teachers whose classrooms are featured in this book, we thank all of the teachers and aspiring teachers with whom we have had the privilege to work over the years—your ideas, your questions, your curiosity, and your excitement keep us committed to furthering the work of *Teaching with Text Sets* (Cappiello and Dawes 2013) and to placing high-quality children's literature at the heart of the curriculum.

This book also could not have come about without the many collaborations that shape our daily work. We are ever grateful to be a part of the Classroom Bookshelf team. Katie Cunningham and Grace Enriquez are ever at the ready for consultation. Our ongoing work of writing and reviewing each other's blog entries feeds our creative energies; we continually model for each other varied and innovative ways to infuse children's and young adult literature into PK–12 teaching and learning. Over the past five years, we have also benefited from ongoing collaborations with the New York City Department of Education's Office of Library Services. Rick Hasenyager and Melissa Jacobs were early supporters of *Teaching with Text Sets* (2013); partnering with New York City teachers and librarians on text set–based, grant-funded projects has expanded our understanding of how we can scale up the work of cocreating curriculum within large and diverse urban school districts. For that privilege, we are so grateful. We thank, too, all of our friends in children's book publishing and marketing. We are particularly grateful to Anne Irza-Leggat, Kathleen Rourke, Adrienne Weintraub, Lisa Nadel, Lisa DiSarro, Jenny Choy, and Donna Spurlock. These dedicated book lovers make sure that we have the most recent titles to share with our students and support us to make connections with authors and illustrators.

We are also incredibly fortunate to have wonderful partners in the many children's and young adult book authors and illustrators we have come to know over the years. In this book, you will read about the ways that Jen Bryant, Melissa Sweet, Melissa Stewart, and Steve Sheinkin gave their time, energy, and creativity to us, to our teacher collaborators, and to their students. We continue to be in awe of what you do and the art that you create—thank you for all that you do to inspire and educate young learners.

We have both been lifelong avid readers and began our careers studying children's literature under the guidance of Barbara Kiefer. In addition to teaching us how to view text and illustration in new and deeper ways, she introduced us to the vibrant and welcoming communities of the Society of Children's Book Writers and Illustrators and the National Council of Teachers of English's (NCTE) Children's Literature Assembly. During the time that we were writing this book, we both served on and as chairs of NCTE book award committees, Mary Ann for the Orbis Pictus Award for Outstanding Nonfiction for Children and Erika for the Charlotte Huck Award for Outstanding Fiction for Children. As we read through stacks of books month after month, year after year, we were able to note publishing trends, discover important new titles, and benefit from the ongoing conversations we had with our fellow committee members about the potential of high-quality children's literature to shape the reading lives of young people and the curriculum that they explore and experience in school. We are so grateful to our fellow committee members for the camaraderie of the work and for their insight into children's literature. Many of the books we discussed together have made their way into this book!

It has been a dream come true to work with our Stenhouse colleagues on this book, and it is stronger because of the collaborative spirit with which they work. Special thanks to Shannon St. Peter, who responded to literally hundreds of emails about figures, photographs, and permissions, to Dan Tobin for bringing us on board, and to Steph Levy for thoughtfully guiding this book to publication. Our editor, Maureen Barbieri, has been a literacy beacon of light for us, long before we ever met her in person. It is an honor to work beside you.

This book also could not have been written without the support of our dear family and friends:

Mary Ann

Since we first met fifteen years ago, Erika and I have always had more things to say to one another than time enough to say it, and more ideas about classroom life than we can write about in a lifetime. We've traveled in cars, planes, and trains with one another, shared countless hotel rooms and presentations, and still always manage to make each other laugh. How lucky we are to have found one another as colleagues, friends, and family.

The steadfast love and support of my parents, siblings, nieces and nephew, and in-laws infuse my life with a sense of wholeness. I depend on my daily walks with Denise Short to balance the juggling act of teaching, writing, parenting, and living in these complicated times. This book could not have been written without the love and care of the Daley and Sloss families, who have invited my family into their own time and time again, feeding us, making us laugh, and ensuring that we get out of the house even when we're under deadline.

When I met Tim Horvath twenty-six years ago, I knew that a life with him would be filled with deep laughter, thoughtful conversations, and piles of books. Tim, you make me a better reader, writer, and person every day. Our daughter Ella has grown up patiently waiting while Tim or I, or sometimes both of us, revise a paragraph, reorganize a chapter, or reconsider a title. Ella—reader, writer, artist, and activist in your own right—you make and remake our world every day. In the poem "Sometimes," Mary Oliver (2008) wrote: "Instructions for living a life: / Pay attention. / Be astonished. / Tell about it." You embody those instructions. It is an honor to be your mother.

Erika

This book was written in the wee hours of the morning and during found moments in between teaching, laundry loads, chauffeuring, and conference calls. I am so grateful for my partnership with Mary Ann. Her determination, practicality, and command of detail keep us ever moving forward, while her vision, sense of humor, and love for learning inspire our process. What a gift it is to have a colleague with such well-aligned commitments and interests who is also such a dear friend. Thank you!

Across my years as an educator, I have been fortunate to have wonderful mentors who have helped me navigate the everyday challenges of balancing work and motherhood. I am particularly grateful for the guidance and inspiration provided by Margery Miller and Rita Gordon during the writing of this book.

My family and friends are ever at the ready to help when life gets extra busy—I so appreciate you all, especially the parents and grandparents. I'm grateful for my home team, Bill, Will and Clara—your patience and willingness to pitch in over the course of many writing deadlines are much appreciated. Will and Clara, I do this work for you—may you always love books and learning and may you always be in classrooms where your teachers and classmates love books and learning, too.

PART 1

DEFINING AND DESIGNING TEXT SETS
Introduction:
Why Teach with Text Sets?

Text Sets and *Our* Classrooms
Mary Ann's Story

Over twenty years ago, at the end of my second year of teaching, after a day filled with juggling all the things an eighth-grade language arts teacher juggles—classroom discussions and debates, stacks of writing (hey, it was the 1990s so there really were stacks of paper on my desk!), competing personalities—I was driving into New York City to discuss the young adult historical fiction I was reading as part of an independent study with my graduate advisor. While I could pretend that this independent study was intended to support my students' reading interests and the cross-curricular work I was doing on my team, the reality was, it was entirely selfish. I love the genre!

As I drove, I started trying to imagine away the modern city, to try and see what it might have looked like during the British occupation during the American Revolution. Then, an epiphany! I was going to research and write a young adult historical novel set in the Hudson Valley during that time. In the forty minutes or so that it took to get from my classroom to Teachers College, I decided to become an author. At the end of our meeting, the remarkable Ruth Vinz approved my decision. The research and writing of a young adult historical novel could supplant the traditional master's thesis.

Where did this audacity come from? I have no idea, really. From sixth grade through college I kept an almost daily journal and wrote a lot of academic papers. When I spent four years working at the U.S. House of Representatives, I learned how to write in the voice of someone else and how to quickly turn around short speeches, statements, and letters. I knew the satisfaction of revision, when the right words fall into place. But I never, ever, ever thought of myself as an "author," let alone a fiction writer. Not ever.

My initial graduate program for certification required a six-credit course, The Teaching of Writing, with four credits of writing workshop and two credits of lecture with Lucy Calkins. I wrote a personal narrative that I can't remember (that's how good it was) and some bad poetry. Two big ideas stuck: kids need to be taught the process of writing, and that to be a teacher of writing, I had to write. But it took until that afternoon's drive for me to claim my writing identity.

What next? I spent the next two years researching and writing. To get started, I mined the author's notes in the historical novels to learn more about the research process. I went to a local historic home connected to the American Revolution and discovered that the family had a daughter born in 1765 who would have been coming of age during the war. Voilà! I had a protagonist. The nearby Rockefeller archives held most of the family papers, from correspondence to accounts to recipes. Voilà! I could do primary source research on my way home from school. I began to read books about the war, books about the lives of girls and women at the time, and books about food and clothing. I went to museums and studied furniture and practiced finding the language to describe everyday objects and artifacts from the eighteenth century. I took open-hearth cooking lessons, and soon starting reenacting *as* my protagonist, Ann Van Cortlandt, during winter holiday tours of her family home. I made timelines and took notes on color-coded index cards. My then-boyfriend-now-husband traveled with me to Albany, searching for Ann's grave on his hands and knees on a damp, cold February morning.

So, what does all of this have to do with teaching with text sets? Everything. In *The Power of Play*, Daniel Elkind (2007) reminds us that "sharing our passions, even by example, is far different from teaching children academic skills or giving them lessons. It amounts to revealing ourselves as people, the things we love to do when we have free time" (185). Throughout my research process, I shared the highs and lows with my eighth graders. I brought my life's passion into the classroom, modeling curiosity and deferred gratification, how one research question can lead to another and how some research questions don't always get answered.

But more than anything, my research on the eighteenth century taught me *how to learn*. Studying eighteenth-century furniture, Enlightenment philosophy, portraiture, women's roles in the social and economic structures of Colonial America, and specific battles of the American Revolution all helped me to understand and recreate that world in my imagination. Looking at objects led me to better understand culture and power in the eighteenth century. Everything was interconnected, and each line of study shone light on the other. From this experience, I realized that we learn best when we use all of our senses. Authentic learning is multimodal.

Knowing this, I knew that I had to transform my teaching. The world is infinitely interesting. School should be, too. The answer wasn't having my students take open-hearth cooking lessons and teaching about portraiture. My passions were not my students' passions. How could I honor theirs? As an English language arts teacher, I was responsible for supporting their literacy learning. What role did music, art, objects, and artifacts have to play in the pursuit of that literacy learning, critical thinking, and creativity?

First, I provided more space and time for individualized research and student decision making about how they demonstrated their learning, influenced by Tom Romano's multigenre research portfolios. But I was not in a school district where individualized explorations could replace the curriculum; nor did I want that. There is tremendous power in whole-class explorations of topics, concepts, and themes. I also made my curriculum more multimodal and multigenre and intentionally positioned my students to "read" a range of text types through which they would create meaning. The meaning was not in any one text. The meaning making was within each and every student. This was the origin of my approach to teaching with text sets.

As educators, we are so busy maximizing the moment and planning our next steps that we rarely take the time to look back and consider how our previous decisions, sometimes made by the seat of our pants, impact our teaching lives in permanent ways. Who would I be as a teacher today if I had not impulsively asked my advisor if I could research and write a historical novel? I had no idea my concepts of teaching and learning would be transformed by that seemingly selfish request to build my historical imagination.

As you read this book, I hope that you think about your passions and how they can make their way into your classroom. You can't love everything you teach, but what you do love can certainly enhance your teaching. How can your passions or what you have learned from them help you design curriculum?

This book will also help you to move your students into the center of the meaning making, by helping you construct curricular contexts ripe for inquiry and exploration through reading, writing, listening, speaking, viewing, moving, and creating with multimodal, multigenre text sets.

And that young adult historical fiction I wrote? It was pretty terrible. A rookie's first attempts at a novel. But now that this book is written, perhaps it's time to find those files on my computer . . .

Erika's Story

I began my teaching journey as a first-grade classroom teacher. A lifelong avid reader, I couldn't imagine teaching without a classroom full of books. Although I was required by the district to use a basal reader, I found every opportunity to bring authentic literature to my students, reading aloud multiple times a day and keeping a well-stocked classroom library. My teacher preparation program had emphasized the power of a thematic, literature-based curriculum, so I sought to enrich my social studies and science instruction with children's books—I made endless trips to the public library and purchased additional titles for the classroom using a portion of my salary. It was easy to see the appeal and power of well-written books and the potential that rich discussion of these books held for extending my students' understanding and inspiring new questions.

One of my fondest memories of these teaching years took place during a unit of study on animal behavior. I had visited a book warehouse sale and had happened on dozens of nonfiction books about animals available for sale for only a few dollars each. I purchased a boxful and brought them into the classroom. My students were, of course, curious about the box. I called them over to our meeting area and upended the box on the rug. We spent the next hour and half, seated on the rug, surrounded by these fascinating books. The students browsed book after book, reading the photographs and text as best they could, and chattering excitedly about what they were discovering and learning. It was a magical stretch of time; we were transported by those books, by wonder at the natural world, and by the joy of curiosity and inquiry. Browsing this collection of nonfiction books, they learned more about animals than a single textbook could ever begin to teach them.

During my first years of teaching, I signed up for a summer course at the University of New Hampshire's Reading-Writing Program. This was a transformative experience. The program, established by Thomas Newkirk, emphasized a workshop approach to writing and reading, describing the processes that writers undertake as they compose as well as the relationship between reading and writing. This program both supported my personal growth as a reader and writer and developed my strategies for fostering reading and writing growth in the classroom. Participating in this community of learners, writers, and teachers (including Susan Stires, Mary Ellen Giaccobe, Linda Rief, Tom Newkirk, and Donald Graves himself) was exhilarating. I signed up for two more summers! The ideas I experienced in these summer sessions were immediately applicable during the school year. I implemented a writing workshop structure and watched my students develop as writers rapidly because this approach honored their voices and their experiences. Choice within reading workshop supported equally rapid growth in reading; selecting their own texts increased motivation and engagement, and consequently achievement. Read-alouds and author studies became forums for us to discuss authors' craft and reading strategies. During this time, I was also introduced to the work of Tom Romano and became interested in his multigenre research approach—sound familiar? This approach aligned with the ways that I was using texts with my first-grade students, in a thematic model for content learning.

After completing my master's degree, I was eager to keep learning. With a desire to remain immersed in literature-based instruction and workshop approach, I began a doctoral program at Teachers College. The core course for the program was taught by four faculty with different areas of expertise, including special education, gifted education, and curriculum, and with different theoretical lenses, including social constructivism and critical theory. Co-constructing the learning experience, these four professors used readings in a way that I had not experienced before in all my years of school. For each topic addressed in the course, we were asked to read a range of texts representing a variety of stances on and explorations of the topic. Provided with these groupings of texts (text sets), I learned how to read critically across the texts, considering, critiquing, and attempting to synthesize a range of perspectives. Experiencing text sets as a learner firmly convinced me of the potential of this approach to transform teaching and learning.

From that point on, in my work as a literacy supervisor then teacher educator, I have coached teachers to use groupings of texts to support student growth in reading, writing, and thinking. Whether this takes the form of author studies, literature circles, genre studies, content-area study, or clusters of course readings, I have seen again and again how the use of multiple texts leads us to think more deeply, to consider more carefully, to empathize more fully, and to take action more deliberately.

Throughout this book, we invite you to consider how teaching with carefully curated collections of multigenre and multimodal texts sets can transform the learning experience for you and your students. The many teachers we have worked with have each approached teaching with text sets from different starting points and from different teaching contexts. We are excited to share their stories with you, and we are confident that the text sets examples in this book will serve as invitations to you and your students.

Teaching with Text Sets Is Both Practical and Aspirational

By hearing our text set "origin stories," you may feel excited to get started or to transition your current work to a deeper level of multigenre and multimodal learning *and, at the same time,* concerned that doing so is a luxury of time and energy you don't have.

Teaching with text sets is not a luxury. It's a possibility. It's an approach to student-centered teaching that allows you to cover what you need to cover while engaging students in perspective taking and sense making. Because of that, it is both practical and aspirational.

Teaching with text sets is practical because text sets allow you to do what you're *already expected* to do. Text sets create structures and contexts in which required learning can take place. It is also aspirational because a text set approach takes you and your students beyond what is merely required and allows you to integrate curriculum to work smarter, to take advantage of students' interests, and to customize curriculum to take advantage of contemporary issues, values, and contexts.

It's Practical
STANDARDS AND BEYOND
Everyone needs to teach to the standards for which they are responsible. We get that. We live in an era of accountability. But we have also learned that when standards are aligned in a progression, such as the Next Generation Science Standards or the Common Core ELA Standards, teams of teachers can plan instruction that builds on prior learning experiences and emphasizes critical thinking and conceptual understanding. This is the exciting by-product of well-written standards. We always consider content standards in science and social studies as the floor, not the ceiling. They are the foundation of what we need to cover, but they do not limit us from using additional content or concepts to frame our instruction, capture student interest, and improve student learning. Teaching with text sets allows you to meet your state and local standards for content and literacy and allows for an integrated approach whenever possible. A teaching-with-text-sets

approach also encourages teachers to use standards from one content area to frame the standards in another content area. For example, how can your social studies standards provide a real-world, local context for your science standards? When you design your curriculum with the standards as the foundation, you don't need to focus on test preparation, since your students are demonstrating that they are meeting standards on an ongoing basis.

READING COMPREHENSION

Over the past two decades, a body of cognitive science research has demonstrated the strong connection between reading comprehension and knowledge. The more students know about a topic, the stronger their comprehension of texts about that topic, and the stronger chance that what they read and comprehend deepen their knowledge of that topic. Much of what students comprehend in a print text is based on their prior knowledge of the content vocabulary and text structure. By design, text sets build prior knowledge on a topic and utilize a range of text structures across different genres and modalities. Audio, video, and visual texts can all be harnessed to introduce topics, prompt inquiry, and build knowledge of content and vocabulary that students can then carry into their reading of print texts of varying levels of complexity and sophistication. By reading, writing, listening, speaking, and viewing, students incorporate vocabulary and knowledge into their receptive and expressive language.

DISCIPLINARY LITERACIES

Practitioners of each discipline use language in ways that reflect the key skills and strategies of the disciplinary area. For example, historians focus on perspective and representation, while scientists focus on inquiry and evidence. When students use text sets from a range of disciplinary areas, they become more fluent in the different ways of reading, writing, speaking, and listening embedded in the disciplines. A focus on literacy within and across the content areas builds student language competencies as well as their content knowledge.

CRITICAL THINKING

Teaching with text sets allows for student learning at a deeper level. When you use this approach, students develop and use critical thinking skills with regularity, as they are constantly negotiating meaning across texts that may represent different information and points of view. When students are mentored into critical thinking, evidence-based thinking can begin to become the norm. A text set approach becomes a force multiplier for critical thinking, as students transfer those thinking skills to each new unit and context. Therefore, with text sets, students are thinking deeply while you are covering what you need to cover.

TAKING TIME SAVES TIME!

Teaching with text sets does ask you to take time to plan. You need to think carefully about what you are teaching, why you are teaching it (beyond "I have to"), and what else about this topic, concept, skill, theme, or strategy is compelling to your students. This allows you to design or revise a more effectively student-centered unit of study. Careful selection and juxtaposition of texts allow you to continue to consider what you are teaching and *why*, what texts optimize that learning, and what ongoing classroom structures and processes allow students to engage deeply. Finding and locating texts for a text set may feel daunting if you are just beginning to use this approach. Ideally, it is done by a team of teachers, with the support of a school or public librarian. The unit begins with structures set up in advance and an end learning product in mind. Thus, the time you take to plan in advance *saves* you time during the unit of study, so that you can focus your time and energy observing students and revising instruction to support them. The focus is on the *learning*, not the planning. Plus, once you've designed a text set for a particular unit, you don't have to reinvent the wheel each year. You can add or subtract texts or use them in different combinations for different goals, focusing again on taking student learning to a deeper level.

It's Aspirational
CONSIDERING MULTIPLE PERSPECTIVES

Our contemporary lives are full of texts of all kinds—we are surrounded by media messages, advertisements, and public commentary. Our democracy depends on our abilities to sift through, sort out, and critique this mass of information in order to take action in our lives. When we bring this same experience into the classroom by using text sets, we are able to hone our students' abilities to read across texts, to consider multiple perspectives, and to begin to synthesize and draw conclusions. Text sets by nature represent multiple perspectives on a theme or a topic. As students read across texts, they engage in critical literacy practices, developing an understanding that all texts are ideological; each text represents the author's worldview. When we use more than one text about the same theme or topic, students understand that there are multiple angles to consider.

CO-CONSTRUCTING UNDERSTANDING

Teaching with text sets repositions the teaching–learning relationship. When teachers and students work together to compare the content, structures, and formats of related texts across different genres and modalities, they engage in the co-construction of new knowledge about the topic/ theme of study. Together they generate new ideas inspired by and informed by the texts that they are experiencing. If you are like us, you became a teacher because you love learning new things—teaching with text sets sustains the excitement and joy of learning alongside your students.

ENGAGEMENT

When teaching with text sets, both you and your students have the opportunity to engage in interesting explorations designed to answer important questions. You learn together and model engagement and enthusiasm for one another. This enthusiasm serves as a positive contagion and force multiplier that maintains a level of engagement that allows everyone to dig in deeper as the work gets more complex. Encouraging students to ask real-world questions and investigate the answers honors their experiences as learners and makes the curriculum relevant and responsive.

AUTHORS, ARTISTS, MAKERS

As students engage with multiple texts, they have the opportunity to experience multiple models (in various modalities and genres) that introduce possibilities for their own work as authors, artists, and makers. After a deep dive into these texts, students can be encouraged to identify the modality and genre that is best suited to express their learning. We are always amazed at what students can write and make when they have choices for how they will express themselves.

Text Sets as Tools to Dig Deeper and to Consider Content

nimated talk fills hallways and classrooms at a New Hampshire elementary school as fourth graders teach one another about the different regions of the United States. Students visit one another's classrooms to learn through interactive maps and presentations focused on the relationships between the economy, geography, natural resources, and agricultural resources of the specific region each class has researched. In another school in Massachusetts, third graders record their classmates interviewing community members, so that the interviews can be transformed into picture book biographies (see Figure 1.1).

FIGURE 1.1
Third graders interviewing a community member.

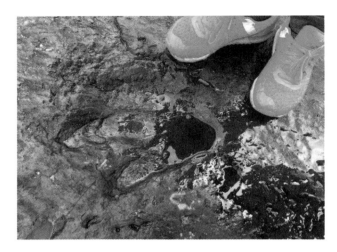

FIGURE 1.2
One third grader's footprint compared with a dinosaur footprint.

In yet another school, third graders take a field trip to examine actual dinosaur footprints and discuss the connections between these dinosaurs and local birds that they have been observing at a feeder attached to their classroom window (see Figure 1.2). They research a favorite bird to discover the adaptations that have sustained this species over time; using a nonfiction picture book as a mentor text, they brainstorm the similes that will help their readers clearly visualize and understand the function of the characteristic they will feature.

What do these diverse scenarios have in common? These students are deeply engaged in content study and are making meaning through their explorations of text sets on different topics, genres, and concepts. A text set approach puts students in the driver's seat to create meaning, sift through evidence, make connections, and then share what they have to say with the world.

Texts as Multiple Voices in the Classroom

Not only were they thinking about perspectives in social studies, but across subjects. When they were reading they had a deeper understanding or had that lens themselves—so what's that character's perspective or why is that character this way? And so it kind of trickled into every unit that we did. Which again just makes the learning, and thinking about learning, much more powerful and deeper than it was before.

—HALEY, Fifth-Grade Teacher

The examples and invitations you will find throughout this book will offer evidence of how multimodal, multigenre text sets enhance the teaching and learning experience. You will see how the teachers that we have worked with used curriculum standards as a starting point, but then went beyond them, extending units of study to explore content that held the most appeal for their students. You'll note how teachers were able to scaffold understandings of complex content by carefully sequencing and layering texts to create pathways to understandings. You'll also note how using multimodal, multigenre texts became a means for teachers to provide appropriate texts for the range of learners in their classroom, challenging students who were ready to learn more and supporting students who needed reinforcement of key ideas. All of these are compelling reasons to bring more texts into our instruction, but we believe the most beneficial aspect of a text set approach is the power that using multiple texts has to propel students to grapple with multiple perspectives.

Text sets present an unmatched opportunity to deepen our students' understandings of the complex world in which we live. Increasingly, we recognize the importance of preparing children to live in a pluralistic and inclusive society. Teaching with text sets allows us to bring diverse new voices into our classrooms. Too frequently, teachers are provided with a one-size-fits-all curriculum in the form of a textbook or a scripted program. Although there are many problematic aspects to this, perhaps the most troubling is that it limits students to a single narrative (Adichie 2009). We know that this can never be an accurate representation of our world. Additionally, we ourselves as teachers can't represent a range of perspectives. A careful curation of texts allows us to bring missing and underrepresented voices into the classroom conversation. Offering students a collection of texts that represent different lenses on curricular content requires students to think critically, to dig deeper, and to consider what they know and don't know, do understand and don't understand, and do believe and don't believe. It sets a stance of inquiry and responsibility, positioning teachers and students together as active learners.

What does it mean to use a text set to bring multiple voices into our classrooms? How do you go about doing this work? In Part 2 of this book, we provide you with examples of teaching with text sets in a range of classrooms. We will also provide invitations, offering you sample text sets to get started with this approach in your school setting in Part 3.

How you read this book is up to you—in this first chapter, we define multimodal, multigenre texts sets and then offer up a framework for designing curricular experiences with text sets. If you learn best by beginning with big picture thinking, you will likely want to read this chapter straight through before proceeding to the classroom examples in Part 2. However, if you learn best by being immersed in examples before unpacking the steps in a process, you might choose to read the examples in Part 2 and then to return to this chapter. Either way, our aim is to provide you with a framework for developing text sets that you can use in your classroom as well as to offer specific examples that help to showcase the versatility and benefits of teaching with text sets. In Part 3 of this book, we offer you additional sample text sets that you can use as scaffolds as you continue to build your text set design skills.

FIGURE 1.3

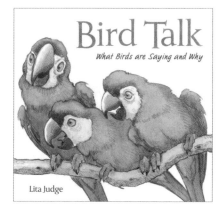

FIGURE 1.4

What Is a Multimodal, Multigenre Text Set?

Let's take a peek into a third-grade classroom where the teacher and her students are using a multimodal, multigenre text set to study the concepts of adaptation and evolution through a study of local birds. As they carry out this science unit, the students experience a variety of texts. A sampling of these texts can be seen in Figures 1.3, 1.4, and 1.5.

The texts in Figure 1.5 comprise a multimodal, multigenre text set: a carefully curated collection of texts that are related by topic, concept, theme, essential question, or genre. You will notice that this text set includes books and articles written for children, a nature guide, and visual opportunities to observe bird behavior firsthand. In addition to using these texts and others, these third graders experienced a presentation that included live raptors, took nature walks, and took a field trip to a museum and site whether they could observe dinosaur footprints firsthand. Having the opportunity to explore the scientific concepts of adaptation and evolution through many different text experiences afforded these students time and multiple exposures and scaffolded access to complex content. You will learn more about this unit of study in Chapter 5; we offer this example here to illustrate the variety of texts in a multimodal, multigenre text set.

Let's further unpack the components of a multimodal, multigenre text set:

FIGURE 1.5 *Sample texts from a multimodal, multigenre text set on birds.*

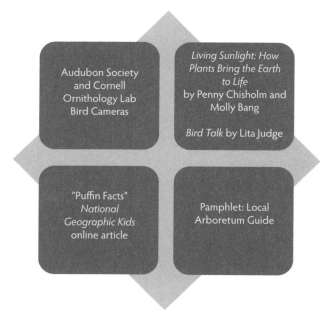

Audubon Society and Cornell Ornithology Lab Bird Cameras

Living Sunlight: How Plants Bring the Earth to Life by Penny Chisholm and Molly Bang

Bird Talk by Lita Judge

"Puffin Facts" *National Geographic Kids* online article

Pamphlet: Local Arboretum Guide

Text. We adopt a broad definition of text, taking a stance that to "read the world" (Freire 1970) one makes meaning from all kinds of objects, not just from books and articles. We read artifacts in our environment, works of art, and symbol systems of all kinds. Anything that conveys meaning or a message is a text.

Multimodal Texts. Given this broad definition of text, you can imagine that texts can take many forms. We encourage the use of texts that draw upon different modalities: visual, auditory, and written. From this stance webcams, videos, podcasts, photographs, speeches, sculptures, and concerts all may be texts that you might include in a text set.

Multigenre Texts. Similarly, we adopt a broad definition of genre, with purpose as a driving factor. This is a definition of genre that depends on social recognition. Any form or format that we recognize as serving a particular purpose or function can be considered a genre. Examples are wide ranging and include things such as travel brochures, tweets, memes, primary source documents, newspaper articles, or advertisements. This expands the concept of genre beyond those typically recognized at school, such as fantasy fiction or nonfiction, and opens up many new possibilities for making meaning and expressing learning.

Practically applied in the classroom, this means that a multimodal, multigenre text set might include text types such as those in Figure 1.6.

We have found that teachers are quite comfortable identifying and collecting a range of texts in connection with a unit of study but often want support identifying how this collection of texts might be used. Therefore, our work has focused on the design aspect of teaching with text sets. The power of this approach lies in the careful juxtaposition of texts. We like to describe this aspect of the approach as placing the texts "in conversation" with one another. As students read across the texts in a text set, the multiple voices of the authors of those texts surface. Reading critically means considering all the voices in this conversation.

Texts sets can be used across all content areas as well as in integrated (interdisciplinary) units of study. Whether you are focusing

FIGURE 1.6 *A multimodal, multigenre text set often contains a range of text types such as these.*

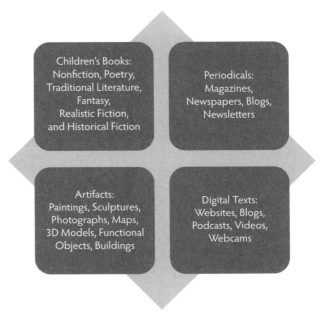

Children's Books:
Nonfiction, Poetry,
Traditional Literature,
Fantasy,
Realistic Fiction,
and Historical Fiction

Periodicals:
Magazines,
Newspapers, Blogs,
Newsletters

Artifacts:
Paintings, Sculptures,
Photographs, Maps,
3D Models, Functional
Objects, Buildings

Digital Texts:
Websites, Blogs,
Podcasts, Videos,
Webcams

on a particular topic, a broad or specific theme, or an essential question or studying a written, visual, or auditory genre, a multimodal, multigenre text set becomes your tool kit for instructional design. We frequently say, "You don't teach a text set, you teach *with* a text set" (Cappiello and Dawes 2015, 16). Taking the time to develop a text set and to design instructional experiences around the texts affords you many benefits (see Figure 1.7):

FIGURE 1.7

Teaching with text sets equips you to explore, scaffold and sequence, differentiate, represent multiple perspectives, and demonstrate literary models.

Explore	Texts can go beyond your guidelines and standards and connect with students' interests to deepen understanding and engagement.
Scaffold and Sequence	Texts can layer complex content and ideas.
Differentiate	Texts in multiple modalities facilitate access.
Represent	Texts include new and underrepresented perspectives that are not found in your textbook or in standard texts.
Model	Texts demonstrate language use and visual literacy across disciplines.

Invitation. Take some time to consider your use of texts in the classroom. What kinds of texts do you use for literacy instruction? For content-area instruction? What kinds of texts compose your classroom library? Do the texts that you use vary in modality? In genre? Set some goals to bring new kinds of texts into your daily use.

Sometimes, a text set comprises a single lesson. Sometimes, a single text set is the whole unit. Sometimes, several text sets are used within a single lesson or within a single unit. A text set approach is flexible and customizable. It all depends on your students, your goals, and the time it takes to work with the texts. Throughout this book, you will see different examples of the duration and timing of various text sets on their own and within units.

Designing a Text Set

> *If we could do that with our driest unit and make it interesting, what could happen if we did it with the units that are already interesting?*
>
> —Tom, Fourth-Grade Teacher

When we began working together at Lesley University, we talked *a lot* about our shared courses. In our K–12 teaching lives, we depended on the collaboration and feedback of our colleagues. We didn't want that shared process to end just because it isn't a typical part of university culture. We consider ourselves lucky to be working partners who are jointly fascinated by the endless possibilities that texts present for enlivening and enriching K–12 curriculum. First and foremost, we see ourselves, and all teachers, as curriculum designers. If you don't have someone to plan with, we encourage you to reach out to find a working partner—either at your school, in your district, or through social media channels.

We first wrote about our text set design process in our book *Teaching with Text Sets* (Cappiello and Dawes 2013). Here, we want to share how our thinking has evolved in recent years to support you and your colleagues in better understanding a text set approach to curriculum design. What follows is an overview of our planning process. In Chapters 3–6, we share specific examples of this planning process in each of the content areas.

Establish Goals: What do you want for your students?

We think all curriculum planning begins with conversation about *what* you are teaching and *why*. When we first wrote *Teaching with Text Sets* (Cappiello and Dawes 2013), we talked about this first step in the text set approach as "Starting with Content." Teachers planning science and social studies units, or integrated units, found this language comfortable. But other teachers found it confusing, since some standards are very content focused and some are skill focused; English language arts teachers had trouble identifying what was "content" beyond genre knowledge. Now, we emphasize establishing your goals (which usually include content-area learning).

Each state has particular standards that need to be taught. You may also have required district standards and outcomes. Although the content and skills codified in these standards may be nonnegotiable, we still think it is important to consider their *value* and their *context* within your school year. After evaluating the standards, consider what else your students might need and establish your goals.

Consider these questions, as a starting point:

- What do these standards indicate that students should know and be able to do?
- Which of these standards seem more important than others? Which ones are worth spending more time on? Why? Which are less important? Why?
- Which standards are knowledge standards, and which standards are action (process and skill) standards?

- How is the scientific or historical knowledge embedded within the standards valuable to our students?

- How is the scientific or historical knowledge embedded within the standards problematic when teaching with a social justice lens? What other voices need to be brought in?

- What about the scientific or historical knowledge embedded within the standards is interesting to us? To our students? What other information can be used to leverage these standards and make them more relevant today?

- What opportunities for curriculum integration are possible? Are there other standards from other subject areas that we can use these standards to access? Or can we use those other standards to help students understand these standards in context?

- Based on the knowledge and actions embedded in these standards, what are some versatile ways that students might be able to demonstrate their learning?

After we do this initial thinking and brainstorming, we consider what might be the most interesting opportunities for student learning. We move past the standards, the "floor" for the unit, to determine our larger goals, which become the "ceiling." Goals are inclusive of and informed by the standards but then go beyond them. They reflect our values and our worldview and our understanding of our school community.

Teachers consider this planning stage critical to the process as a whole. Although it takes time to talk through the standards, as Brooke told us, "Once you have an idea of where you are going, it's much easier." Tom, another member of Brooke's fourth-grade team, told us that the hardest part was trying to find out what you want kids to learn from those units, but that once you distill those units, you can plan. Everyone on the team has to be committed to the process, knowing that it will look a little different in everyone's classrooms.

Invitation: On your own or with your teaching team, select a unit of study to teach using a text set approach. Perhaps this is a brand-new unit for your grade level that you are creating from scratch; perhaps it is a unit you want to revise to better capture student interest or move more students toward mastery of knowledge or skills. Use our questions to consider what is important for you and your students to explore and take this opportunity to draft your goals for the unit.

Find Texts: What are the best texts to help you meet your goals?

The next step in the process is to find and locate print and digital texts that can be used in your text set. If you are revising a unit, you may have some texts that have worked well in the past that you would like to continue to use. That's great. You might also have some texts, such as a textbook or even a basal reader, that you are required to use. Text sets are flexible. You can incorporate the latest middle-grade novel and a textbook or a basal reader and a recent podcast.

Finding new texts for your curriculum is an exciting part of the process and one that has tangible benefits. As you introduce multiple texts into a unit of study, the responsibility of meaning making shifts from teacher to students. This process is described by Haley, a fifth-grade teacher:

> *Last year we worked a lot on the Revolutionary War text set, and we spent a lot of time finding different resources, books, podcasts, videos, different things . . . Watching the kids learn last year through different perspectives through different books, different podcasts we found, it was amazing to see them making meaning out of their learning. Instead of me just standing up there delivering information, the kids were in the driver's seat of their learning. They were making all the connections. They were understanding why things happened in the Revolutionary War, the different perspectives of different people involved, and it was just such a deeper understanding level I think than I ever could have achieved just simply teaching from a book or from a worksheet or something like that . . . that really inspired us this year.*

If you are lucky enough to have a school librarian, we encourage you to collaborate with that colleague. There may be resources right at your fingertips about which you are unaware!

TRADE BOOKS

We believe that high-quality children's, middle-grade, and young adult books are at the heart of a text set approach to curriculum design. Authors and illustrators who write and illustrate for children, tweens, and teens know and understand their audience; high-quality fiction and nonfiction books present diverse protagonists and reflect cultural authenticity and multiple perspectives. Typically, we build our text sets around what trade books are available and appropriate for our audience and topic or theme. Trade books are the heart of text sets.

Some days, you may feel bombarded by all the new books that you hear about on Twitter, and you just can't keep up with them all. Other days, finding the right book for your classroom needs can feel like the proverbial needle in a haystack. If you feel like you need more support in finding, selecting, and evaluating children's, middle-grade, and young adult literature of all genres for curricular use, we recommend our second book, *Teaching to Complexity* (Cappiello and Dawes 2015). For our purposes here, we share some of our favorite resources and direct you to a more extensive list available on our website at **www.teachingwithtradebooks.com**.

Here are some of our recommended resources for finding and locating great books for classroom use.

The Classroom Bookshelf, a *School Library Journal* Blog*
www.theclassroombookshelf.com
*We coauthor this blog with Grace Enriquez, Katie Cunningham, and Denise Davilá.

We Need Diverse Books
https://diversebooks.org/

Notable Books for a Global Society
http://www.clrsig.org/nbgs-lists.html

American Library Association Youth Media Awards
http://www.ala.org/awardsgrants/awards/browse/yma ?showfilter=no

National Council of Teachers of English Charlotte Huck Award for Outstanding Fiction K–8
http://www2.ncte.org/awards/ncte-childrens-book-awards /charlotte-huck-award/

National Council of Teachers of English Orbis Pictus Award for Outstanding Nonfiction K–8
https://ncte.org/awards/orbis-pictus-award-nonfiction -for-children/

Notable Social Studies Trade Books for Young People
https://www.socialstudies.org/notable-social-studies -trade-books

Outstanding Science Trade Books for Students K–12
http://www.nsta.org/publications/ostb/

 Follett Titlewave Search Engine (create free account
http://www.titlewave.com/

DIGITAL TEXTS

Once we have discovered a range of trade books that *could* be used in our text set, we begin our search for digital texts that may also play a role. This, too, can sometimes feel initially overwhelming, given all the digital content that is generated daily.

Sometimes, these sites are curated for you. For years, we relied on the American Library Association's Great Websites for Kids (**gws.ala.org/**), which curated websites for elementary teachers searching for age-appropriate material. Although this website is no longer being updated, it remains useful. ALA has replaced the site with an annual Notable Children's Digital Media list (**www.ala.org /alsc/awardsgrants/notalists/ncdm**).

Often, though, we find ourselves searching strategically for digital multimodal texts using our different categories of resources.

News Organizations

- We search the websites of print newspapers, both nationally and locally, not only for text-based news stories but for short video clips, photographs, interactive maps, graphics and infographics, and podcasts.

- We also look at National Public Radio stations for short podcasts, interviews, and photographs.

Museums, Historical Societies, Zoos, and Nonprofits

- History, science, and art museums as well as historical societies, zoos, and nonprofits also provide invaluable resources for text sets in their digitized collections. Not only do they have original art, artifacts, and documents, but they sometimes have web cameras (think zoo cameras!) that you can use. Organizations such as the Audubon Society and the Cornell Ornithology Lab provide research reports and extensive information about bird habitats, birdcalls, and identification, plus webcams. The National Constitution Center provides teachers and the general public with extensive primary and secondary materials for understanding this seminal document. Local nonprofits, nature centers, art museums, and historical societies sometimes have documents, photographs, or text-based information that provides local insight on a topic that you are exploring that makes the learning even more personal or relevant to your students.

Government

- Local, state, and federal agencies have a treasure trove of information on their websites, from research reports to artifacts to primary source documents and photographic collections. For example, the Library of Congress and the Federal Archives have millions of digitized items in their collection; the Department of the Interior has research reports, public service announcements, videos, and graphics from the National Park Service and the U.S. Fish and Wildlife Service. From our perspective, you could teach K–12 science just by using the NASA site alone!

Databases from School, Local, County, or State Library Systems

- You may not realize that you have many children's and young adult magazines available to you in digital format through one of the subscription services paid for by your school, public, or state library system. You may be able to curate a range of age-appropriate magazine articles for your text set with the help of a local librarian.

Typically, we start saving links to digital texts in a Google document. The more we find, the more we begin to categorize them by the subtopics they represent. Once you have found and read, viewed, or listened to your range of multigenre, multimodal texts, you will find that some stand out, ripe for certain roles in the classroom. Our next step explores these roles more closely.

Invitation. Think about the unit for which you established new goals. What texts would you like to keep? Why? Next, using the types of sources that we have recommended here, try to find new trade books and digital multimodal texts that you can consider using in a text set approach.

Identify Roles: Is a text a scaffold, an immersion, or an extension of learning?

We find that as we search for texts, we automatically begin to group them into certain "piles" either literally or figuratively. Although we like to sort our digital texts by subtopic, to make sense of the content of those texts and to keep ourselves organized, we subconsciously begin to identify some based on the ways in which we can harness their potential in the classroom.

As we consider the texts, we ask the following questions:

- What perspectives are included and excluded? Do the texts represent diverse authors, experiences, and locations? Are more diverse representations needed?
- Do the texts have content that is well matched to our topic, theme, and goals? What gaps exist?
- Which texts maximize student interest and engagement?
- What texts help to fill in gaps in students' prior knowledge?
- Do any text model disciplinary practices and disciplinary ways of thinking?
- Which texts might be scaffolds? Which texts are best for immersing students in learning? Which texts would be extensions, only comprehensible after students have done some learning on the topic or theme?

Our last set of questions becomes an important step in constructing our text set, so we want to explain our thinking in greater depth for you.

SCAFFOLDS

Short texts, such as picture books, podcasts, video clips, poems, webcams, and songs are often well suited to begin a unit of study or a new stage within a unit of study, pique student interest, and to prompt inquiry. As such, we think of these as *scaffolds* to student learning. Such texts are usually easy to access. Students don't need prior knowledge to understand them. Often, they are great at front-loading important prior knowledge. Sometimes, we use them to introduce contrasting perspectives on a topic or theme. With short texts, we can do that relatively quickly, but we draw upon the "heft" of those texts throughout the unit. Scaffolds help to frame a text set.

IMMERSIONS

Immersion texts are often the ones that have the most to say about whatever topic or theme we are exploring. These texts are most closely matched with our goals for the unit of study. Given our belief that trade books are at the heart of texts sets in elementary and middle school, these immersion texts are most often fiction, nonfiction, and poetry trade books. They immerse students in the topic or theme. Some texts may be used by all students, some texts by only a few.

EXTENSIONS

Finally, students read, view, or listen to extension texts after they have learned a great deal about the topic or theme. These texts often take us beyond the required curriculum standards but help to frame and contextualize them. Extension texts can be differentiated, allowing you to stretch those who are ready to be stretched.

This process is quite recursive. As you think about each text, you realize that you can't really think about any one text in isolation, because you are always thinking about the texts in relation to one another and how the students will "use" them. Depending on how you organize your unit, some texts might be scaffold or immersion texts, depending on what other texts are being used.

After you have considered the texts as scaffolds, immersions, or extensions, another step is needed to strategically sequence the texts: organizing them into our five instructional models.

Invitation. Consider the trade books and digital multimodal texts that you assembled. What are some of the opportunities these texts provide? Apply our guiding questions to determine if you have a diverse enough range of experiences represented, and then sort the texts by which ones could be scaffolds, immersions, and extensions.

What are our instructional models?

After considering the ways in which texts may be scaffolds, immersions, and extensions, you want to think more intentionally about the order in which you share the texts with students. As you organize texts for instruction, you consider how to position texts to build knowledge and encourage critical thinking. In a text set approach, the order in which students access the text is critical to how they understand and view the topic or theme that you are exploring with them.

Consider the following questions:

- How are the texts "talking to" one another?
- What subtopics of a topic are represented by the texts?
- What perspectives are represented by the texts?
- Which texts connect with one another and are ideal to compare?
- Which texts contradict one another and are ideal to contrast?

The answers to these questions will position you to place the texts into our instructional models. These instructional models arose in our early stages of defining our text set work with teachers, as well as our own K–12 classroom practices and our use of texts in our graduate children's literature classes. Again and again, we observed similar patterns as we organized texts for instruction.

As we observed students working with texts, we realized that these repeating patterns of organization were the blueprints for specific types of critical thinking. Therefore, we named our instructional models as metaphors, to make it easier for other teachers to foster specific types of critical thinking. Our names may feel a little strange to you. They are! We want the metaphors to be clear to K–12 students, so that they can, over time, connect the instructional model with a specific ways of thinking. So far, we have discovered that teachers are more comfortable using the names of the instructional models as they plan units and create text sets but less comfortable using the names with students. Perhaps you can help us change that!

DUET

Duets can be sung, danced, or performed on instruments, and they encompass all moods and types of music: jazz, classical, pop, hip-hop, and more. A Duet text set (see Figure 1.8) comprises two texts paired together to compare and contrast their content or theme. Sometimes, Duet models ask students to think about similar content across two texts. Sometimes, Duet models ask students to contrast themes or perspectives across two texts. Sometimes, Duet models suggest that students do both. This is the easiest text set model to implement and perhaps the most common. One text might be a scaffold for the other or both are scaffolds for the unit as a whole or both texts may be immersion or extension texts.

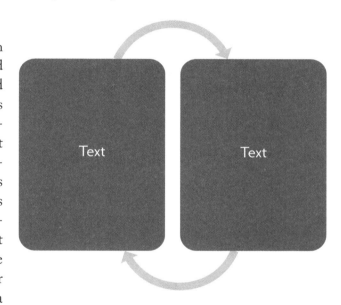

FIGURE 1.8 *The Duet model contains two texts and invites comparison and contrast.*

SUNBURST

Think of an old-fashioned drawing of the sun, a simple circle with rays emanating from the center. Our Sunburst model (see Figure 1.9) has this sun as its metaphorical origin. One text, such as a required textbook or trade book, is the core text. It takes the place of the sun in that drawing. The other multigenre, multimodal texts explored help students better understand the single core text. Each of those additional texts is like one of those "rays" in the drawing. The single core text is the immersion text; the other texts are scaffolds and extensions. The strength of this instructional model

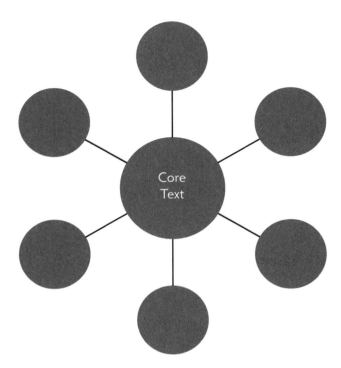

FIGURE 1.9 *The Sunburst model has one single core immersion text and a range of other texts that serve as scaffolds and extensions.*

FIGURE 1.10 *In the Tree Ring model, the core text is the scaffold, the texts used to research and create the text are the immersion texts, and other texts on the same topic or genre are extensions.*

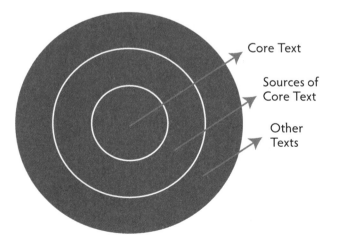

is that it allows you to use the text required by your district, but also to differentiate to meet the diverse needs and interests of your learners and bring in multiple perspectives. It is likely that your teaching now might look a little bit like the Sunburst model, particularly when you think of the phrase *supplementing the curriculum*. Our model just asks you to think even more strategically about the role each text plays. In a text set, every text serves a purpose; nothing is merely a supplement.

TREE RING

Imagine a piece of wood sliced off a freshly fallen tree trunk. Look at the concentric circles emanating from the center that reveal the age of the wood. Using concentric circles as the metaphor, the Tree Ring model (see Figure 1.10) has students again reading a common core text. But after accessing the core text, the students then move onto another concentric layer surrounding the text and investigate the texts used to write and illustrate it. As a teacher, you can mine the author's and illustrator's notes at the back of the book to find their sources and determine which ones your students can examine. This allows students to see what is included and excluded in the core text. From there, students can look at other texts on the topic and begin to see a range of representations of information and perspectives. In this model, the core text is the scaffold; texts used to research and create the text, the immersion; and the other texts, the topic extensions. A focus here is on author and illustrator process; examining the sources and choices made by the author or illustrator supports students as they make their own compositional choices.

SOLAR SYSTEM

Consider again that old-fashioned drawing of the sun, but now put it in the center of a drawing of the solar system. Now, the sun is no longer a single core text that everyone examines, but rather a single topic, concept, theme, genre, or essential question that the class is examining. In the Solar System model (see Figure 1.11), like the solar system itself, the planets move around the sun, the center of gravitational force. In this case, the topic, concept, theme, genre, or essential question serves as the center of gravity. The various "planets"—the texts—serve as scaffolds, immersions, and extensions. But they all contribute to understanding the topic, concept, theme, genre, or essential question.

MOUNTAIN

The reward of hiking up a mountain is the view you get from the top, right? But it is also the fascinating glimpses that you get along the way, and the satisfaction that comes with pushing yourself harder, even when the path gets steep. The research process is somewhat similar, and the Mountain model (see Figure 1.12) typifies the process used when a whole class, small group, or individual is conducting research on a topic. You start off broadly and then slowly begin to narrow the focus of your texts. In this model, the whole class may start off looking at a topic together, and then small groups make take over the research process of a particular aspect of the topic. Or it could be individualized from the start. In this model, the base of the mountain contains the scaffolds; the middle, the immersion texts; and the peak, the extension texts.

The more you work with these models, the more comfortable they get. The most important takeaway is that the different instructional models position learners in specific and intentional ways that allow them to make meaning across a range of texts. You'll see that more specifically when you look at the examples in Part 2 and consider the invitations in Part 3.

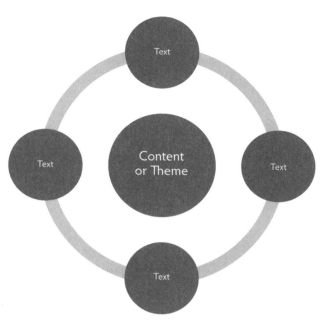

FIGURE 1.11 *In the Solar System model, the topic, concept, theme, or genre is the "center of gravity." Some texts are scaffolds, some are immersions, and some are extensions.*

FIGURE 1.12 *In the Mountain model, reflecting the research process, the base of the mountain contains the scaffold texts; the middle, the immersion texts; and the peak, the extension texts.*

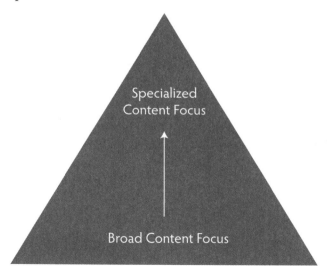

Invitation. What is the instructional model that you feel most comfortable starting with? Are your texts ideal for that model? What are some of the opportunities these texts provide? Apply our guiding questions to determine if you have a diverse enough range of experiences, and then start to sort the texts by the labels of scaffold, immersion, and extension. Will your unit use just one instructional model, or several?

Create New Texts: What are the new texts created by students?

What new texts are created by students? In the examples that we offered at the beginning of the chapter, students expressed their learning by creating and sharing new texts. As we map out text set experiences, we keep in mind this question: What kind of texts will the students create to demonstrate their new learning? In your initial goal planning conversation, our final guiding question asked you to consider some versatile options students could use to show what they have learned. As each text set fosters multiple pathways to explore content, concepts, genre, and themes, we think it is important to provide students with choices as to the genre and modality through which they demonstrate their learning. We recognize that this can't always be possible, but we encourage it as much as possible.

But before students are ready to tackle the creation of new texts, we have to give them ways to document their learning as they make their way *through* texts.

FIGURE 1.13
Two third graders taking notes.

Taking Notes

Note taking is a vital part of the teaching with text sets process (Figures 1.13 and 1.1.4). As one teacher shared, "I feel like they did more writing this year than they ever have, simply because we had them take so many notes in science and social studies. That was a huge benefit of doing text sets, that they could learn to take notes."

Over the years, we have found graphic organizers to be critical in helping students hold their important thinking when making their way through a text set. We have some examples in which students used the same graphic organizer, with a specific yet open-ended structure,

Characterization in Biography

Your Name: _____   Title of Biography: _____

Directions: Write down what you know about the subject of your biography (the person the biography is about). What is he or she like? How do you know? Find evidence in the word and pictures, and write that down.

What Do We Know?	How Do We Know It? What Do the *Words* Say?	How Do We Know It? What Do the *Pictures* Show?
whthe he was over he wnat to london	"where he was older he whnt to londen"	Tonys going to londen
he got elafent and camals and bears	"Mays even bring in elefents and camals"	it shens bears and camals
becose they worked ther thay maby holiday	"Thay missed thoe"	
He is joyful		he smiles

FIGURE 1.14
Notes on Balloons over Broadway *(Sweet 2011).*

with all or most of the text sets within the unit. Other examples have a different graphic organizer attached to each text set within the unit because each stage of the exploration served a specific purpose that the graphic organizer helped to highlight. When we ask our students to do complex thinking, we think we need to offer them clear and consistent structures in which to do that complex thinking.

Some teachers have found that teaching with text sets allowed them to give more control over to their students. One fourth-grade teacher told us, that "just teaching them how to take notes in fourth grade has been amazing. I don't think I printed out one worksheet. I just always had them make a graphic organizer on their own in their notebook . . . They actually did know how to take notes, and that's a skill that is going to carry on next year and all the years following that."

Another fourth-grade teacher gave students even more choice to help them "synthesize information across the board." Rather than dictate any one way of taking notes, he suggested that they learn about themselves as learners and make that decision. "One kid may say, 'I really work best making charts,' while another might do better making a list, and that artistic kid is going to do some drawing. Allowing them some of that student choice is powerful as well."

While teaching with text sets allows teachers and student to customize their note taking based on the texts selected and the purposes for which they are exploring those texts, we have found some consistent alignment over the years with the type of graphic organizers that are most frequently made when using particular instructional models. In these cases, it's because the graphic organizer matches the goal of the unit and the purposes for exploring a particular text or set of texts.

In Part 2, you will see specific graphic organizers for different instructional models in all four of the core content areas. However, we thought you might find the chart in Figure 1.15 a handy guide for designing graphic organizers to reinforce the specific critical thinking that each of our instructional models supports.

FIGURE 1.15 *The different instructional models suggest different types of graphic organizers for note taking.*

If using this model...	Graphic organizers will generally...
Duet Two texts paired with one another	• prompt comparison and contrast • focus on genre, content, or both at once
Sunburst One core text and a range of other texts that support comprehension of the core text	• demonstrate the relationship between the shorter texts and the core text • anchor content/genre information gleaned from texts that serve as scaffolds
Tree Ring One core text, some of the texts used to create the core text (author's sources), and other texts related by topic or genre	• demonstrate the relationship between the source texts and the core text • illuminate any differences between the source material and the core text • shape students' understanding of author's craft and the choices the author of the core text made • serve as a foundation for student writing on the topic or within the genre
Solar System A range of texts that work together to support understanding of a topic, theme, or genre	• be structured on the content/theme/genre study that is the focal point that holds the text set together • identify commonalities and differences across texts
Mountain A range of texts on a topic that become increasingly more specific to support the reader's interests and purposes	• help students keep track of source material and document bibliographic information • provide a parallel structure for taking notes across a range of texts on a topic or within a genre

FIGURE 1.16
Third-grade students conducting an interview of a community member.

Creating New Texts

There are times when you want to plan very intentionally from the start the final product that students will create. But there are also times when you may want to co-construct that with your students as they make their way through text sets and different text types and modalities speak to different students. Providing students with the opportunity to co-construct how they will demonstrate their learning can be an exciting part of the text set approach.

A great deal of thinking goes into the initial planning of the unit, the curation of texts, and the organization of texts into models. Planning out possible student text production before you begin teaching the unit makes a lot of sense. You may stick to one or two genres or modalities as you have originally mapped it out, but you might also see new possibilities as you watch the students work and listen to their conversations.

As you move toward concluding the unit, you might wind up having all the students work on the same text type and modality as response as originally planned. For example, in a biography genre study that you'll read about in Chapter 3, all students conducted interviews of community members (see Figure 1.16) and then wrote and illustrated picture book biographies of those community members. The text set approach allows you to focus on the specific writing outcomes that you need all students to demonstrate. But a text set approach also allows you to respond to the needs and interests of your students. You may allow the students to choose what text type and modality everyone uses. Or you may allow students to pick from a list of options that you have constructed together. Teaching with text sets supports such flexibility. Student choice accompanies deep learning. It's a natural outgrowth. In Part 2, you will see examples of each.

As fifth-grade teacher Taylor shared with us, "It's important to remember that they [students] are capable of coming up with ways to demonstrate their learning. It may be hard to let that go, or to accept that, but when you do let go, they are capable of coming up with things that are just as good if not better than the things we could have thought of, because when they come up with it, they are passionate about it and the outcome is far superior." In Chapter 4, you will read about the ways in which Taylor turned some of that decision making over to her students.

Invitation. Think about the instructional models that you may plan on using for your unit of study. What are some of the text types and modalities that are modeled in the text sets you have designed? Which ones make the most sense to offer students as choices? Is there a specific writing standard that you must align with this unit? Can students demonstrate that they have mastery of that standard and still have choice on another student-created text?

Conclusion

As we shared in our introduction, teaching with text sets takes time up front. But, as Tom has told us, "I think in the long haul, it saves time. It also allows you to teach things that are not necessarily in the science and social studies curriculum . . . making connections, defending your thoughts, and looking beyond the surface . . . I think a lot of those things are forced with the sources that you use in a text set, whereas in a textbook, it is just laid out there for kids to see and there is no necessity for them to look at those sources a little deeper." The planning takes time but allows you and your students to dig in more deeply, and such careful planning allows you to be flexible in your teaching, so that you can respond to student needs and, as Tom suggests, go "beyond the surface." In the next chapter, we will talk about some of the ways in which text sets work across the different content areas.

CHAPTER 2

How Do Text Sets Cultivate Disciplinary Literacy and Critical Thinking?

As educators, we believe it is important to give students the opportunity to see the work of the real world in school and the work of school in the real world. Students need to wrestle with the complicated history of their community, to study the earth below them, the skies above them, and the water that flows around them. Students deserve access to robust social studies and science curriculums and the opportunity to learn and understand how these disciplines operate. They also need to see literacy and math not only as discrete subjects worthy of their own exploration but also as the tools to do all the other work there is to be done in the world. You can't do science or social studies without literacy and math.

Providing students with the opportunity for integrated instruction as much as possible captures the richness of our interconnected world. All four core content areas, plus the integrated arts, reinforce one another, and that reinforcement plays an important role in developing students' agency and their ability to draw upon their learning from multiple disciplines.

To maximize students' learning across the disciplines, it is helpful to understand the specific ways in which each of the disciplines operate. In this chapter, we will draw on current thinking about approaches to teaching content with a disciplinary literacy lens. Our goal is to highlight the critical thinking skills specific to particular disciplines and across disciplines. Understanding these skills and strategies supports the design process when teaching with text sets.

Disciplinary Literacy

Over the past decade, the concept of disciplinary literacy has taken on an important role in our conversations about literacy. Disciplinary literacy has been defined as "the idea that we should teach the specialized ways of reading, understanding, and thinking used in each academic discipline, such as science, history, or literature. Each field has its own ways of using text to create and communicate meaning" (Shanahan and Shanahan 2014, 636). Teaching with a disciplinary literacy lens allows us to support students' thinking and decision making as scientists, historians, writers, and mathematicians. "We should teach students the way reading in various fields differs rather than only expecting students to apply the same general lens across everything they read" (Shanahan and Shanahan 2014, 637).

Although disciplinary literacy has been discussed more frequently at the secondary level (Moje 2008; Shanahan and Shanahan 2008), we believe that disciplinary literacy is also a way for elementary students to engage in the big conversations that take place within the disciplines. "Building disciplinary knowledge is intertwined with the literacy practices of a particular discipline. By coupling content with domain-specific literacy practices, students engage in the same process used by disciplinary experts" (Spires, Kerkhoff, and Graham 2016, 151). When we ask young people to *do* the work of a discipline, rather than simply read information, they grow their disciplinary knowledge and fine-tune their diverse literacy practices.

Does this concept of literacy feel overwhelming to you? It might, particularly if the last time you formally studied history, mathematics, or science was in college. But if we think about it at the textual level first, it is less complicated. All texts are constructed with a purpose. Whether a text is a street sign, a poem, or a new environmental law, each has a particular purpose for which it was constructed. The street sign could signal an important stop for pedestrians to remain safe in a busy intersection; the poem might convey the writer's feelings about the death of a loved one; the environmental law could allow for stronger drinking water protections.

Each text also follows certain genre expectations. A stop sign won't be effective if it is too small or too dim or written upon material that will decompose. A poem isn't a poem unless it conforms to certain expectations of how space and line are used. An environmental law has to fit into the code of law already in place within its area of jurisdiction, drawing upon specialized vocabulary and a rigid written format. We already teach upper elementary students to recognize and understand literary genres. Teaching with a disciplinary lens asks us to think about how all texts are constructed from the larger context of discipline and genre. A chef writes a cookbook in ways that are totally different from a sports reporter's story covering the World Series. Scientists write certain kinds of texts, historians write another. We use cookbooks for different purposes than we use sports stories.

Teaching with text sets draws upon a framework of disciplinary literacy, as we ask students to think like scientists or historians, fiction writers or mathematicians, as they comprehend, construct, and critique a range of children's literature and authentic texts. Shanahan and Shanahan (2014) suggest that at the elementary level, a "way to prepare students for disciplinary reading is to introduce and guide the reading of multiple texts on the same topic, much the way experts in history, science, or English think about and evaluate what they read across sources" (638). Let's take a deeper dive by looking at the disciplinary literacies and critical thinking skills within each of the content areas with which we are most familiar. We teach each of the four core content areas not merely because they are required on state standards, although state standards certainly provide a foundation to the content and skills addressed at each grade level. But there are bigger, more powerful reasons to explore each content area in school, and those reasons are tied to the critical thinking and literacies inherent in each associated discipline.

Genre, Voice, and Theme in Language Arts

Why do we teach language arts in the intermediate grades? It's not merely to decode words, to bubble in multiple-choice answers, to construct open responses on standardized tests, or to recall elements of plot or characterization. But all too often, that is what literacy instruction looks like, particularly for marginalized students attending underfunded schools. Historically, literacy education has been withheld from oppressed populations as a means of control by those in power. As literacy educators, it is important for us to recognize that part of our work is to grow our students' reading and writing *identities*. Being able to skillfully read and write, knowing and understanding the different ways that you can choose to read and write, is a foundation for emancipation and empowerment whether you are ten or twenty-five or fifty-five.

We teach language arts because we want students to learn about themselves and others in the present, past, and future and to live vicariously through the fiction, nonfiction, drama, and poetry they read. To see, as Dr. Rudine Simms Bishop (1990) has suggested, through "mirrors, windows, and sliding glass doors." We want students to see their own lives reflected in texts, to learn about the lives of others, and to interact with other cultures through their reading experiences. We also want students to understand the power of writing, to find their voices as human beings first and foremost. We want them to know that they can be agents of change in the world by shaping their ideas, arguments, and feelings into words. We also want to empower students to be full participants in society, with the skills necessary to ask and answer questions through careful research and informational literacy, with the ability to make informed decisions, and with the capacity to advocate for themselves and others.

Disciplinary Literacies in Language Arts

Our graduate students will sometimes ask us to identify the disciplinary literacy at work in language arts. Everything? When we think about the real-world literacies that fall within language arts, it can feel overwhelming—the professionals who use language as part of their work are varied and far-reaching. Novelists and poets, yes. But also advertising copywriters and political speech writers, journalists and editors. What unites this disparate group? We believe that a focus on genre, voice, and theme, as they relate to an understanding of purpose and audience is the disciplinary literacy at work in the language arts.

Rainey and Moje (2012) suggest that the disciplinary literacy at work in English language arts focuses on students' ability to identify author's craft and theme; synthesize texts connected by topic, theme, or genre; and critique texts. We believe students need to identify author's craft and theme within and through their own writing as well as by reading and critiquing the writings of others. This focus on the art and craft of writing and the critical thinking required to explore genre, voice, and theme is at the heart of disciplinary ways of thinking in language arts.

Building Curriculum in Language Arts

A deeper dive into the goals of language arts is not possible within the pages of this book, but we encourage all of our readers, novice and veteran educators alike, to read or reread the National Council of Teach-ers of English/International Literacy Association Standards for the English Language Arts K–12, originally published in 1996, updated in 2009, and reaffirmed by NCTE in 2012 (**www.ncte.org/standards/ncte-ira**).

One particularly important element of the standards is the Interactive Model for Language Arts. This model puts students at the center of three interconnected dimensions of learning: the content (the what), the purpose (the why), and the development (the how) (NCTE/ILA 1996/2012,

10). "Because the standards are learner-centered, they focus on the ways in which students participate in their own learning, acquire knowledge, shape experience, and respond to their own particular needs and goals through the English language arts. This reflects an active rather than a passive process of language use and learning—a process in which students' engagement is primary" (9). This model of active learning is at the heart of literacy curriculum and instruction. If you are not already a member of one of these two professional organizations, we recommend joining.

There are twelve standards for English language arts K–12:

1. Students read a wide range of print and non-print texts to build an understanding of texts, of themselves, and of the cultures of the United States and the world; to acquire new information; to respond to the needs and demands of society and the workplace; and for personal fulfillment. Among these texts are fiction and nonfiction, classic and contemporary works.

2. Students read a wide range of literature from many periods in many genres to build an understanding of the many dimensions (e.g., philosophical, ethical, aesthetic) of human experience.

3. Students apply a wide range of strategies to comprehend, interpret, evaluate, and appreciate texts. They draw on their prior experience, their interactions with other readers and writers, their knowledge of word meaning and of other texts, their word identification strategies, and their understanding of textual features (e.g., sound-letter correspondence, sentence structure, context, graphics).

4. Students adjust their use of spoken, written, and visual language (e.g., conventions, style, vocabulary) to communicate effectively with a variety of audiences and for different purposes.

5. Students employ a wide range of strategies as they write and use different writing process elements appropriately to communicate with different audiences for a variety of purposes.

6. Students apply knowledge of language structure, language conventions (e.g., spelling and punctuation), media techniques, figurative language, and genre to create, critique, and discuss print and non-print texts.

7. Students conduct research on issues and interests by generating ideas and questions and by posing problems. They gather, evaluate, and synthesize data from a variety of sources (e.g., print and non-print texts, artifacts, people) to communicate their discoveries in ways that suit their purpose and audience.

8.	Students use a variety of technological and information resources (e.g., libraries, databases, computer networks, video) to gather and synthesize information and to create and communicate knowledge.
9.	Students develop an understanding of and respect for diversity in language use, patterns, and dialects across cultures, ethnic groups, geographic regions, and social roles.
10.	Students whose first language is not English make use of their first language to develop competency in the English language arts and to develop understanding of content across the curriculum.
11.	Students participate as knowledgeable, reflective, creative, and critical members of a variety of literacy communities.
12.	Students use spoken, written, and visual language to accomplish their own purposes (e.g., for learning, enjoyment, persuasion, and the exchange of information). (NCTE/ILA 1996/2009)

In language arts, a focus on disciplinary literacy emerges organically, as students are positioned to explore texts as writers. In language arts, we examine genre, voice, and theme within and across fiction, nonfiction, poetry, and drama. Students read, listen, and view texts with an eye for composition. They unpack themes as independent human beings, experienced with the world around them. When we ask students to read and respond to texts as literary and visual artists do, we give them the opportunity to practice and strengthen their abilities, and they develop agency as readers and writers.

Selecting Texts for Text Sets in Language Arts

Regardless of the purpose for which you are selecting the book, you are first going to determine its quality. Is it a good book, worth taking time to explore in the classroom? What makes it so? What have reviewers said? Are characters represented authentically? In nonfiction, can you tell where the author found source material? Is the language interesting and engaging for your students?

Next, you will consider the utility of the text. Why are you going to use it? What role will it have in your classroom? Is the book an outstanding version of its genre? Does the book have the theme that you want to frame a unit around? Does the book cover the content that you need it to cover? How will the book be read? By everyone? Just a small group? As a read-aloud?

Finally, you will consider the match between quality, instructional purpose (why it is being read), practice (how it is being read), and the complexity of the book. If the book is challenging, is that less important because you are planning on reading it aloud? If the book is going to be for a guided reading group, is the vocabulary and syntax within the range that your students can handle? If the book is well written, how might it be easier for your students to navigate in small groups because the language makes it so engaging, despite having a lot of content-specific vocabulary?

Because of the important role selecting texts has in the process of teaching reading, as well as literacy learning as a whole, a more comprehensive process is beyond the scope of this book. In our previous book, *Teaching to Complexity: A Framework to Evaluate Literary and Content-Area Texts* (Cappiello and Dawes 2015), we articulated a process for selecting texts for a range of curricular purposes based on these three considerations: quality, utility, and complexity.

What are some of the ways that a book can model the disciplinary practices of genre, voice, and perspective? Let's explore *Poet: The Remarkable Story of George Moses Horton* (see Figure 2.1). Specifically, let's take a look at this two-page spread from the conclusion of author-illustrator Don Tate's picture book biography (see Figure 2.2).

On the left, we have the conclusion of the primary text, a chronological narrative of Horton's life. We see how Tate incorporated Horton's written words in a banner running across the illustration. Horton writes

FIGURE 2.1

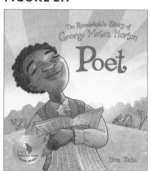

FIGURE 2.2

in a tent, Union Army soldiers visible behind him. Tate uses the stylistic choice of repetition to affirm Horton's agency: "Words made him strong. Words allowed him to dream. Words loosened the chains of bondage long before his last day as a slave" (n.p.). Students reading Horton's story and Tate's words experience the power words have to create change within people and the world.

On the right, the back matter begins; Tate shares his book creation process with readers. He makes visible the sources used to research the book, including Horton's autobiography. Tate also offers his readers a lesson on sourcing and publishing, by referencing that Horton's works are now in the public domain and guiding his young readers to the origin of the quotes used in the book. Tate treats his readers as peers, respecting their intelligence and including them in the conversation about book production.

This two-page spread is followed by another, the author's note, in which Tate reveals more about his own life and evolution as an author and illustrator. At first, he did not want to write or illustrate books about slavery. By admitting this, he makes himself vulnerable to his audience. "But as I read the stories and studied the history of my people, I had a change of heart. I decided that there was nothing to be ashamed of, and much to feel proud about. I fell in love with stories that demonstrated the resilience of African-American people." Tate goes on to discuss his process of researching Horton, filling in the larger context of the time and place in which he lived. Tate models the process of doing historical research. Thanks to Tate's back matter, readers have a road map for writing a picture book biography.

Tate concludes the author's note with a connection to today, when "statistics show that far too many African-American students graduate from high school functionally illiterate." Tate makes the past relevant to the present, connecting the dots across time for his readers. In doing so, he raises a call to action for contemporary readers, who he hopes "will see themselves in the story of George Moses Horton." By the end of this book, we have learned about Horton's important life and Tate's research and writing process. But we have also learned something equally important: *why* Tate felt the need to share this life story with the world.

Selecting texts for language arts invites student into the power of words to reflect reality or to create new realities. You will be able to see that work up close in Chapter 3, when we describe a third-grade biography genre study. You can go read that right now and then come back or read it after you've finished this chapter.

Invitation. Think about your language arts curriculum. What are some of the ways in which the organization of your units fosters a sense of authentic reading and writing experiences? Now, think about one particular unit you teach. Perhaps it is one that feels challenging to you. What are some of the ways that you would like to deepen students' agency as readers and writers of authentic texts?

Perspective and Representation in Social Studies

It is not enough to be able to find certain places on a map, to identify the rivers in your community, or to know the difference between agricultural and natural resources in your state. It is not enough to memorize dates and names or string together a list of causes of the American Revolution. That is not to say that any of that content is unimportant, or those skills are unnecessary. Rather, there is more to it.

The past few years have been turbulent ones in the United States and around the world. We are facing the largest humanitarian refugee crisis the world has ever known (U.N. Refugee Agency 2018). Gun violence is the largest contributor to premature death in the United States (American Public Health Association, n.d.). Almost a quarter of American children are growing up in poverty (Gould and Schneider 2018). The human race may not survive climate change without significant policy reforms in the next decade (National Aeronautics and Space Administration 2019). In recent years, the brutality of systemic racism has been made even more visible. And yet, in many elementary schools, social studies curriculum barely exists, since, unlike science, literacy, and math, mandatory testing of the subject is not required by federal law.

We teach social studies not just to cover basic skills, but, as Doug Buehl likes to say, to "apprentice" young people in the disciplines of history and geography and the social sciences, to give them the tools to understand the past and its impact on the present, and to develop solutions for the future. In 2010, the National Council of Teachers of Social Studies published the revised *National Curriculum Standards for Social Studies*. The document states that "the aim of social studies is the promotion of civic competence—the knowledge, intellectual processes, and democratic dispositions required of students to be active and engaged participants in public life. By making civic competence a central aim, NCSS emphasizes the importance of educating students who are committed to the ideas and values of democracy" (9).

Disciplinary Literacies in Social Studies

What does disciplinary literacy look like in social studies? The majority of writing on disciplinary literacy connected to social studies focuses almost exclusively on history. Rainey and Moje (2012) tell us that history "is something to be interpreted rather than observed" (75). One of our favorite professional books for teaching social studies is Linda Levstik and Keith Barton's (2015) *Doing History: Investigating with Children in Elementary and Middle Schools*. We love the verb at the heart of this title: *doing*. How exactly does one "do" history?

> History is not made through an accumulation of facts, but rather through examination and interpretation of multiple artifacts of the past. Students of history thus need to be able to read across multiple texts, not only to gain information about the nature of historical research that has already been conducted about an event or a person, but also to interpret those artifacts—those data—and draw conclusions about them. Students reading and writing history need to develop skill in synthesizing the perspectives and voices of many different observers, none of whom they can interview. (Rainey and Moje 2012, 75)

As Shanahan and Shanahan (2014) tell us, "When historians create historical accounts, they rely on documents from the period under study (primary documents) and on what others have written about the event (secondary documents). Because their study is limited to existing sources and there can be disagreements among these sources, historians expect their interpretations to be contested as new documents come to light or alternative perspectives are weighed" (636–637).

To teach with a disciplinary lens in social studies at the elementary level is to invite students into this conversation about source material and the process of interpretation, giving them introductory access to primary sources, and engaging in conversations about how secondary sources are constructed and composed. It's about immersing students in the artifacts and texts of the past and asking them to build meaning and interpret multiple perspectives.

Building Curriculum in Social Studies

The 2010 National Curriculum Standards for Social Studies contain ten themes, which you may see visible in your state social studies standards:

- Culture
- Time, Continuity, and Change

- People, Places, and Environments
- Individual Development and Identity
- Individuals, Groups, and Institutions
- Power, Authority, and Governance
- Production, Distribution, and Consumption
- Science, Technology, and Society
- Global Connections
- Civic Ideals and Practices

In 2013, the NCSS also participated, along with many other organizations, in the creation of the College, Career, and Civic Life (C3) Framework for Social Studies State Standards. You may wonder why, on the heels of the standards revision, another document was produced. The C3 Framework is an attempt to help align the Common Core Literacy Standards and the development of new individual state social studies standards. In part, the document was created in response to the "marginalization of the social studies" and the fact that children "quickly become disengaged when instruction is limited to reading textbooks to answer end-of-chapter questions and taking multiple-choice tests that may measure content knowledge but do little to measure how knowledge is meaningful and applicable in the real world" (NCSS 2013). Additionally, the impetus was in response to the fact that "abundant research bears out the sad reality that fewer and fewer young people, particularly students of color and students in poverty, are receiving a high-quality social studies education, despite the central role of social studies in preparing students for the responsibilities of citizenship" (NCSS 2013).

The C3 Framework identifies four disciplines within the social studies—civics, history, geography, and economics—and articulates a process for teaching social studies that rests on the "inquiry arc." Although it is easy to identify the role of perspective and representation in the discipline of history, geography, economics, and civics also require a consideration of perspective and representation. By way of example: just think about the history of mapmaking over the years. Prior to global imaging, maps reflected the biases of the mapmakers.

The inquiry arc happens over four "dimensions." Dimension One focuses on developing good questions, ideally teacher- and student-generated ones. Dimension Two is the process of exploring curricular content, using the habits of mind from the four disciplines as a lens. Some content requires you to pull from all four areas, while other content may focus on just one of the disciplines. Dimension Three asks students to gather sources and evaluate evidence. Finally, Dimension Four asks students to communicate what they have learned and what conclusions they have drawn and to "take informed action." In this structure, you can see close parallels to the process that we have developed, ending with student-created texts that demonstrate learning.

Within Dimension Three, when students are gathering sources and evaluating evidence, a text set approach is most visible. When we ask students to examine primary source documents, artifacts, historic newspaper accounts, or political music and popular culture, we are asking them to consider multiple perspectives. Think about what happens when you compare and contrast just two news stories. So much of what we hear and read is framed by the perspectives of the authors, and the selection of supporting materials that contributes to the representation of the event.

Selecting Texts for Text Sets in Social Studies

When selecting texts for social studies, we consider the ways in which primary and secondary sources can bring perspectives and events to life for learners. First and foremost, we look for books that students will connect with, books that will get them excited or engaged, books that will prompt further inquiry.

Children's nonfiction has changed dramatically over the past fifteen years. We seek out books that make the process of "doing history" visible, looking for nonfiction and historical fiction with robust author and illustrator notes that explain their research and sense-making processes. We vet these texts for their accuracy, ensuring that appropriate back matter demonstrates research on the part of the author and illustrator. We read professional book reviews and look to see that the books have been reviewed by experts in the field. As Kathleen Issacs (2011) notes, "whether they are chronicling their own investigations, using primary sources, or recasting information from titles published for adults, authors of books for school-aged readers now take the time to describe their research. They note choices they've made and areas where information is contradictory" (15). The conversation about the process of doing history that happens in the author and illustrator notes is often as powerful a teaching tool as the rest of the book.

Additionally, we seek out books that reflect the experiences of underrepresented and marginalized populations to bring their voices into historical conversation. In reading those books, we consider the identities of the authors and illustrators to see whether they are a part of the cultures reflected in the books and, if not, who vetted their manuscripts. Overall, as we consider different titles, we consider who has power and agency within the books, and we determine how the information in one confirms, extends, or challenges the information found in others. To draw on the expertise of those in the field, we seek out the recommendations made by the National Council for the Social Studies and the Children's Book Council in their annual "Notable Social Studies Trade Books for Young People."

We also look for primary source documents that reveal the ways that people have communicated in the past and art or artifacts from the time that reveal how people dressed, what they looked like, and how they went about their everyday tasks. We seek a diverse range of identities and perspectives for primary source documents. We strive to find photographs of objects and artifacts in museums and research libraries—when we can't bring them in—that help students consider the everyday lives of people in different time periods.

What are some of the ways that a book can model the disciplinary practices of perspective and representation? Let's explore Laurie Halse Anderson's (2008) nonfiction picture *Independent Dames: What You Never Knew About the Women and Girls of the American Revolution*.

The first two-page spread in the book shows a school staging a play about the American Revolution. Anderson's casual tone points out the perspective to the reader immediately: "Look, another school play about the heroes of the American Revolution. How sweet." After listing some Founding Fathers, otherwise known as "famous guys who did important things" (4), Anderson's sarcasm grows. "Wonderful. Just wonderful. Of course, you're missing part of the story. In fact, you're missing about half of it" (4). Immediately, the reader is reminded of the dominant narrative of this important time in American history, and then further reminded of the misrepresentation at work in that dominant narrative.

Within the second two-page spread, there are several levels of meaning making for young readers to unpack. First, there is a primary text, which demands the reader answer a few questions: "Hello? How about the women? What about the girls?" (6). Anderson's questions may be ones that students have already been asking about history. But, as Levstick and Barton (2015) suggest, children are not always critical readers of historical narrative. When a book asks them to think about who has been included and excluded from the narratives they have read and/or are reading, new understanding of the process of doing history emerges. History is constructed by people. Historians and writers make choices about who gets included and who gets excluded. Including women's stories in history isn't adding an additional layer; women have always been present. As Anderson notes, women and girls "worked, they argued, they fought, and they suffered—just like the men and the boys" (6).

The illustration across the spread reveals the shock and surprise of the Founding Fathers and the school play participants as they witness who has emerged on the stage: two women on horseback, one loading a cannon and one dressed as a male soldier, holding guns. In smaller font, encased in a circle, Anderson writes about the two women on horseback: sixteen-year-old Sybil Ludington, delivering an important message to militiamen, and Deborah Champion, who acted as a spy for George Washington. Over the course of the book, readers learn more about a diverse set of women, including African American and Native American women. Anderson provides a running timeline of the war at the bottom of the page, so that readers can absorb the individual stories of women's bravery into the larger context of political events and battles.

The book concludes with four pages of back matter devoted to snapshots of additional women who did not make it into the primary text. After sharing those stories about which she has verifiable evidence, Anderson writes that much of women's history survived through the oral tradition. Under the banner of "Fact or Fiction" she writes about women's stories that she cannot fully verify. She then discusses some of the roles of Loyalist women, African American women, and Native American women. Following these four pages are author and illustrator notes that explain the process of doing the required research and the bibliography. Like Don Tate's work discussed previously, Anderson and illustrator Matt Faulkner make the process of doing history and responding to history visible. They model process, from asking questions to decisions involved in composing text and illustrations. Anderson's discussion of the role of primary source documents in revealing women's history allows students to see the challenges, and the opportunities, historians face.

Selecting texts for social studies text sets invites student into the cacophony of the past and the present. Linda Levstik (1993) suggests that when crafting social studies curriculum, teachers must explore "how young learners use literary texts to build historical understanding, how the texts themselves structure history, and how teachers mediate among children, texts, and history" (67). You'll be able to see how children engage with texts up close in Chapter 4, when we describe a fifth-grade exploration of the American Revolution. You can go read that right now and then come back or read it after you've finished this chapter.

Invitation. Think about your social studies curriculum. What are some of the ways in which it is designed to focus on multiple perspectives in the present and the past? To what extent do you ask students to consider how various perspectives are represented? Now, think about one particular unit you teach. Perhaps it is one that feels challenging to you. What are some of the ways that you would like to deepen students' agency, and their ability to sift through evidence, to come to their own conclusions?

Evidence and Inquiry in Science

Turn on the news, scroll through media, listen in to conversations on public transportation and you will hear evidence for the urgency of science learning and active participation in the scientific community. Climate change demands our attention and action; we are on the cusp of new and significant treatments for cancer; new discoveries alter our understanding of our place in the universe; and the amazing diversity of humanity compels design and innovation for the improvement of daily life. During the Covid 19 pandemic,we watched scientific understanding evolve at a historic pace, allowing students to witness the power of collaboration in real time. Imagine what might be possible when students' abilities to observe, to ask questions, and to problem solve are fostered in classrooms that value scientific inquiry, discourse, and communication.

Curiosity about the phenomena of everyday life is the driving force for learning in the sciences for both children and for adults working in science-based professions. From birth, children demonstrate their natural capabilities for inquiry as they observe, experiment, and test their emerging ideas and theories through interactions with their caregivers, their physical surroundings, and the natural world. The National Academy for the Sciences (2012) presents a framework for K–12 science learning that "rests on a view of science as both a body of knowledge and an evidence-based, model and theory building enterprise that continually extends, refines, and revises knowledge." When this orientation permeates the school science curriculum, teachers invite their students into an ongoing conversation in the scientific community—a conversation grounded in inquiry, evidence, and ideas.

Disciplinary Literacy in Science

Scientists and engineers engage in disciplinary literacies that emphasize the critical thinking skills of inquiry and evidence. As scientists carry out their work, they are engaged in broad conversations with members of the scientific community. Scientists read, consider, adapt, and build upon the work of others; write to disseminate their investigations and theories; and participate in lively debates with other scientists, describing their work and defending their ideas with evidence (Ebbers 2002; Ippolito et al. 2018; Cervetti and Pearson 2012).

The National Academy of Sciences identifies eight essential practices for K–12 science instruction. Although all eight involve reading, writing, speaking, and listening, five of them fall clearly into the realm of disciplinary literacy: asking questions and defining problems; constructing explanations and defining solutions; engaging in argument from evidence; analyzing and interpreting data; and obtaining, evaluating, and communicating data (National Research Council 2012). For the full listing, see the NAS's helpful infographic at **www.nap.edu/visualizations /practices-for-k-12-classrooms/.** As they seek to understand the phenomena of our world, scientists use language and literacy practices to formulate and substantiate their ideas within the context of a scientific community engaged in constant communication and debate.

Building Curriculum in Science

Like social studies, science inquiry is often neglected in elementary programs with a heavy emphasis on math and literacy. Science instruction may consist of textbook readings, a series of recipe-like experiments, and/ or read-alouds of trade books that focus on science topics. Often, science is portrayed as a fixed body of knowledge, facts that students need to memorize.

The Next Generation Science Standards (2013) espouse a more comprehensive approach, one aligned with the definition of science above. These standards comprise three interwoven strands:

- *Crosscutting Concepts* in the four domains of science:
  - Physical science
  - Life science
  - Earth and space science
  - Engineering design
- *Science and Engineering Practices*—the processes used by scientist and engineers as they engage in inquiry and design; and
- *Disciplinary Core Ideas*, established and key understandings across the four domains.

Taken together, the three strands of this framework are "designed to help realize a vision for education in the sciences and engineering in which students, over multiple years of school, actively engage in scientific and engineering practices, and apply crosscutting concepts to deepen their understanding of the core ideas in these fields" (National Research Council 2013). This model emphasizes the doing of science, but this doing also involves work with texts. Reading across the Next Generation Science Standards, you will find specific mention of scientific literacy, framed as knowledge of the nature of science. A helpful matrix in Appendix H outlines eight basic understandings and how these can be developed across the grade levels (NGSS 2013):

- Scientific Investigations Use a Variety of Methods
- Scientific Knowledge Is Based on Empirical Evidence
- Scientific Knowledge Is Open to Revision in Light of New Evidence
- Scientific Models, Laws, Mechanisms, and Theories Explain Natural Phenomena
- Science Is a Way of Knowing
- Scientific Knowledge Assumes an Order and Consistency in Natural Systems
- Science Is a Human Endeavor
- Science Addresses Questions About the Natural and Material World

An inquiry orientation and hands-on learning are primary in science, but well-written texts and text sets play an important role. In their excellent resource on science and literacy in elementary classrooms, Worth and her colleagues (2009) describe instruction that provides "a balance of open interaction with phenomena, carefully designed hands-on experiences, and the structured and intentional use of oral and written language" (xi). As we frame it for our students, you can't learn science by reading about it. Like history, science is something that you do, and our understanding of the field is constantly evolving based on new inquiry and new evidence. Cervetti and Pearson (2012) reassure us that in science teaching, placing inquiry and experiential learning at the forefront results in literacy learning, as well. When students have the opportunity to engage in meaningful exploration and dialogue in science, they are building their abilities to comprehend and communicate in the discipline.

As students combine inquiry with text sets, they enact the disciplinary literacies of science, describing their observations, recording data in science notebooks, constructing and debating theories with their fellow students, and reading the history of scientific discovery. A focus on inquiry, claims, and evidence permeates the classroom.

Selecting Texts for Text Sets in Science

When selecting texts in science, we are particular about finding texts that model inquiry—texts that illustrate the ongoing processes of learning about our world and how it works. We look specifically for texts that describe how science theories have changed over time by offering a historical and contemporary framing. We also seek texts that describe scientists and engineers as they engage in their work. The Scientists in the Field series published by Houghton Mifflin is an excellent example. Additionally, we look for what Zarnowski and Turkel (2013) refer to as "literature of inquiry." They pose the important question: "Do children's books reveal science as a way of thinking and learning that scientists would find authentic?" (295). Books of this nature support student learning about science processes and the disciplinary literacies of science by describing how and where scientists carry out their work. Ebbers (2002) describes the potential well-curated science texts sets hold for revealing the nature of science:

> With careful selection, teachers provide children with windows into a welcoming scientific community. These windows include stories about its current and historical members, explanatory frameworks, descriptions, and examples of scientific practices. They also include the social and political contexts and historical stories that describe the development of current understandings. (49)

Because we are not science experts, we look to those who are for support with text selection in science. We read reviews of science titles, knowing that the review journals are deliberate in selecting reviewers who have subject matter expertise. Additionally, we draw on annual lists of high-quality titles selected by professional organizations. The National Science Teachers Association and the Children's Book Council annually (revised in reference list) publishes a listing of "Outstanding Science Trade Books for Students K–12" organized by topic. The annual winners of the Orbis Pictus Award for Outstanding Nonfiction for Children, a book award sponsored by the National Council of Teachers of English, typically include science titles. When we select books from these lists, we know the books have been vetted for accuracy, reviewed for stereotypes, and elevated for recognition due to their quality and appeal.

We also select science texts with consideration of the accessibility of their content. We carefully consider what background knowledge a young reader would need to understand the concepts in the book. We look at the organization of the book to determine whether the text structure helps to scaffold students understanding across the content of the book. We also consider the language use in the book: Are explanations clear? Is less familiar vocabulary defined in context? Does the author employ devices such as simile and metaphor to help readers construct meaning?

What are some of the ways that a book can model the disciplinary practices of inquiry and evidence? Let's take a look at *Giant Squid* written by Candace Fleming (2016) and illustrated by Eric Rohmann (see Figure 2.3). This award-winning nonfiction picture book has a unique opening with several double-page spreads of text preceding the title page. Accompanied by dramatic illustration, these pages have a cinematic quality. White text scrolls down the page, set against an inky black background. Across three-page turns, red and white tentacles emerge, creeping upward from the bottom right-hand corner of the book. With her opening line, Fleming sets a tone of mystery and wonder: "Down, / down / in the depths / of the sunless sea, / deep, / deep / in the cold, / cold dark, / creatures, / strange / and fearsome, / lurk" (n.p.). The use of repetition in this poetic text reinforces scientific understandings, developing a sensory image of the cold dark ocean depths that are the habitat for this yet unnamed creature. The text on the following double-page spread further piques readers' interest, describing the animal's eyes, movement, and size—"some large as buses." Fleming notes the contradiction that these animals are "So big yet rarely seen." She then poses a series of questions, highlighting how little we know about these elusive undersea inhabitants.

FIGURE 2.3

FIGURE 2.4

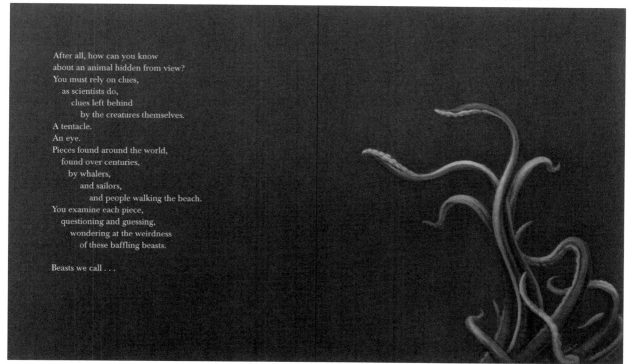

If we look at the two-page spread in Figure 2.4, the third spread in the book, we see a clear emphasis on the disciplinary literacies of inquiry and evidence. Fleming poses a key question, rooted in the inquiry process: "After all how can you know / about an animal hidden from view?" She then answers this question with a focus on evidence and an explicit mention of how scientists carry out their work: "You must rely on clues, as scientists do, clues left behind by the creatures themselves." These clues are then described—what they are, where they have been found, and most important, that these clues have been found over "centuries." Readers are left with a sense of scientific inquiry as a process of culling and considering accumulating evidence over time.

Fleming's emphasis on questions is sustained throughout the main text of *Giant Squid*. With poetic descriptions and careful use of figurative language, she notes what is known about the behaviors of this mysterious creature. Rohmann's illustrations provide an accompanying visual narrative, immersing readers in a close-up view of the squid's interaction with other ocean animals. A wordless double gatefold spread finally reveals the giant squid in all its glory—a quick glimpse and then on the following, concluding page: "It's gone."

The back matter of *Giant Squid* further illuminates the process of science inquiry. A large diagram of the squid describes the animal's unique adaptations. Fleming includes her sources in the back matter and acknowledges her consultation with Dr. Edith Widder, a marine scientist who captured the first film footage of a giant squid. She also includes a listing of resources for readers who want to learn more about this intriguing animal. In a section titled "The Mysterious Giant Squid," Fleming describes how scientists have used evidence over time to construct an evolving understanding of this animal: "So how do we know about these mysterious creatures? From the bits and pieces of them discovered on the ocean's surface or washed up on the world's beaches." Describing how scientists have dissected these pieces to learn about internal organs, Fleming concludes with a list of unanswered questions. The processes of the scientist are clearly visible to young readers.

When selecting texts for science, we consider a book's potential role in a text set. You'll be able to see how children engage with texts up close in Chapter 5, when we describe an integrated science and language arts unit, focusing on the concepts of adaptation and biological evolution. We illustrate how text sets can support students' development of a concept that is not easily observable. In this unit, text sets accompanied the observation of animals in their natural habitats, with an emphasis on the observable characteristics that make these animals suited for survival within this particular ecosystem. Texts provided additional support for the abstract concepts of adaptation and evolution. You can go read that right now and then come back or read it after you've finished this chapter.

In other units of study, science texts may play different roles, such as offering additional examples of design principles at work, describing geographically significant but remote areas, relaying the life story of a scientist, providing reference information, narrating a scientific discovery, or describing a phenomenon (Ebbers 2002).

Invitation. Think about your science curriculum. How do you incorporate both primary and secondary research? How are students encouraged to use inquiry processes and to find evidence for their emergent scientific understandings? Does your science curriculum present scientific knowledge as fixed or ever evolving? Select one particular unit that you teach—either a unit that you love or one that feels challenging to you. Consider the balance of experiential learning and learning through texts within the unit. What are some ways that you could heighten your emphasis on inquiry and evidence, encouraging your students to think like scientists?

Problem Solving and Visualizing Data in Mathematics

We don't often hear people say, "I can't do history" or "I don't do science." But for some reason, it is very common to hear people say, "I don't do math." Or for teachers to declare, "I'm no good at math." Do you experience this as well? Why is that? What is it about mathematics that makes it socially acceptable for us to talk about it in that way? What allows people to disassociate from it? We know what a joy it is to work with passionate math educators. You may, too. You may be one of them! They shine a light on what is beautiful about mathematics. They speak the language of mathematics to and with children.

We need mathematics. We need it to design buildings and bridges, determine budgets, analyze data, create art, write metered poems, compose music, and much, much more. Math allows us to understand how the world works. Consider the Fibonacci sequence, a mathematical representation of a pattern within nature. Math is *everywhere*, all around us.

Disciplinary Literacy in Mathematics

The disciplinary literacy of mathematics has not been investigated by educational researchers to the same extent that the other disciplines have. Mathematics requires that students—or professionals—navigate two symbol systems at once: the alphabetic code and the numeric code. Doing math requires students to have an understanding of certain processes, identified by the Wisconsin Department of Public Education as the following "critical thinking experiences":

- Construct viable arguments through proof and reasoning.
- Critique the reasoning of others.
- Process and apply reasoning from others.
- Synthesize ideas and make connections to adjust the original argument.

These critical thinking experiences require the application of mathematical knowledge as well as specific communication skills. When we think about doing mathematics, we may have a vision of students working quietly at their desks practicing problem solving and completing worksheets in much the same ways that we may have learned ourselves years ago. But applied mathematics opens up venues for students to use mathematics to solve real-world problems or to consider and compute real-world information. All of this requires students to be in conversation with one another, comparing and contrasting information, identifying strategies, and doing close reading of words, sentences, numbers, and symbols.

Building Curriculum in Mathematics

In 2000, the National Council of Teachers of Mathematics published the *Principles and Standards for School Mathematics*. This comprehensive set of K–12 standards comprises ten standards. Some of the standards are content based, and others are process based:

Content Standards

- Numbers and Operations
- Algebra
- Geometry
- Measurement
- Data Analysis and Probability

Process Standards

- Problem Solving
- Reasoning and Proof
- Communication
- Connections
- Representation

In 2006, the National Council of Teachers of Mathematics published *Curriculum Focal Points for Prekindergarten Through Grade 8 Mathematics: A Quest for Coherence* (Schielack et al.) to better support teachers' ability to construct curriculum rooted in the *Principles and Standards for School Mathematics*. The Common Core Standards for Mathematics were informed by these professional standards.

In 2014, the National Council of Teachers of Mathematics published *Principles to Actions: Ensuring Mathematical Success for All*, to help situate teachers in "the essential elements of teaching and learning, access and equity, curriculum, tools and technology, assessment, and professionalism" (p. vii). Within the "essential elements of teaching and learning," eight actions are encouraged:

- Establish mathematics goals to focus learning.
- Implement tasks that promote reasoning and problem solving.
- Use and connect mathematical representations.
- Facilitate meaningful mathematical discourse.
- Pose purposeful questions.
- Build procedural fluency from conceptual understanding.
- Support productive struggle in learning mathematics.
- Elicit and use evidence of student thinking.

As the title makes clear, mathematics instruction is all about taking action, all about doing. It is not a passive process of rote memorization and repetition. Mathematical thinking is fostered though a range of experiences that include reading, writing, drawing, listening, and evidence-based argumentation.

Despite our understanding that math is everywhere, students may often be aware of math *only* during mathematics instruction. Isolated math instruction does not always celebrate the beauty and coherence of mathematical thinking. Instead, students experience math as a set of discrete and unrelated problems. Narrative thinking is often absent. Although we don't always want to privilege narrative, story gives us tools to make sense of and talk about the world around us. We explore this further in Chapter 6, when we discuss the use of nonfiction texts in a third-grade unit on multiplication. Math is visual. Numbers are a symbol system, operating much like the alphabet. Numbers and operations symbols represent mathematical concepts. So do pictures, charts, and graphs. Wedding mathematics to narrative and grounding mathematics in visual representation are two ways to embed mathematics in the real world.

A text set approach in mathematics allows teachers and students to engage in problems and strategies in community and conversation with one another beyond a worksheet or a set of problems on the page of a textbook.

Selecting Texts for Text Sets in Mathematics

When we select texts for math text sets, we think on multiple levels. First and foremost, we consider what we are already reading and exploring in science, social studies, or language arts. We examine the texts anew, seeking to identify the mathematical opportunities they present to students. This integration of content strengthens students' critical thinking, allows for additional pathways through texts they are already using, and contextualizes the math within the real world. It can also provide that narrative lens for mathematics. We also explore texts that visually represent mathematics. We seek out developmentally friendly and clearly written charts, graphs, and infographics to share with students. If we can select these texts on content that matches what the students are studying in science, social studies, or language arts, that is ideal. If we can't, then we seek out graphics that mirror students' personal interests and experiences or those of the school community.

We want to make the math as relevant and utilitarian as possible. Ultimately, the mathematical concepts with which the students are working toward have to take center stage in the text set. Text sets are another tool for doing math, even if some of the texts are also embedded in text sets that are focused on work in other content areas.

What are some of the ways that a book can model the disciplinary practices of visual literacy and numerical representation? Let's take a look at *Animals by the Numbers: A Book of Animal Infographics* by Steve Jenkins (2016) (see Figure 2.5). This nonfiction picture book offers readers a variety of infographic models to explore. Each infographic reveals a difference "slice" of information about animals.

On the first two-page spread of the book, Jenkins grounds his readers in an initial conversation about the power and potential of numbers. He writes: "Numbers help us understand our world. We use numbers to measure and compare things. Numbers help us explain what happened in the past and predict what might happen in the future" (3). Numbers allow us to do the work of science and history. What's more, as Jenkin cautions, our big questions about the world "would be difficult to answer . . . even to ask them—without numbers" (3). Finally, Jenkins introduces infographics to his readers: "In this book, facts and figures about animals are presented visually as graphs, symbols, and illustrations. These infographics give us

FIGURE 2.5

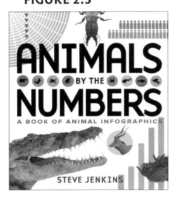

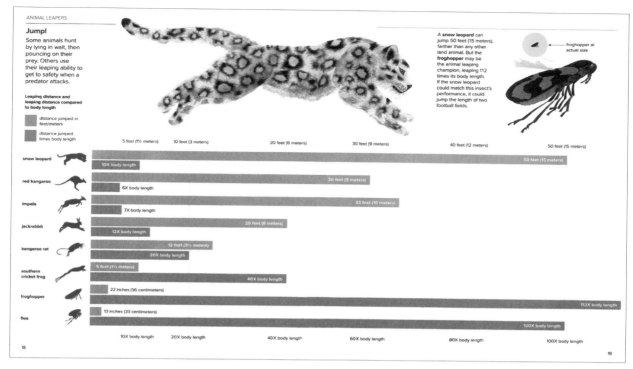

FIGURE 2.6

another way of looking at animals and understanding some of the amazing things that they can do" (3). The next two-page spread contains a visual table of contents, which reveals snapshots of the illustrations that appear on the pages of the book, along with the topics covered. Jenkins honors the importance of numbers by providing infographic images in the table of contents.

How does Jenkins represent numbers visually in infographics? Let's look at Figure 2.6, from pages 18–19 in the book. The section, entitled "Jump!," explores how far animals can jump as compared with their body length. Multiplication, which we will explore more deeply in Chapter 6, is required to create this infographic. Jenkins highlights the animal that jumps the farthest, the snow leopard, and the animal that jumps the farthest as a representation of body length, the tiny froghopper. This infographic allows readers to compare and contrast animals across the classes of mammals, reptiles, and amphibians. Because the infographic relies on comparing different measurements, it includes another math standard. Jenkins's appealing graphics affirm that numbers allow us to understand animals and the natural world and that multiplication is an essential tool in the study of science.

Integrating math instruction into the other content areas to harness multiple perspectives, and to emphasize the visual nature of mathematics, is at the core of a text set approach to math. We examine visual literacy and explore how multiple perspectives become visible when you read across different graphs, charts, and statistics. You'll be able to see that work up close in Chapter 6, when we describe a third-grade exploration of multiplication. You can go read that right now and then come back or read it after you've finished this chapter.

Invitation. Think about your mathematics curriculum. To what extent does your math curriculum remain isolated from other content areas? To what extent do you already build upon real-world applications of mathematics? What role does visual literacy have in your math curriculum? Consider the balance of experiential learning and learning through texts within the unit. What are some ways that you could heighten your emphasis on visual representation, encouraging your students to think like mathematicians or other professionals who use math in their daily work?

Critical Thinking Within the Disciplines

When we teach with text sets, we ask students to use their identities as scientists, historians, critics, writers, and mathematicians to *think critically* as they examine voice, perspective, and representation within and across texts of different genres and modalities. Yes, we always want to support them as developing readers and writers. But we know the act of inquiry and the comparison and contrast of interesting and engaging texts provide a deep and nurturing "ecosystem" in which they can go beyond mere comprehension. Comprehension is the starting point, not the end point. And comprehension doesn't happen in a vacuum. When we deliberately juxtapose texts within a text set model, we create fertile ground for critical thinking to develop.

Our hope is that students push beyond an understanding of vocabulary, sentence structure, and text structure toward deep engagement with the author's ideas, purpose for writing, and underlying ideology. We want students to be able to analyze, to compare, and to critique. As we described in Chapter 1, we believe that a text set offers a unique opportunity for students to compare and contrast perspectives, writing techniques, and the impact of genre structures. This provides students with a foundation for writing, composing, drawing, performing, and building in response to their learning. The creative work is an outgrowth of their critical thinking. Students' original and unique products, the creative responses to the texts they investigate, are generated from the critical and aesthetic thinking about the content they have learned and the texts they have explored.

When we do this critical thinking across the disciplines within a text set approach, something even bigger often happens. The close examination of multiple perspectives also develops students' critical literacy skills. We like to draw upon the work of Mitzi Lewison, Amy Seely Flint, and Katie Van Sluys (2002), who, after reviewing thirty years of research, constructed a model of critical literacy comprising four parts: "disrupting the common-place, interrogating multiple viewpoints, focusing on sociopolitical issues, and taking action and promoting social justice" (382). When we immerse students in meaningful questions and tasks, when we ask them to approach a topic with a lens that is different from how they might normally approach it, when we ask them to consider multiple viewpoints concurrently, and then do something about it, we are *doing* critical literacy. When students create authentic texts, they are communicating not just within the classroom but beyond it. If they have learned something important in the world, it is vital to give them the opportunity to do something about it. This is the heart of the text set approach.

In the chapters that follow, we will describe our work in four classrooms, implementing a text set approach across the content areas of language arts, social studies, science, and mathematics.

PART II

EXAMPLES
How To Read Part Two

I n the next four chapters, you're going to read about teachers using text sets in language arts, social studies, science, and math. In most cases, these are integrated explorations, merging and blending literacy and content-area learning. You can expect to read a lot about using texts of all genres and modalities in all of the content areas. Students will be reading, writing, listening, speaking, and engaging with meaning making throughout all four chapters. All of these chapters are about literacy learning, even when they are about teaching the American Revolution, adaptation, or multiplication.

Three different schools are represented in Part 2, and we partnered with teachers over the course of different school years, with slightly different, but parallel, structures for working together. Some units have been revised since we first worked on them. Some units are brand-new. You'll notice that regardless, at the conclusion of each chapter we have a "Notes for Next Year" section, because teaching with text sets is an ongoing process of reflecting and revising from year to year. We try to model that in this section, in naming the ways that teachers adapted the unit in the second year or the ideas they have for revision if they have not yet had a chance to reteach it.

We close each chapter with "Voices from the Classroom," where you have the opportunity to hear directly from the educators with whom we worked. No unit is perfect, and different students need different levels of support year to year. There are always going to be new ideas, new texts, and new ways to frame a unit. Hearing the educators' evolving thinking on each unit can give you and your teaching team a lens for your own curriculum trajectory.

Material in chapter 3 originally appeared in "Portraits of Perseverance: Creating Picturebook Biographies with Third Graders," by Erika Thulin Dawes, Mary Ann Cappiello, and Lorraine Magee with Jen Bryant and Melissa Sweet. *Language Arts* 96.3 (January 2019), pp. 153–166. Copyright 2019 by the National Council of Teachers of English. Used with permission.

Genre and Theme in Language Arts
Examining Life Story Through Picture Book Biography

I learned the steps of writing a biography, like notes, interviewing, watching over your interview, the writing and illustrating. I also learned that writing about someone is fun because it has a lot of steps and interesting facts that you can learn about the world and that person.

—Alex, Third-Grade Student

We have long been fascinated by picture book biographies, as an art form and as a powerful curricular tool. Crafted with careful attention to research, language, and image, picture book biographies are ideal mentor texts with high appeal for elementary students. To learn more about the potential of this genre, we collaborated with one of our graduate students, a third-grade teacher, to research this question: How can child readers' glimpse into the research and artistic processes related to picture book biographies deepen their understanding of the art and craft of biography and influence their writing of biographies?

This question shaped a six-week genre study of biography that we implemented in Charlotte's inclusive third-grade classroom composed of socioculturally, economically, and academically diverse students. The genre study included a deep dive into the work of award-winning author Jen Bryant and author-illustrator Melissa Sweet; an examination of a range of titles drawn from NCTE's Orbis Pictus Award for Outstanding Nonfiction and ALA's Robert F. Sibert Informational Book Medal and other valuable book lists; and student research and writing of original picture book biographies. Jen Bryant and Melissa Sweet agreed to collaborate with the students in a Skype interview and to participate in the analysis of student work to explore connections between the student creations and their own.

Establish Goals: What do you want for your students?

In this unit, the standards did not drive our instructional goals (see Figure 3.1), but we were confident that, throughout this genre study, students would be working toward meeting many language arts standards. If you review the ILA/NCTE Standards in Chapter 2, you will see that this project, in fact, meets all of these standards. Additionally, the study of biography is a recurring topic across the elementary school curriculum. But most important, we were confident that Charlotte's third-grade students would be fascinated by the life stories they would read across the unit and that exposure to these beautiful and interesting books would offer strong motivation to try writing their own.

FIGURE 3.1

A listing of the goals and outcomes for this unit.

GOALS	OUTCOMES
To conduct a genre study of picture book biographies, exposing students to a collection of quality picture book biographies representing diverse subjects	Students will read and analyze picture book biographies by author/illustrator collaborators and others representing underrepresented subjects
To present picture book biographies as constructed objects created through research and deliberate choices for text and illustration	Students will analyze the development of character, context, theme, and back matter across a range of picture book biographies
To engage students in writing and illustrating picture book biographies	Students will select a subject, interview their subject, and compose a picture book biography representation of their subject's life story

Find Texts: What are the best texts to help you meet your goals?

Books

We decided to focus on Jen Bryant and Melissa Sweet's collected work for a variety of reasons. For beginning third-grade readers, their picture book biographies are engaging, kid-friendly, and relatively accessible. After years of reading and reviewing picture book biographies, using them in classrooms, and teaching with them in our graduate courses, we know that their books

FIGURE 3.2

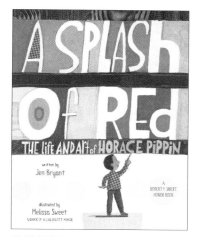

FIGURE 3.3

FIGURE 3.4

represent a high level of research and artistic decision making, as evidenced by their back matter. We have also watched their back matter develop over time, providing readers with greater insight into the research and creating processes with each book. Consistently, their picture book biographies provide equal space for the author's note and the illustrator's note. This recognition of equivalency is something that we have long admired; the illustrations are not just an "extra," but an inherent part of a well-researched picture book biography. These exceptionally well-written, well-crafted works of art have also been vetted by the field and have received numerous awards and honors, such as NCTE's Orbis Pictus Award for Outstanding Nonfiction. Finally, we have gotten to know both Jen and Melissa over the years, and we were excited to see what would happen when we brought their actual voices, not just their books, into the classroom.

We recognized that by selecting Jen and Melissa's picture books (see Figures 3.2–3.4), plus Melissa's (2011) *Balloons over Broadway: The True Story of the Puppeteer of the Macy's Thanksgiving Day Parade* (see Figure 3.5)

FIGURE 3.5

FIGURE 3.6

FIGURE 3.7

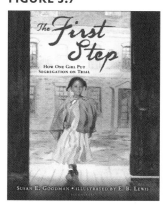

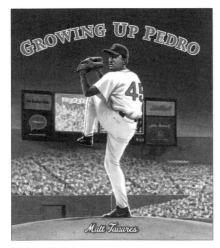

FIGURE 3.8

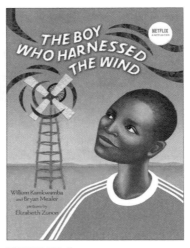

FIGURE 3.9

FIGURE 3.10

and doing a read-aloud of Melissa's (2016) chapter-length *Some Writer! The Story of E. B. White* (see Figure 3.6), we were focusing on five men, four of whom were white. In today's diverse classrooms, it is more important than ever to ensure that students have access to life stories that represent a full range of diversity and experiences. To balance the focus on white men in the mentor texts, we included a broader range of biography subjects to extend the set of mentor text (see Figures 3.7–3.10). We reviewed the lists of the NCTE Orbis Pictus Award for Outstanding Nonfiction for Children and the Association for Library Service to Children Robert F. Sibert Informational Book Medal to select a diverse range of picture book biographies to incorporate. Throughout the unit, these books extended the whole-class lessons. Students worked in partners, small groups, and individually to read and examine these texts as additional models.

Digital Texts

To supplement the books used across the unit, we sought digital texts that would support students as they crafted picture book biographies. We sought resources that would illuminate the processes involved in the composition of biography. The University of Michigan's Kerlan Collection includes an online exhibit of Melissa's process of creating *Balloons over Broadway* (**gallery .lib.umn.edu/exhibits/show/balloons-over-broadway**). We knew students would be fascinated to see the sketches and drafts that are included. The narrative structure of this online exhibit features the trial and error involved in the creation of a picture book biography.

We also searched for and found resources that would help the students prepare to interview community members (see Figure 3.11). We

Kirkus TV Interview with Melissa Sweet
www.youtube.com/watch?v=zEiJJIBC_ww

Mackin Educational: Jen Bryant: Melissa Sweet Collaboration: Interview on Process www.youtube.com/watch?v=PXlHKyXVESg

Reading Rockets: Bryan Collier on Process
www.readingrockets.org/books/interviews/collier

FIGURE 3.11
A collection of digital resources to support students as they prepared to conduct interviews.

located three online interviews that students would watch to learn more about interviews (as well as more about writing biographies).

Organize Texts for Instruction: How can we arrange the texts for critical thinking?

When mapping out this six-week genre study, we planned to engage these students with picture book biographies on multiple levels, embedding the study of biography into the reading and writing workshop structures with which they were familiar. We used two-hour-long (plus) time blocks during the day. Although we initially used the first block of time for reading activities (teacher read-aloud, small-group and partner reading) and the second to focus on writing (modeled writing and student independent writing), this became more fluid as the unit evolved. During the first few weeks, we focused more heavily on reading; then, as the focus shifted to student-written biographies, writing took on a stronger role (see Figure 3.12).

FIGURE 3.12 *This figure outlines the sequence of instruction for this six-week genre study of biography.*

WEEK	KEY QUESTIONS	READING WORKSHOP	WRITING WORKSHOP
1 **Scaffold**	What is biography? What is characterization? How do authors of biography develop character? Who can a biographer write about? What are we learning about how biographers do their research?	Anchor chart for character development Small-group reading of biographies using character cards and graphic organizers Character mapping	Quick write: someone you admire Examination of back matter: choosing a subject Teacher modeling of choosing a subject Selecting a subject and making a character map

WEEK	KEY QUESTIONS	READING WORKSHOP	WRITING WORKSHOP
2 Immersion	How do authors of biography develop historical context? How do authors of biography learn about their subjects? What are you learning about the process of conducting an interview? How do interview questions reveal details about subjects' lives?	Anchor chart examining historical context in text and illustration Small-group reading of biographies, making notes on historical context Timeline of biographies Creating a new illustration for a biography that includes historical context	Listening to online oral history interviews Examining author interview transcripts Teacher modeling of the development of interview questions Developing a list of possible interview questions Interviewing a classmate
3	What do we notice happening in the back matter? What can back matter tell us? How can back matter help us to know what to do when we are writing?	Anchor chart examining back matter Examining elements of back matter and finding examples: author's note, illustrator's note, timeline, etc. Developing interview questions for Jen and Melissa Skype interview with Jen and Melissa	Selecting and organizing questions for interviewing their subjects Model interview with the principal Practicing interviews with classmates
4	What did we learn about the writing and illustrating process from the interview with Jen and Melissa and an online exhibit of Melissa's process? What big ideas (or themes) emerge from Bryant and Sweet's books, and how does this connect with what we are learning about how they do research?	Using a video clip from the interview with Jen and Melissa to practice note making Explore an online exhibit of Melissa's notes, sketches, and drafts for *Balloons over Broadway*	Identifying a process for working on student-composed biographies Conducting interviews Making notes from videos of interviews Discussing big ideas or theme

WEEK	KEY QUESTIONS	READING WORKSHOP	WRITING WORKSHOP
5–6 Extension	How do authors of biographies use words in engaging and exciting ways to teach readers about their characters? How does back matter reflect the processes of researching, writing, and illustrating?	Developing and sharing a character map for the subject of your biography Anchor chart to examine how authors begin and end their biographies Rereading biographies to notice "great sentences" Revisiting back matter	Drafting and revising biographies Teacher modeling of developing back matter Writing back matter Illustrating biographies

Scaffold: Identify Biography

Within the reading workshop structure, we mapped out three kinds of reading experiences, moving from teacher modeling to small group to individual reading experiences. To foster whole-group discussion, Charlotte engaged in a read-aloud of *Some Writer!*, Melissa Sweet's 2016 chapter-length biography of E. B. White (see Figure 3.6). Spreading the reading out over a three-week period, she used a document camera to project the text as she read. As she read each chapter, she focused discussion on a particular aspect of life story and recorded student responses on chart paper. This whole-group introduction to biography, the characteristics of the genre, and the processes of composing and illustrating biographies laid the foundation for a broader exploration of picture book biographies.

Immersion: Exploring the Genre of Picture Book Biography

Each day, following the whole-group read-aloud, students moved into small-group or partner activities. To immerse students more fully in Jen and Melissa's books in the Solar System instructional model (Figure 3.13), we obtained multiple copies of *A River of Words: The Story of William Carlos Williams* (Bryant 2008), *Balloons over Broadway: The True Story of the Puppeteer of the Macy's Thanksgiving Day Parade* (Sweet 2011), *A Splash of Red: The Life and Art of Horace*

FIGURE 3.13 *The Solar System model consists of the Jen Bryant and Melissa Sweet's picture book biography collaborations.*

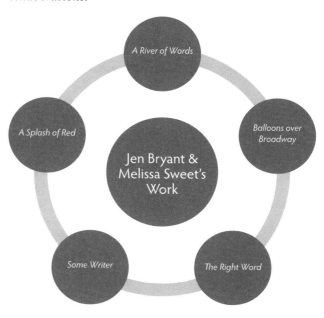

FIGURE 3.14 *Students read a variety of picture book biographies during reading workshop.*

Pippin (Bryant 2013), and *The Right Word: Roget and His Thesaurus* (Bryant 2014) (see Figures 3.2–3.5).

These titles were initially read aloud, then students worked in small groups, reading and rereading these books and making notes about the information they gleaned from the text and illustrations. During independent reading time, students made selections from the collection of diverse picture book biographies (see Figure 3.16). Students most often read these books with partners, using the same graphic organizers to note how the authors and illustrators of these picture book biographies used text and words to convey life story (see Figures 3.14 and 3.15).

From an initial analysis of Jen and Melissa's titles, we knew we wanted to unpack four essential elements of life story with these third graders: character, context, theme, and back matter. Character and theme are strongly conveyed through words and pictures and each of these biographies provides just enough historical context to understand the subject without overwhelming the reader with background

FIGURE 3.15
Students analyze characterization in Balloons over Broadway.

Characterization in Biography

Your Name: _____   Title of Biography: _____

Directions: Write down what you know about the subject of your biography (the person the biography is about). What is he or she like? How do you know? Find evidence in the word and pictures, and write that down.

What Do We Know?	How Do We Know It? What Do the *Words* Say?	How Do We Know It? What Do the *Pictures* Show?
whthe he was oller he wnat to londen	"where he was oller he whnt to londen"	Tom's going to londen
He got elaten anz camals anz bears	macys even oghne to bring in bears eleten and camals	It shows bears and camals
becase thay yorked ther thay nad to miss ther holoday	"Thay missed the...	
HC is Joyful		he smiles

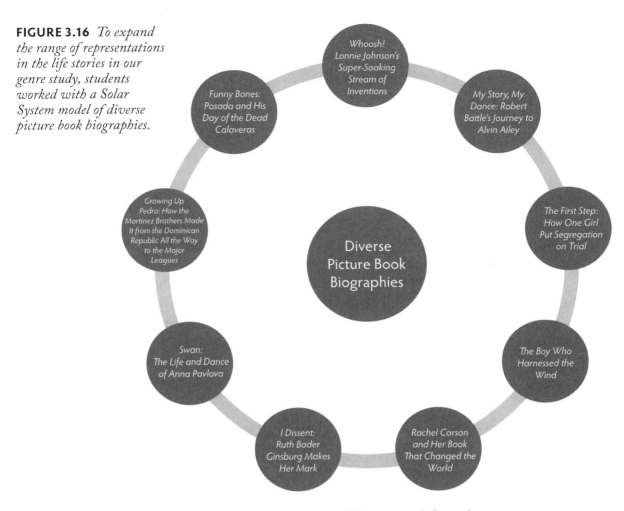

FIGURE 3.16 *To expand the range of representations in the life stories in our genre study, students worked with a Solar System model of diverse picture book biographies.*

information. For young readers, the development of Bryant and Sweet's back matter widens the window into their research and artistic processes. The more that they can learn about how the book they just read was created, the more they can understand picture book biographies as a series of decisions made by the writer and illustrator. This concept lies at the heart of our work with third graders. How much can they learn as readers by reading the back matter of picture book biographies? What do they absorb from the back matter as researchers and writers that informs their own writing and illustrating processes, both consciously and unconsciously?

CHARACTERIZATION

Characterization is at the heart of biography. Betty Carter (2003) writes that "as a reviewer, I look for books that present individuals as people readers might *want* to know rather than those they *should* know" (170) and that "the best children's biographies inspire curiosity" (171). Collectively, Bryant and Sweet make William Carlos Williams, Tony Sarg, Horace Pippin,

How do authors develop character?

What do we know?	What do the words say?	What do the pictures show?
Tony was creative and inventive.	• "His dad, so impressed, never made Tony do another chore." • "Tony Sarg loved to figure out how to make things move."	• Tony connected a pulley to the door. • Tony used a pulley to control a puppet. • Diagram
Tony was careful.	"Tony did not know if everything would go as planned."	The thought bubbles showed him thinking a few steps ahead.

FIGURE 3.17 *An anchor chart noting character development in* Balloons over Broadway

Peter Roget, and E. B. White fascinating *and* appealing while they share valuable information about each man's achievements and character.

To begin, we posed this question to the students: "How do authors of biography develop character?" Their responses were recorded on an anchor chart (see Figure 3.17). Each of Jen and Melissa's biographies starts with the subject's childhood and moves forward in time. Three adopt a chronological narrative, in which the climactic moment highlights the most well-known achievement: Sarg's successful balloon puppets after several years of trial and error; Pippin's ability to paint after losing the use of one arm during World War I; and Roget's (2008) publication of his lifelong lists in the form of his thesaurus. *A River of Words: The Story of William Carlos Williams* differs slightly in that it primarily follows a chronological exposition, detailing Williams's work as a doctor and a poet. For each subject's childhood, we are introduced to interests or characteristics that play an important role in his adult life. Through words and images, readers observe the innate curiosity of these men, the questions they asked, and the trial and error embedded in their work. The four picture book biographies end not with death but with the subject at work.

When we moved from whole-group read-aloud to small-group and individual reading of additional biographies, it became evident that students needed additional modeling of language to describe character traits. Noting that the concept of character was either too abstract or that students lacked descriptive language to reflect their understandings, we developed a deck of character cards (for example, *hardworking, persistent, brave, kind*). Students used the cards as prompts to consider whether these descriptors could apply to the subject of a book. Charlotte wrote about the character cards in our reflection journal:

> Students loved using the character trait cards to support their thinking, and it seemed to be exactly what they needed to focus on how the author/illustrator was using words and pictures for characterization. The discussions about the traits that did not match were so helpful and pointed students in the right direction.

FIGURE 3.18 *Students created a character map to explore the character traits of Horace Pippin.*

FIGURE 3.19 *Students created a character map to explore the character traits of Tony Sarg.*

> I overheard things like "He definitely wasn't lazy . . . do we have one that's kind of the opposite of that?" Many of the students elevated their thinking today in a way that will benefit them as readers and writers.

At the end of the first week, we also introduced character mapping, inviting small groups to create large portraits of Horace Pippin or Tony Sarg and to surround their portrait with text that described the subject, as well as illustrations of objects that were significant for the subject (see Figures 3.18 and 3.19). The character maps drawn by the students addressed both details about the characters (appearances, favorite activities, and artifacts) and character traits, previewing our discussion of theme to follow.

Charlotte noted the success of the character mapping activity in the Reflection Journal:

> The character mapping was such an engaging activity, and so many students demonstrated thinking in a new way using the visuals. Some highlights:
>
> • Written on a poster: "He was a problem solver because he figured out how to use his hurt arm."

- Written on a poster: "perseverant: he had to start over many times."
- A group added red dots to their design of Horace Pippin's shirt because "we just had to add a splash of red!"
- Students drew the first paint set Horace Pippin received because "we think that sort of started him being a real artist."
- Students drew balloons near Tony Sarg to represent the idea he had to put the strings on the bottom of the puppets and fill them with air.

The engagement level today felt totally different. Students who had previously had difficulty writing down their thinking showed it in new ways using the visuals.

CONTEXT

Historical context plays an important part in bringing the past to life in biography. "Many children may find life in another era as strange and foreign as life on Mars. Consequently, biographers must help them understand the historical context that sets the stage for the story" (Carter 2003, 166). How much context is needed within the words and pictures and book format to help young readers make sense of the subject? When there is not enough context, the subject cannot be fully understood. Too much context drowns young readers in details.

During the second week of the unit, we focused on context, inviting students to consider how authors of biography offer readers a sense of the events and conditions at work in the lives of their subjects. To consider written and visual techniques, we again used anchor charts, this time posing the question: How does the author/illustrator use text and illustration to provide readers with information about the time period? (See Figure 3.20.) During read-alouds, small-group work, and partner reads, students examined the texts, noting language use, how characters dressed, artifacts, and text references that provided evidence of the time period. The students' conversations often focused on the differences between the lives of the subjects and

FIGURE 3.20 *An anchor chart noting the development of context in* Some Writer!

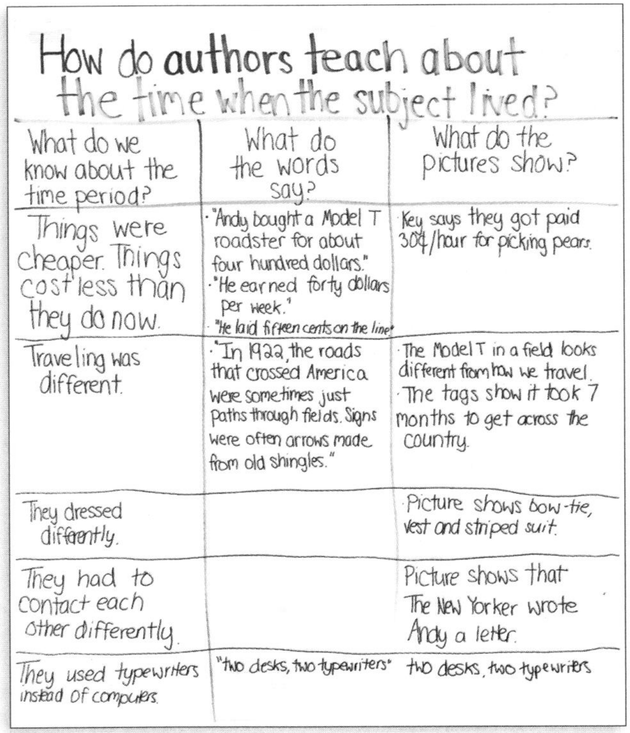

their own; for example, typewriters were compared with the laptops of today (see Figure 3.21). Because we were not examining a set of books to explore a time period or understand a single event, we did not go further than noting the differences that established a historical context; as new third graders, they had little experience studying history in social studies in the primary grades. For young readers, historical context gives them a larger world into which they can situate their understanding of the subject.

Charlotte's notes in the Reflection Journal indicated that students were using context to make connections across Jen and Melissa's biographies:

> It was great to see students exploring the timeline in *A River of Words*. My favorite quote came when a small group read about the Model T being created. They then said, "Hmm, who else do we know who had a Model T?" and connected to *Some Writer!* In this way, they determined that White and Williams could have been alive at the same time based on the cars that existed in both texts.

FIGURE 3.21 *Students had a chance to explore a typewriter just like the one E. B. White might have used.*

THEME

In the final weeks of the unit, we focused on theme. All four picture book biographies share the theme of perseverance, exemplified by subjects who pose questions, take risks, experiment, and overcome challenges from childhood to adulthood. Because the students had very firmly latched onto the idea of characterization, their conversations circled around the commitments, values, and key moments for the subjects of the biographies—what we ultimately named as "the big ideas" of the book. These discussions grew out of a focus on process, which included a look at back matter and our interview with Jen and Melissa. Students considered which aspects of the character's life were *selected* by the author/illustrator to be included in the biography. They discussed the role of choice in the composition process— what to put in and what to leave out. We were striving toward the idea that author's choices reflect the aspects of their subjects' lives that they view as most compelling. Theme emerges from the synthesis of the book in its totality: words, images, front and back matter, and book design. Although theme can be very abstract for young readers to label, they are often able to understand the theme of a text intuitively. In this unit of study, understanding theme grew out of understanding characterization; there was a clear connection in these biographies between the character development offered by the authors and the themes that emerged in the subjects' lives.

BACK MATTER

Jen and Melissa's combined work provides a fascinating overview of the development of back matter in picture book biographies over the last decade. From the start, their books provide equal attention to the author's note and the illustrator's note. Over time, they move from a reporting stance, sharing additional information about the subject, to a more nuanced discussion of the process: their personal connection to the subject, shared collaborative research, wide range of source materials, and the experts who supported their work. For young readers, the development of Jen and Melissa's back matter provides a widening of the window into their research and artistic processes. The more that they can learn about how the book they just read was created, the more they can understand picture book biographies as a series of decisions made by the writer and illustrator. Charlotte noted in the Reflection Journal:

FIGURE 3.22 *An anchor chart reflecting students' understanding of what back matter may consist of.*

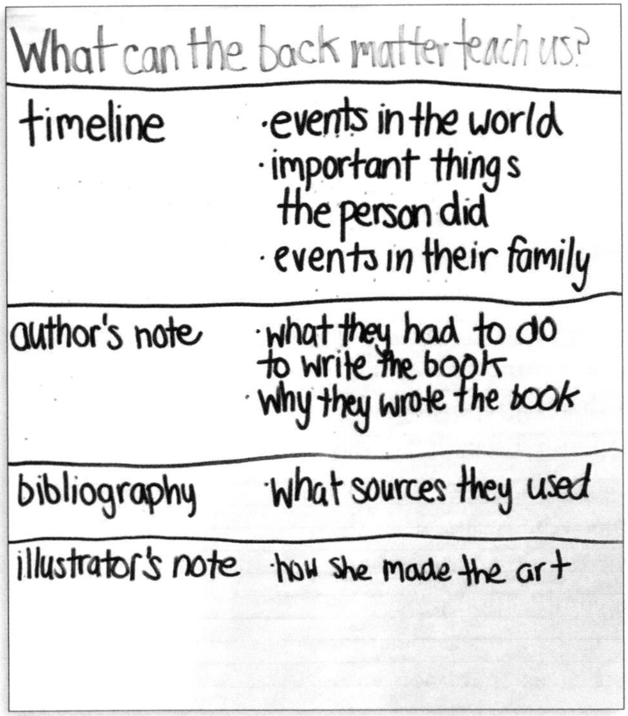

> Students enjoyed exploring the back matter in the books they had already read. They really enjoyed returning to the familiar "friends" that are Horace Pippin, Tony Sarg, and Peter Roget. They noticed many ways in which Jen Bryant had to do research for her writing—especially in *A Splash of Red*. They enjoyed the descriptions of her travel to different museums and important places.

Throughout the unit, we drew students' attention explicitly to the back matter of the texts that they were exploring in reading workshop. We asked them to notice the kinds of information that the back matter provided and to think about how this information was related

FIGURE 3.23
Students examine the back matter, recording notes on a graphic organizer.

FIGURE 3.24
Students sort segments of back matter, identifying sections that discuss authors' and illustrators' processes.

to the primary text of the book (see Figure 3.22). We framed this discussion by our now familiar concepts of character, context, and theme development (see Figure 3.23). During the third week of the unit, we asked students to categorize the kinds of information provided in Jen and Melissa's back matter (see Figure 3.24).

Charlotte notes in the Reflection Journal:

The students did an excellent job sorting the back matter from *Balloons over Broadway*, *A Splash of Red*, and *A River of Words*. I made two copies of each element of the back matter (because many of the elements belonged in more than one category), passed them out, and asked kids to find the partner who had the same piece of back matter as them. They had great conversations about what they noticed, and really enjoyed returning to the same books again. They were very easily able to distinguish between back matter that taught about character and

back matter that told about the writing process. They had more difficulty spotting back matter that told about context, aside from a timeline. We talked about how the author's notes in both *A River of Words* and *Balloons over Broadway* talked about what life was like during that time period, so the author's notes belonged in both the character and context sections.

Extension: The Processes of Biographers

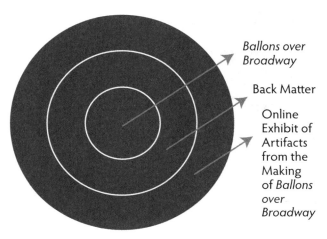

Ballons over Broadway

Back Matter

Online Exhibit of Artifacts from the Making of *Ballons over Broadway*

FIGURE 3.25 *A Tree Ring model for* Balloons over Broadway *engages students in a close examination of Melissa's source matter and process notes.*

Charlotte also gave the students the opportunity to explore *Balloons over Broadway* in a Tree Ring model (Figure 3.25) with the goal of expanding students' understandings of how biographers craft life story. Students moved from the primary narrative of the book, to the back matter, and then to the online exhibit curated by the Kerlan Collection in Minneapolis, with materials donated to the collection by Melissa Sweet.

Some students simply enjoyed looking at the digital notes, the sketches, and the questions that Melissa posed as she brainstormed, researched, and wrote and illustrated the book. Others were able to identify that some of the early sketches helped her to move her thinking forward on the manuscript.

Create New Texts: What are the new texts created by students?

As students read, discussed, and analyzed Jen and Melissa's titles and the additional books included in the unit, they engaged in rich discussions of the process of writing biographies. While these experiences unfolded, we used the writing block as a time to model the steps that students would undertake to write their own picture book biographies.

In our initial conversations about the unit of study, we explored two options for student-composed biographies. Students might select a contemporary local subject with whom they could schedule an interview or they might select a historical or a less accessible subject about whom they would need to conduct research. During the first week, Charlotte asked students to brainstorm a list of people about whom they would like to write a biography. When their list focused primarily on community members, Charlotte immediately took steps to schedule interviews with local people who fit the descriptors offered up by the students: the town historian, high school athletes, authors, musicians, and so on.

To prepare students to conduct their interviews, we modeled the process of asking questions through several pathways (see Figure 3.26). As students developed their list of questions in preparation for interviewing the subjects of their biographies, Charlotte had one student interview her. Watching the interview allowed students to see the difference between their weak and strong questions. We also used multimedia resources, watching videos of children interviewing adults and following along with online transcripts of author interviews. Charlotte offered additional modeling by bringing in the school principal. While she interviewed the principal, students practiced recording with iPads. Students even made cue cards for themselves, reminding them to look their interview subjects in the eyes while asking questions (see Figure 3.27).

Charlotte described these practice experiences in the Reflection Journal:

> The mock interview in the afternoon went very well. Students generated some great questions for a student to ask me. After the interview, students were able to decide which questions had been really helpful in giving them information as biographers and illustrators. They were also able to decide which questions hadn't given them much information. I was thrilled that they were able to see that questions like "What's your favorite animal?" may not be worth asking during

Types of Questions
We can ask about...

- age when you started
- why they chose that job
- family
- challenges
- how they got that job
- special objects
- where they grew up
- inspiration
- favorites
- things in history (what life was like)
- job

FIGURE 3.26 *An anchor chart created as students brainstormed the kinds of interview questions they could ask.*

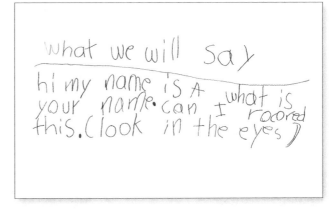

FIGURE 3.27 *Students created cue cards to prepare for their interviews.*

FIGURE 3.28 *Our Skype interview with Jen and Melissa.*

FIGURE 3.29 *Students interview a high school athlete.*

the interviews (unless, of course, it's relevant for that subject). The students seemed to be engaged in watching the mock interview, and I hope they hold on to their takeaways!

Students prepared for their Skype interview with Jen and Melissa by developing a list of questions; when their initial draft yielded questions that again felt too generic to be useful, Charlotte skillfully guided them back to the books they had read. Revisiting the books resulted in a much more refined list of questions that focused on the writing process and how/why Jen and Melissa developed a deep interest in the subjects of their books. The Skype interview was fascinating, lasting just over an hour and offering students great insight into how Jen and Melissa carry out their work (see Figure 3.28). A transcript of the Skype interview became yet another model for students as we referred to their advice for writing biographies.

All this practice with question writing and interviewing contributed to the success of the student interviews. Students were well prepared and confident when they sat down with the community members who were the subject of their biographies (see Figures 3.29 and 3.30). Students worked in teams to ensure that the interview was properly documented and that all the planned questions were asked. Charlotte described the experience in the Reflection Journal:

> The students spoke with their subjects for a long time, and most ended up asking far more questions than they had previously listed. One group said, "We only had twelve questions, but we ended up asking thirty-two!" This was due to the great conversations that developed and the ability of students to add questions as they went. These additional questions did not seem superfluous, but instead seemed more targeted to the lives and experiences of the subject.

During the final weeks of the unit, the students focused fully on drafting and revising. Because we had recorded the interviews, students were able to watch and listen a second time, making notes about important content. Throughout their composition process, they served as models for each other, sharing drafts and offering suggestions. Charlotte continued modeling by discussing how she moved from interview data to written text. The students further explored the character traits they hoped to convey about their subject by drawing more character maps (see Figure 3.31). Some students then chose to include these maps in their back matter. Students had constant access to all the biographies used in the

FIGURE 3.30 *An interview with the town historian.*

FIGURE 3.31 *Character mapping as a prewriting strategy.*

FIGURE 3.32 *Using her interview notes as reference, a student creates a draft.*

FIGURE 3.33 *Notes and drafts reflect a biography in process.*

FIGURE 3.34 *Charlotte holds a writing conference with the mentor text close by for easy reference.*

unit for further inspiration. They frequently referred to these mentor texts as they worked (see Figures 3.32–3.34).

Becoming Biographers

As the unit progressed, students grew as both readers and writers of biography. Students who read one or fewer biographies over the past year were soon reading multiple picture book biographies each week. Students self-selected biographies during independent reading time and engaged in deep thinking as readers of biography during reading workshop. As the volume of students' reading grew, the volume of their writing grew as well. For many students, their biographies were the largest writing projects they had ever completed; some wrote upward of twenty and thirty pages.

At the conclusion of the unit, Charlotte administered a survey and conducted individual interviews with the students. Compared with their responses at the beginning of the unit, students had a changed understanding of what biographies can be. Their reflections also revealed ways students had grown as researchers. Many students named the interview process as an area where they had learned new skills. Students spoke to the importance of listening skills while interviewing. Kylee explained that "it's really important to listen to what the person is saying and pay attention because if you don't pay attention you won't know what to write." Travis said, "You need to listen to the person that you're interviewing." Preston focused on the types of questions to ask during an interview: "I learned that in an interview, you don't want to make them feel so pressured that they don't tell you what you want them to tell you." Students recognized the key role of research as the first step in creating a biography.

Within their biographies, students emulated motifs and craft moves shown in Jen and Melissa's works. Kylee noted the ways in which mentor texts helped her to craft a stronger biography: "Reading biographies can really help you if you're planning to write one because they can teach you about back matter and if you want it to be interesting. Real authors teach you that from books, and if you read biographies, you can have a better biography." Reagan explained that a step for authors is "reading other biographies for advice" and a step for illustrators is "looking at pictures in other biographies for advice." The value of mentor texts was tangible for students as they navigated the process of becoming biographers.

> It was evident that the students were familiar with the parts
> and concepts of a book: title page; dedication; table of contents;
> chapters; story; back matter including thank yous, author notes,
> and timelines. Each of these components help organize a book,
> and give layer and depth to the story. It took me decades of making
> books before I understood how to craft a biography, and it was
> inspiring to see how the students gleaned these concepts from
> existing biographies. (Melissa Sweet , personal communication,
> December 29, 2017)

After we completed the unit, we reviewed the student-composed biographies, looking to see whether we could identify literary devices and visual and written motifs in the student writing that were similar to those identified through our analysis of the titles. At the same time, we asked Jen and Melissa to read the biographies. We were curious whether our review and their review would align. As we read across the student biographies, we identified common elements in the students' writing that could be directly connected to their models they had experienced. These elements included titles, narrative structures, characterization, theme, illustrations, conclusions, and back matter.

The use of Jen and Melissa's collected works as mentor texts is visible in many of the student-written biographies. These instances of imitation appear as early as the title pages. Prior to this unit, students had primarily been exposed to biographies that used the subject's name as the title. The mentor texts we had used modeled other possibilities. Students worked to emulate these titles in their own writing. Student-written titles included *Books in the Library*; *Get the Scoop, Billy!*; *Counseling with Fun*; *Books, Books, and More Books*; and *A Little Girl's Dream*. Demonstrating similarities to *Balloons over Broadway: The True Story of the Puppeteer of the Macy's Thanksgiving Day Parade* (Sweet 2011) and *The Right Word: Roget and His*

Thesaurus (Bryant 2014), the student-written titles often hinted toward the narrative through which the biography would be framed.

Students also emulated the chronological narrative format seen in Melissa's *Balloons over Broadway: The True Story of the Puppeteer of the Macy's Thanksgiving Day Parade* and Jen and Melissa's *A Splash of Red: The Life and Art of Horace Pippin* (2013) and *A River of Words: The Story of William Carlos Williams* (2008). Their narratives included sequencing words to indicate the timing of each event they featured. Students also used visuals to show their characters growing older, which demonstrated an understanding of the role illustrations can play in conveying the passage of time.

During their interviews, students had asked about turning points in their subjects' lives. These key events became climactic moments in the student-written biographies. Gemma wrote about the moment her subject realized she could combine her love of science and her love of writing by composing nonfiction texts. Leah wrote about when her subject received a phone call with her first job offer. Alex wrote about the moment his subject decided he wouldn't let his disability stop him from pursuing his dream. This emphasis on key moments as a component of narrative storytelling is drawn directly from what students saw in Jen and Melissa's collected works.

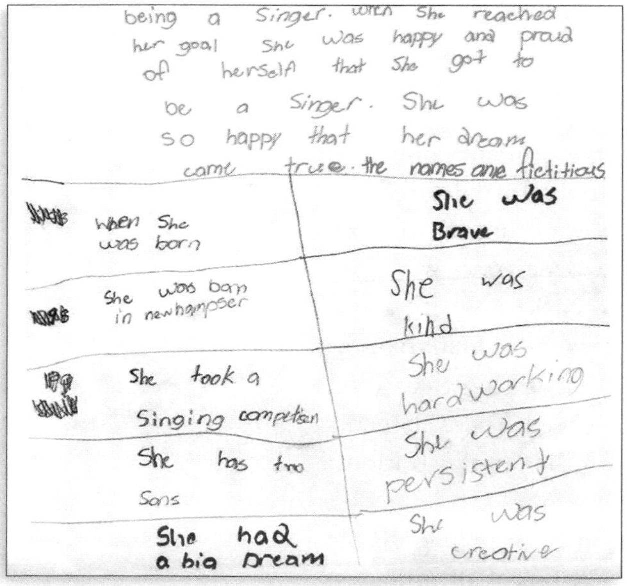

In life story, character and theme are intertwined. Characterization is typically more descriptive, while themes are more abstract representations of patterns in a subject's life. Authors help readers to understand their subjects by offering descriptions of everyday actions; everyday actions build into life trajectories and give rise to themes. In the mentor texts used in this unit, themes were frequently represented in character traits, such as creativity, perseverance, persistence, and resilience. Discussion about characterization and theme during reading workshop influenced the students' development of interview questions as they prepared to compose biographies themselves. Students crafted questions that would help them get to know their subjects' interests, habits, and key moments. In her author's note, Lainey reveals her thinking about character, both at the level of informational detail and stretching from character traits toward theme (Figure 3.35).

FIGURE 3.35 *Excerpt from an author's note reflecting character development and theme.*

Jen and Melissa's biographies used throughout the unit featured characters who lived in past time periods. Because the third graders' subjects

FIGURES 3.36–3.37 *A student captures a turning point in the life of her subject.*

are alive now, context was more subtle and less necessary for the readers' understanding of their subject. Context was provided through details about their subjects' life trajectories and circumstances, often through illustrations.

Students used Melissa's illustrations as mentors for accomplishing context. Many of their illustrations emulated her artistic style. Student-created illustrations included the motifs of circles and swirls (see Figures 3.36 and 3.37). This illustration includes a depiction of the tools of each occupation being considered by the subject, providing additional context for this important choice. Reviewing the students' work, Melissa observed:

> As an illustrator, I'm always looking for different ways to impart information to make the book and subject come alive. In [the students'] books, the illustrators used perspective, points of view, sequential art, varying spot art, and full-page pictures, large and small lettering, speech bubbles—all visual and storytelling devices that keeps the reader's interest. They captured exactly what I do every day in illustrating picture books. (personal communication, December 29, 2017)

FIGURES 3.38– FIGURE 3.39 *Establishing context through the use of illustration*

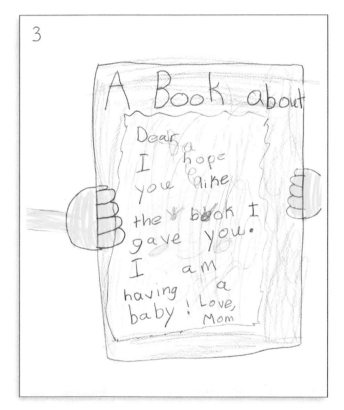

To establish the context of one subject's life, a student carefully embedded a context clue in an illustration before she included the details in text. In one illustration, the subject, a future librarian, is a child reading on the floor of her bedroom. In her doorway stands her pregnant mother. On the next page, the reader discovers, through both text and illustration, that the subject's mother used a book to tell her that she was going to be an older sister. (See Figures 3.38 and 3.39.)

Students drew further on Jen and Melissa's works by incorporating the theme of perseverance. In their interviews, students asked about times their subjects experienced challenge. This overarching theme became visible in the student-written biographies through narration, dialogue, and illustration. In the narration and dialogue, student words included:

- "She had to go to school again which really worried her because she thought if she wouldn't be up to the challenge. But after a lot of work-work-work she finally reached her goal." —Gemma

- "She had to do lots and lots of practice. Even with so much practice she still wasn't perfect. But she kept on practicing for a long time and now she's a professional singer." —Ava

- "When he was on the team he was the smallest on the team and he said it's not about the dog in the fight it's about the fight in the dog." —Andrew

In visuals, students drew situations in which the subjects faced obstacles and then kept going. Reagan illustrated the moments of stage fright leading up to her subject's first concert performance (see Figures 3.40 and 3.41). Devin illustrated the grueling physical exercises his

FIGURES 3.40–3.41 *In this student example, the illustrations highlight the subject's perseverance in carrying on despite experiencing stage fright.*

subject completed while trying out for a sports team. Students made use of facial expressions, thought bubbles, and physical stances to demonstrate perseverance. With the words and illustrations working together, students were able to convey theme in their stories.

Students had noticed how Melissa's illustrations accomplished two goals: first, conveying theme, context, and characterization in conjunction with the text, and second, making each page visually appealing. Students used her illustrations as mentors for accomplishing the same work in their own biographies. As a result, many of the students' illustrations echo Melissa's artistic style. Some even included the motifs of circles and swirls (see Figures 3.36 and 3.37). Students also made the choice to include illustrations that zoomed in on the subject's hands. Other illustrations zoomed out to provide more context for a scene. Sweet's illustrations in *A Splash of Red: The Life and Art of Horace Pippin* (Bryant 2013) provided models for both of these illustration strategies.

After students were exposed to Jen and Melissa's recurring motif of ending with the subject at work, many of them chose to use a similar craft move to end their own biographies. Visuals on the final pages show a librarian smiling behind a desk, a singer on stage at a concert, an author holding a pencil, and a newspaper reporter typing up his latest story. The accompanying narration reminds readers of typical actions or catchphrases of the subject:

- "And if you go to Code Institute Library you might just see Mrs. Donna at her desk helping kids, typing, or just reading." —Kylee

- "And if you see Billy Baker he just might say 'don't stop at challenges'" (see Figure 3.42). —Alex

- "If you look at his office you will see him writing his stories." —Blake

Each of these endings are reminiscent of *A Splash of Red: The Life and Art of Horace Pippin* (Bryant 2013), which ends with "If you stood outside his house, late at night, you might see him leaning toward his easel, his left hand holding up his right, painting the pictures in his mind" (n.p.) (see Figure 3.43). By ending with the subjects at work, students make a deliberate choice to provide characterization of their subjects and to echo theme as they conclude their narratives.

Students' perceptions of the purpose of back matter also changed over the course of the unit. Prior to our exploration of Jen and Melissa's back matter, many students had skipped over the back matter upon finishing a nonfiction text. By the end of the unit, students saw back matter as a place to learn more about both the biographer's process and the subject. As Blake explained in a post-unit interview, "I learned that in back matter

FIGURE 3.42 *The theme of perseverance is expressed in the final page of this student's biography.*

FIGURE 3.43 *The conclusion of* A Splash of Red: The Life and Art of Horace Pippin, *written by Jen Bryant and illustrated by Melissa Sweet.*

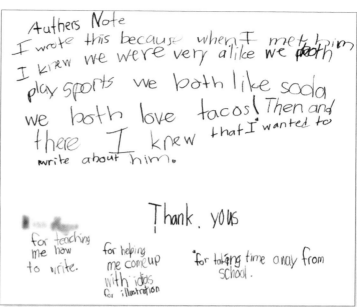

FIGURES 3.44–3.45 *In these author's notes, the students describe their research process and thank their collaborators.*

you can tell more stuff about the book if it doesn't fit in. If it was about when Ruby Bridges went to school, in the back matter you could tell stuff about what happened after she went to school or her job or her husband." Students included back matter in the biographies they composed. In most cases, students included an author's note. These author notes offered additional information about their subject and acknowledgments of classmates with whom they worked as they interviewed, made notes, and drafted their biographies (see Figures 3.44 and 3.45). Students continued to reference back matter in new nonfiction books throughout the school year.

> Every student writer seemed to understand that they needed to give credit to their sources and to share their research paths and experiences with their readers. Their methods and structure varied greatly, but all of them acknowledged some combination of their illustrators, the cooperation of the subjects themselves and their family members. I think this is such a valuable writing experience for them to have, because now they fully realize that no one creates a biography alone . . . it's always a matter of trust, communication, relationships, and working together as a team. (Jen Bryant, personal communication, December 28, 2017)

Back matter in picture book biographies can show the large number of people that play a part in creating just one book. As we engaged with

Bryant and Sweet's back matter, students grew their understanding of the writing process. When writing their own back matter, students thanked their interview partners, the students who filmed the interviews, and peers who reviewed their work. Although reading Bryant and Sweet's back matter and interviewing them showed students that collaboration is a key part of the writing and illustrating process, writing their own biographies allowed students to experience collaboration firsthand.

Mentor Processes

We began our work with Charlotte with the goal of formally researching the role of mentor texts and back matter in student writing. The students' writings confirmed that they could and did use well-written picture book biographies as models for their own writing. But it also went one step further, affirming the importance of the mentor *processes* modeled by children's authors and illustrators. Over the weeks of exploration, the students developed deep connections with Jen and Melissa's four picture book biographies. Through the repeated readings of the four core biographies, students had the opportunity to know the books deeply. The appeal of these books helped to spark students' curiosity to learn more about the subjects' lives and how the creators of these biographies carried out their research, writing, and illustrating. Our conversations repeatedly explored *what* the writing conveyed; *how* the author/illustrator employed text and image to create meaning; and *why* the text and images moved us as readers. Students considered voice and theme across the genre, developing the disciplinary literacies of language arts.

In this unit, texts served as mentors, but we also drew upon the author and illustrator's descriptions of their craft. The close study of Jen and Melissa's picture books over time, the students' familiarity with the texts, their examination of the back matter, and an opportunity to ask questions directly to the author and the illustrator offered students insights into the decision-making *processes* of the biographers. These insights offered students strategies for composition. They were immediately able to apply what they were learning to their own writing. In effect, the authors and illustrators became their writing coaches. We were fortunate to have access to these authors, and although direct contact is ideal, it is important to note that in addition to back matter, we often have access to authors and illustrators through online interviews, blog entries, and examples of their work in process.

As a consequence of this unit, the students reached a deeper understanding of the processes *involved in* creating biography, not just *the attributes of* biography. Perhaps even more compelling is that in the process of learning how to write biography, these students also learned more about their community and about the human experience. As Melissa observed,

> Ultimately, [the students'] stories showed me the students not only understood the process of making a book, but had empathy and compassion for the people they interviewed. To have these insights as young writers and artists is a gift to all of us. (personal communication, December 29, 2017.)

This is truly what we hope for in language arts instruction, that students will learn the power of language it all its forms to support us to make sense of our world and to honor our experiences and those of others.

Notes for Next Year

Although we were all significantly impressed by what these beginning-of-the-year third graders were able to accomplish in their reading and writing across this biography genre study, we considered what changes we might make to enhance the experience when repeating the unit the following year. Our reflections centered around writing instruction that would best support students as developing writers.

In the final weeks of the unit, Charlotte noted in the Reflection Journal:

> Looking ahead to Thursday's lesson on language, I'm thinking about what I would do differently if I were teaching this unit again! Along the way, many different students noticed language that stood out to them. Just today, a student pointed out the phrase in the lead of *The Right Word* in which Jen Bryant uses the word "clattered"—the student focused on this word and discussed with her group how it made her feel like she was in Switzerland with Roget. If I were teaching this unit again, I would have had students add those sentences/phrases to a "reading graffiti" chart where we could collect sentences we admired. Then, we could revisit them for a language lesson.

Charlotte's reflection highlights the fact that we had focused so thoroughly on character, context, and theme that we had not paid explicit attention to language use in the way that we might otherwise have done when using mentor texts. Her suggestion of posting an anchor chart for interesting and effective language use that could be added to across the unit strikes a good compromise. The characteristics of biography writing could remain the focus of the unit and more general stylistic choices could be recognized and explicitly discussed. In the example we shared, we focused on the language arts disciplinary literacies of theme and genre. In the future, we would include more attention to voice.

We also wondered about the timing of this unit during the school year. The curriculum for third grade includes a personal narrative unit. What would have happened if this unit preceded the biography writing? Were there strategies for voice and theme that students could have learned about and practiced when writing about their own lives that could have strengthened their biography writing? It's hard to know. We often assume that children can learn more about the writing process when writing about their own lives, but we suspect motivation to write plays a strong role. Charlotte's students were all in for this project—the opportunity to interview and represent the life stories of their community members challenged and engaged them. The length and depth of their writing reflects their interest in the project. We had a timeline for this project, but it would be interesting to see what would happen if this were one of the last units for the school year rather than the first.

The next time Charlotte teaches this unit, she plans to collaborate with the art teacher at school. At the onset, we had big plans to support students to create multimedia illustrations, as Melissa does. Time constraints prevented us from achieving this goal, but we look forward to seeing what students might create next time around.

VOICES FROM THE CLASSROOM *Charlotte, Third-Grade Teacher*

When our biography genre study began in the fall of third grade, I never imagined the lasting impact it would have on my students' journeys as readers, writers, and researchers. At the conclusion of the school year, I moved to fourth grade with the same students, which allowed me to see firsthand the ways the study of biography paid dividends throughout future reading and writing units.

Prior to the start of our genre study, many of the readers in my classroom had minimal exposure to biography. Through an exploration of high-quality texts, they fell in love with biography as a genre. Students were enthralled by life stories. Exploration of biographies became widespread during independent reading time. This love of life story continued as students moved on to fourth grade, with many students seeking out new biography releases and asking me for biography recommendations.

Within their reading of biographies, students found an opportunity to consider what back matter can teach us. Students demonstrated the same attention to back matter in later nonfiction units. Readers placed value in authors' explanations of their research processes and saw back matter as a tool for exploring both content and author's craft. Although back matter had previously been skipped by many readers, students began to see the value in exploring the additional information and insight authors chose to include.

As writers, students carried lessons from the biography unit into their composition of other genres. Students infused theme into the narration and dialogue in personal narratives and fictional pieces. They included back matter in nonfiction compositions. The most significant change, however, was in students' awareness of their own writing processes. After exploring the back matter in Bryant and Sweet's collected work and Skyping with them to discuss their stories, students had a new understanding of the ways in which writers use the world around them to inform their creativity. Through their back matter, Bryant and Sweet were able to model curiosity and inquiry for their readers. They successfully explained how wondering turns into deliberate actions by writers and researchers. Students then had a road map for engaging in these processes themselves.

Beyond their growth as readers and writers, the biography study led to growth in my students' roles as engaged citizens of our community. The students who had connected with a children's librarian began to visit the library more frequently. Students who interviewed a newspaper reporter began writing their own stories to share news with the community. The subjects of students' biographies were living examples of how to engage productively with the community at large. By capturing the subjects' stories, and then following in their footsteps, students began to contribute positively to our neighborhood and town.

At the end of elementary school, students are asked to share a favorite memory at an assembly with family and friends. When one student approached the microphone, he shared, "My favorite memory was interviewing people from our town in third grade and getting to tell their stories." Through engaging in this biography study, my students had the opportunity to use their voices to celebrate others. They learned how to be avid nonfiction readers, deliberate writers, accurate researchers, and engaged citizens.

Comprehensive Text Sets

To help you design your own biography genre study, Figure 3.46 shows a comprehensive listing of the text sets that we used within ours.

FIGURE 3.46 *A listing of the texts used in this genre study of picture book biographies*

SCAFFOLD TEXT	
Some Writer! The Story of E. B. White. Written by Melissa Sweet (2016).	
IMMERSION TEXTS	
Bryant/Sweet Picture Book Biographies	*The Right Word: Roget and His Thesaurus.* Written by Jen Bryant and illustrated by Melissa Sweet (2014).
	A Splash of Red: The Life and Art of Horace Pippin. Written by Jen Bryant and illustrated by Melissa Sweet (2013).
	A River of Words: The Story of William Carlos Williams. Written by Jen Bryant and illustrated by Melissa Sweet (2008).

IMMERSION TEXTS	
Bryant/Sweet Picture Book Biographies *continued*	*Balloons over Broadway: The True Story of the Puppeteer of the Macy's Thanksgiving Day Parade.* Written and illustrated by Melissa Sweet (2011).
Picture Book Biographies with Diverse Representations	*Whoosh! Lonnie Johnson's Super-Soaking Stream of Inventions.* Written by Chris Barton and illustrated by Don Tate (2016).
	My Story, My Dance: Robert Battle's Journey to Alvin Ailey. Written by Lessa Cline-Ransome and illustrated by James Ransome (2015).
	The First Step: How One Girl Put Segregation on Trial. Written by Susan Goodman and illustrated by E. B. Lewis (2016).
	The Boy Who Harnessed the Wind. Written by William Kamkwamba and Bryan Mealer and illustrated by Elizabeth Zunon (2012).
	Rachel Carson and Her Book That Changed the World. Written by Laurie Lawler and illustrated by Laurie Beingessner (2012).
	I Dissent: Ruth Bader Ginsburg Makes Her Mark. Written by Debbie Levy and illustrated by Elizabeth Baddeley (2016).
	Swan: The Life and Dance of Anna Pavlova. Written by Laurel Snyder and illustrated by Julie Morstad (2016).
	Growing Up Pedro: How the Martinez Brothers Made It from the Dominican Republic All the Way to the Major Leagues. Written and illustrated by Matt Tavares (2015).
	Funny Bones: Posada and His Day of the Dead Calaveras. Written and illustrated by Duncan Tonatiuh (2015).
EXTENSION TEXTS: CREATING PICTURE BOOK BIOGRAPHIES	
Digital Texts	Scholastic Author Interview Videos and Transcripts **www.scholastic.com/teachers/books-and-authors/#author-interviews**
	Scholastic Kid Reporters' Notebook **kpcnotebook.scholastic.com/** (landing page for Scholastic News Kids Press Corps) **kpcnotebook.scholastic.com/search/node/interviews** (links to their interviews)
	Interview Tips from What Kids Can Do Organization **(whatkidscando.org)** Tips: **www.whatkidscando.org/featurestories/2007/maine_students /tip_sheets/INTERVIEWING%20TIP%20SHEET.pdf**
	Tell Me Your Story—Interviewing Tips for Kids **www.youtube.com/watch?v=SWRYIAfojqk**
	Bryan Collier Video Interview on Process of Illustrating *Rosa* **www.readingrockets.org/books/interviews/collier**
	Digital Exhibit of the Making of *Balloons over Broadway* **gallery.lib.umn.edu/exhibits/show/balloons-over-broadway/book**

Perspectives and Representations in Social Studies
Stories of the American Revolution

*Students are thinking about multiple perspectives,
not just in relation to the Revolutionary War but
in other aspects of their lives and learning.*

—HALEY, Fifth-Grade Teacher

The American Revolution is a commonly taught topic in elementary schools across the country. Here in New England, where we live and work, colonial history is intertwined with the state and local history explored in fourth grade and fifth grade. In this chapter, we explore the ways in which a fifth-grade team used texts sets to layer their students' understandings of different perspectives during the American Revolution. Together with teachers, we cocreated a unit of study in which students examined a range of multimodal and multigenre texts and engaged in conversations about various points of view from men and women, children, spies, soldiers, free and enslaved African Americans, and Tories and Whigs. These conversations shaped the ways in which students explored primary and secondary sources and articulated their own perspectives on the war through the texts they created.

Establish Goals: What do you want for your students?

When we began talking about goals for a revised unit on the American Revolution, fifth-grade teacher Marie shared that each year, she and the students found the unit enjoyable and interesting. Yet, she never felt as if she was doing the topic justice. She knew there was so much you *could* cover, asking the group, "If you can spend a year teaching it, how do you narrow things down?" Both Marie and Haley, another member of the fifth-grade team, felt that they had a lot of resources available to them already. In fact, as we sat amid the piles of books they brought in, they wondered if they had *too* many.

Because of the local appeal of the topic and the wide range of books available, the team previously approached the unit through inquiry, allowing students to do individual research. Although they saw the merits of this more exploratory orientation, they felt that the students were just "on the surface" with their thinking. Each questioned how specific their instruction should be on the major events within the war, knowing that their students would study it again in eighth grade. Ultimately, both Marie and Haley felt that a big idea was missing. Something needed to hold the content together, and teaching with text sets would allow them to get deeper, by providing a more focused class exploration of that big idea across multiple texts.

Our work on the American Revolution is an example of how state content standards provide the content and skills that have to be covered but not *how* that content or skills should or could be covered. We knew that the school's curriculum required that the American Revolution be studied and that students were expected to write persuasive pieces before the end of the school year. The New Hampshire K–12 Social Studies Curriculum Frameworks (2006) guided the content and skills from the grades 5–6 standards used at the fifth-grade level. We looked at these standards to ground ourselves. Those standards are easily mapped back to the C-3 Framework as well as the Common Core State Standards (CCSS) literacy standards, as shown in Figure 4.1.

FIGURE 4.1 *This chart documents the standards this unit was designed to meet.*

NEW HAMPSHIRE SOCIAL STUDIES CURRICULUM FRAMEWORK GRADES 5–6	
SS:HI:6:1.2:	Explain how the foundations of American democracy are rooted in European, Native American, and colonial traditions, experiences, and institutions.
SS:HI:6:5.2:	Describe the impact of major national and state events on everyday life, e.g., the Industrial Revolution or the World War II home front.
SS:HI:6:5.3:	Examine changes in the roles and lives of women and their impact on society, e.g., the family or the workplace.
NATIONAL CURRICULUM STANDARDS FOR SOCIAL STUDIES GRADES 3–5	
Time, Continuity, and Change	*Knowledge* • We can learn our personal past and the past of communities, nations, and the world by means of stories, biographies, interviews, and original sources such as documents, letters, photographs, and artifacts.

| Time, Continuity, and Change *continued* | *Knowledge* continued
• People view and interpret historical events differently because of the times in which they live, the experiences they have, and the point of view they hold.
• Historical events occurred in times that differed from our own but often have lasting consequences for the present and future.
Processes
• Use a variety of sources to learn about the past.
• Compare and contrast differing stories or accounts about past events, people, places, or situations, and offer possible reasons for the differences.
• Describe how people in the past lived, and research their values and beliefs.
• Use historical methods of inquiry and literacy skills to research and present findings. |
| Power, Authority, and Governance | *Knowledge*
• Learn the fundamental values of democracy: the common good, liberty, justice, equality, and individual dignity.
Processes
• Analyze conditions and actions related to power, authority, and governance that contribute to conflict and cooperation among groups or nations or that detract from cooperation. |

NEW HAMPSHIRE LITERACY STANDARDS	
RSI. Craft and Structure.5.6	Analyze multiple accounts of the same event or topic, noting important similarities and differences in the point of view they represent.
CCSS.ELA-LITERACY.RI.5.9	Integrate information from several texts on the same topic in order to write or speak about the subject knowledgeably.
CCSS.ELA-LITERACY.RI.5.8	Explain how an author uses reasons and evidence to support particular points in a text, identifying which reasons and evidence support which point(s).
CCSS.ELA-LITERACY.RI.5.7	Draw on information from multiple print or digital sources, demonstrating the ability to locate an answer to a question quickly or to solve a problem efficiently.

But in all honesty, our planning did not center on these standards, and we considered those standards the floor, not the ceiling. It was more important to wrestle with the teachers' goals for a deeper understanding of the big picture, with an emphasis on multiple perspectives, without sacrificing the student interest and engagement that came with the exploratory and more individualized approach.

Teachers Haley and Marie both wondered out loud what criteria to use when narrowing down a unit of study as big and as important as this one. This led our whole group to have a valuable conversation about what was *important* historically. Why does the American Revolution matter?

What about it matters to fifth graders? These conversations about the value of the content and which content is more important than others need to happen *before* you can determine your goals. The conversation about the content helped us to identify different subtopics and themes, which led to identifying different structures we could use for the unit. We live history every day, and none of us knows the outcomes of the actions we witness or take part in. The team wanted students to understand that about the lead-up to and the events of the American Revolution. No one knew how things would turn out. This would be at the heart of student learning.

We actually began looking for new trade books and multimodal texts *before* the team landed specifically on their essential question. Presenting the planning process here in this book makes it look very linear and clear. But we had a lot of messy, recursive conversations as part of the planning. The text selection process allowed us to work toward identifying the larger goals and essential questions. The process of naming larger goals and developing essential questions helped us to be even more specific about text selection.

The essential question grew out of the search for more diverse curricular materials and the desire to have a more specific focal point for the unit. As Haley shared, the most challenging part was "having a multitude of resources and ideas and not knowing how to weave them together." By looking at and exploring the texts, the essential questions and the organizational structures for the unit emerged. This is a great example of teamwork, which requires listening, patience, compromise, and flexibility. Creating engaging and thoughtful curriculum is not always easy, quick, or simple. Strong planning in advance saves time during implementation. Because Haley and Marie were grounded in their goals, the planning was coherent

FIGURE 4.2 *This chart documents the goals and outcomes for the American Revolution unit.*

GOALS	OUTCOMES
To integrate language arts and social studies	Students will understand the complexity of different identities during the American Revolution.
To emphasize critical thinking	Students will understand how a person's perspective influenced their interpretation of the American Revolution.
To expose fifth graders to multiple perspectives, including marginalized voices not always included, such as those of free and enslaved African Americans, women, children, and indentured servants	Students will understand how a person's social context and location impacted their experiences during the American Revolution.

week to week, and they could then focus on responding to students needs in their instruction.

The goals that Haley and Marie articulated (see Figure 4.2) reveal what they wanted to make happen in the classroom; the outcomes are what students would be able to do as a result.

To meet their goals and outcomes, they created a simple question, with subquestions that served as concrete pathways to complex answers to that simple question. These questions not only emphasized the significance of multiple perspectives for the students throughout the unit but helped us in mapping out the unit trajectory when we got overwhelmed.

Big Question
- What is "the story" of the American Revolution?

Follow-Up Questions
- From whose perspective?
- What's the evidence?

In reality, there is no single story of the American Revolution. There are many perspectives, many stories. Historians continue to reinterpet the American Revolution through different lenses. We wanted students to arrive at this realization on their own, through their navigation of a range of primary and secondary texts and perspectives.

As students read, listened to, and viewed the various primary and secondary sources that they were exposed to throughout the unit, they participated in a process of extracting evidence from texts. In applying the disciplinary literacies of a historian, they compared and contrasted different representations of events, and they began to understand that perspective always shapes how information gets shared. Historians must always be mindful of who has written a piece of historical evidence and how an individual's perspective shapes their representation of their lived experiences.

Find Texts: What are the best texts to help you meet your goals?

We began with too many texts, and we still went on to look for more. Why? As we found books and digital texts that seemed worth exploring further, new ideas for how to shape and organize the unit were generated. The more texts we discovered, the more opportunities we had to consider previously used texts in new ways. This is a great reminder that a text set approach allows you to see texts themselves from multiple angles: it's not just what the single text offers in terms of content that's important, it's how the text fits together with others to create meaning. The same texts, used in a different order or in different combinations, can lead to different learning experiences and outcomes.

Not all of the books that Marie and Haley inherited or purchased were equal in their potential to pique students' interest and curiosity or frame the unit in ways that would activate critical thinking. Some were great. Some contained valuable information but were dated. Some were just dated. They were energized to find texts with the most potential for instruction.

Books

The team had access to historical fiction novels set during the American Revolution, available to them in their book room. Expanding the list of historical novels would allow for each child to read one historical novel as part of a literature circle. Knowing that we were interested in adding text sets based on various identities, we used Titlewave, the digital resource from Follett Library Services we discussed in Chapter 2, to search for additional historical novels as well as nonfiction and historical fiction picture books that focused on smaller events, marginalized perspectives, or multiple perspectives. Because the school's library uses Titlewave for collection development, we were able to see which books were available within the school library. We went broad initially with our searches, reading book reviews and making lists of subtopics the books might fit into. Book reviews helped us to weed out books that had misrepresentations or inaccuracies within them, as well as oversimplifications. One goal was to find texts that reflected Native American experiences during this turbulent time. The students had already studied the colonization of North America by Europeans. We were hoping that we could discover well-written fiction or nonfiction by Native American authors that authentically reflected the perspectives of individuals in various nations during the American Revolution. The dearth of available texts speaks to a troubling gap in the publishing industry. As we were concluding our revisions of this book, Debbie Reese and Jean Mendoza's Young People's Edition of *An Indigenous Peoples' History of the United States* (2019), by Roxanne Dunbar-Ortiz, was published. Although the book is written for middle and high school students, teachers could use portions of Chapter 5 with students to bring Native nations more directly into the conversation about the American Revolution.

Digital Texts

In previous years, the team had used *Mission US: For Crown or Colony?*, an online video game created by WNET, a New York public television station.

The game takes players to 1770 Boston, seeing the political unrest through the eyes of a fictional teenage printer's apprentice Nat Wheeler. Because of our proximity to Boston, the fifth graders annually walk the Freedom Trail, exploring the sites connected to the Revolution. Haley and Marie knew that this should continue to be an important part of the unit for the interest and energy it generated. But we knew we needed more texts, and the team was eager to consider primary source documents and artifacts. We did a giant brainstorm of all the organizations—history museums, cultural institutions, libraries—that could offer access to primary sources and high-quality secondary sources, such as the National Park Service, Colonial Williamsburg, and the Massachusetts Historical Society. From there, we began to explore the options, considering the broadest possible reach in terms of perspectives and points of view. Again, we were confronted by a paucity of digital texts to support student understanding of the various roles different Native American nations played during the American Revolution. What is available is mostly too difficult for fifth graders to comprehend and unpack, and without strong print texts to support students' introduction to the material, we felt we had minimal choices to draw upon.

Synthesizing Our Consideration of Texts

Because we searched for nonfiction, biography, historical fiction, and multimodal texts on the experiences of specific groups of people, including marginalized populations, texts that focused on those groups were obvious choices as immersion texts in the unit. These were texts that could be used in flexible combinations with one another to support a deep exploration into multiple perspectives. Some of these texts were useful in multiple text sets, as the identities of the subjects of the picture book biographies overlapped. For example, some spies were women or African American. The teachers thought seeing the same historical figures repeat in the different text sets would be a valuable lesson in identity for the students. We all have many identities. They also knew that due to time, not every student would necessarily explore each text set personally, and this maximized student exposure to certain individuals. The historical novels used in literature circles were also immersion texts, because they offered more in-depth explorations of the tensions of the time, the lived experiences of diverse boys and girls from different regions, social classes, and political beliefs.

We considered using primary source material—documents, art, artifacts—in a range of ways. Artifacts from the time period are compelling, and they could be of interest to students as a scaffold. Portraits from the time period could also be effective scaffolds. Looking directly into the faces of some of the actual people who bore witness to the Revolution could easily hook students' interest! But those portraits might also be more valuable once students have read about some of these people. Hearing the voices of the people of the American Revolution, through letters, broadsides, and newspapers could also engage students as scaffolds. More complex documents, such as correspondence, were easy to see as extensions, texts that the students could only explore after learning a bit about the conflicts of the time.

Organize Texts for Instruction: How can we arrange the texts for critical thinking?

Because Haley and Marie wanted an integrated language arts and social studies unit, they could use two time blocks during their day, allowing for more time and deeper exploration than they would have if they were just trying to do this work during the time allotted for social studies/science exploration within their schedule.

FIGURE 4.3

Not all units need a single core text that every student reads. This one did. Without a clear and obvious "spine" for the unit, such as the cause-and-effect chronology often outlined in a social studies textbook, Haley and Marie sensed that freedom could lead to chaos. The students needed *something* to hold the big picture together, even if they would get that big picture reinforced three years later in eighth grade. Steve Sheinkin's (2015) *King George, What Was His Problem? Everything Your Schoolbooks Didn't Tell You About the American Revolution* (see Figure 4.3) became the clear and obvious choice as a core text. Both teachers felt that Sheinkin's humorous narration, effective use of the second-person perspective, and engaging questions would hook their students. His complete coverage of the American Revolution would give students the full story as outline.

Therefore, in this unit, we have one core stand-alone text that is read alongside a range of various text sets focused on different perspectives and events. See Figure 4.4 for an overview of the unit as a whole. A comprehensive text set can be found at the end of this chapter.

FIGURE 4.4 *This chart provides an overview of the American Revolution unit*

SCAFFOLD TEXTS	
Introducing the Critical Thinking for the Unit	Duet Text Set • Contemporary news story from Dogo: "Pittsburgh Woman Creates Gender Pay Gap Awareness by Asking Men to Pay More," June Liu, May 2015 • Historical newspaper from Massachusetts Historical Society: *The Boston Gazette*, October 7, 1765b

IMMERSION TEXT:	
Exploring Multiple Perspectives	Steve Sheinkin's *King George: What Was His Problem? Everything Your Schoolbooks Didn't Tell You About the American Revolution* (2015)
	Solar System Multimodal, Multigenre Text Sets (Topic/Theme-Based) • Women in the American Revolution • Free and enslaved African Americans during the American Revolution • Children in the American Revolution • Journeys during the American Revolution • "Behind the scenes" actions during the American Revolution • Political perspectives during the American Revolution
	Solar System Text Set (Genre-Based) • Historical fiction novels
EXTENSION TEXTS:	
Students' Independent Research	Primary and secondary sources for student-based research on topics of interest

Scaffold: Introducing the Critical Thinking

To begin the unit, Haley and Marie knew that they needed to teach vocabulary up front, to support their student's understanding of the essential questions so that that students could explore all texts through the lens of multiple perspectives. Specifically, they wanted to pre-teach the words *event*, *identity*, and *perspective*. As part of that preteaching, they wanted to introduce the essential questions and a graphic organizer they had designed based on the essential question. Their goal was to have all students use that graphic organizer as a method of note taking with every text that they read, primary or secondary, digital or print, assuming that through multiple applications of the graphic organizer, students would then begin to read primary and secondary sources with the lenses of the essential questions automatically. They launched the unit working closely with their individual classes in parallel ways.

FIGURE 4.5 *Marie and her students created this anchor chart to document their thinking about identity and perspective.*

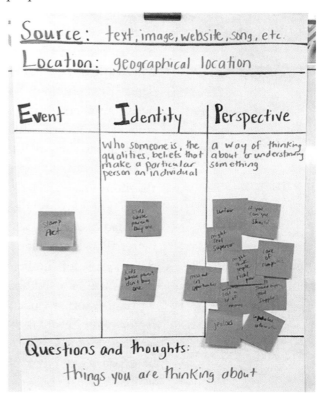

FIGURE 4.6 *This Duet model was used to introduce key vocabulary for the unit.*

Marie sat at the rug with her class next to a version of the graphic organizer on chart paper on the easel beside her (see Figure 4.5). She went over the different parts of the graphic organizer and asked students what they thought the words meant. Students defined what a source would be and talked through how they might fill out the complete organizer. She next zeroed in on the interconnections between event, identity, and perspective. To do so, she employed the power of oral storytelling. She asked the students to brainstorm all the things about a person that make someone an individual. Students were able to share many identifiers, from as scientific as DNA and fingerprints to more culturally oriented signifiers like hobbies, jobs, national heritage, and religion. She next asked them what *perspective* means, and students summed it up by saying that it was "someone's way of thinking or understanding something." (See Figure 4.6.)

Marie then used a story about an event to help tease out the complexity of perspective with students: the principal of another school announces that students can only use a computer in school if their family buys it for them. Because the students were in a school where every third through fifth grader had access to a Chromebook, they knew this scenario was hypothetical. Marie asked the students to name the identities involved in this event. Students listed children, boys, girls, kids who have computers, kids who don't have computers, teachers, the principal, and parents. Next, Marie asked the students to identify different perspectives on this situation. Students were easily able to share that some parents would be angry because they pay money in taxes already to support the school, while others expressed concern over the money, saying that "parents are struggling with financial issues and computers cost a lot." Students saw that some students might be jealous of those who had computers, while those who had computers might think they were better than those who didn't. They then started to get more nuanced with the conversation, noting that they can sometimes do better work with a computer, making a slideshow that looks more polished than something handwritten. Another student noted that at the beginning of the year, when the laptops were new to the school, that "a lot of people were dropping computers and breaking the chargers. You said that was very expensive and it might be expensive to buy more chargers. I think if it belongs to you, the teacher wouldn't scream but your parents probably would."

From there, Marie had the students return to their desks, and she projected the October 7, 1765, *Boston Gazette* front page on the whiteboard for the students to examine. She asked the students to broadly share what they noticed about this primary source. One student noticed that "there is no color and it is old." Another noted the name and identified it as either a newspaper or magazine. Another noted the date, and Marie confirmed that they were looking at an actual newspaper. The students then began to dissect the first few paragraphs of an article on the Stamp Act. Marie modeled how they might fill out the graphic organizer using this document, and as a group they went through the process of naming the source, the text type, the location, and the event. Marie read aloud a portion of the article, and the students did a close reading together in pairs and then as a whole class, identifying the words that seem important, the perspective of the writer, and the mood and tone of the piece.

In contrast, Haley paired a contemporary news story about a pop-up shop in Pittsburgh, Pennsylvania, where the store owner tied prices to people's wages, with the historic newspaper article. As a result, men paid more than women, because in Pennsylvania, men get paid 24 percent more on the dollar than women. Haley began with this actual news event as a way to see how her students could apply the same vocabulary words. From there, she, too, had her students look at the historic newspaper to practice the note taking. Both teachers employed the Duet model but using different contemporary texts: one a fictional anecdote, the other a contemporary news story.

Immersion: Exploring Multiple Perspectives

CORE TEXT

Both Marie and Haley read aloud *King George: What Was His Problem? Everything Your Schoolbooks Didn't Tell You About the American Revolution* (Sheinkin 2015) to their classes. Often, this took place in the morning at the start of the day. They knew that the book would be too difficult, and too long, for most of their fifth graders to tackle independently as readers. But they also knew that the students were capable of hearing the book, understanding it, and using the information from it to help them make sense of the rest of the texts they were exploring. To hold their thinking, students constructed a timeline, which will be discussed later in this chapter.

TEXT SETS ON PERSPECTIVES

During the first year of this unit, Marie and Haley planned to have the students explore text sets on perspectives for one week, moving students

FIGURE 4.7

through different text sets each day in small groups that combined students from both classes. Some texts focused on the perspective of one individual, and others focused on a range of people, such as *Colonial Voices: Hear Them Speak* by Kay Winter (2008/2015) (see Figure 4.7). The following week, they planned for students to explore text sets that focused on major events of the Revolution. Throughout the text set work, students used the graphic organizer to take notes. Sometimes students read books as a whole group, and sometimes students read books in pairs and swapped them with one another. Students self-selected podcasts, videos, and primary source material. The first year Marie and Haley used Pinterest Boards to share the digital resources; starting the following year, with students accustomed to using the Google platform for work, they located all the text set links within Google Slides.

In Figure 4.8 through Figure 4.18, you will find the various Solar System text sets focused on different perspectives and experiences.

FIGURE 4.8 *This text set focuses on the experiences of different women during the American Revolution.*

FIGURE 4.9

African Americans During the American Revolution
Answering the Cry for Freedom
Prisoner for Liberty
The Untold Story of the Black Regiment Fighting in the American Revolution
Samuel's Choice
Portrait of Phillis Wheatley
No Master over Me video

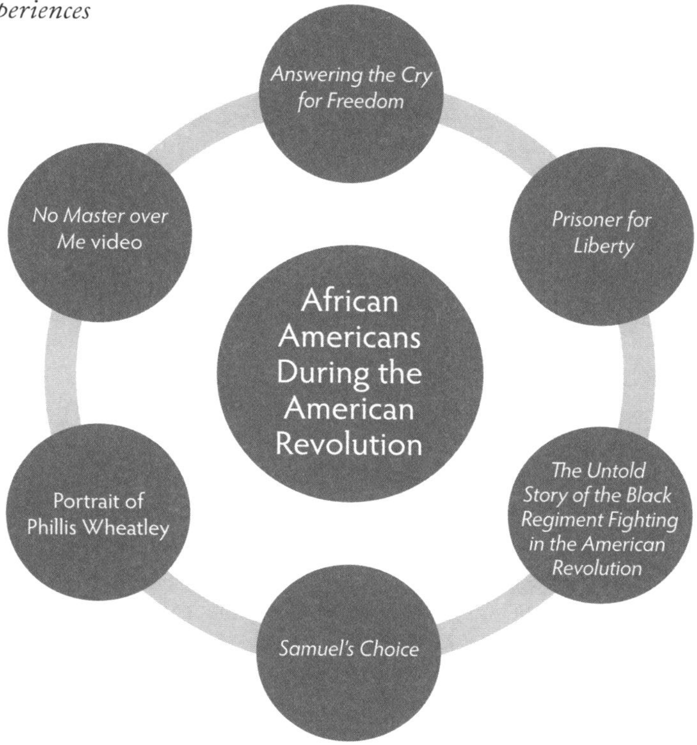

FIGURE 4.10 *This text set focuses on the experiences of different African Americans during the American Revolution.*

FIGURE 4.11

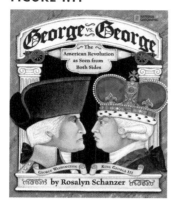

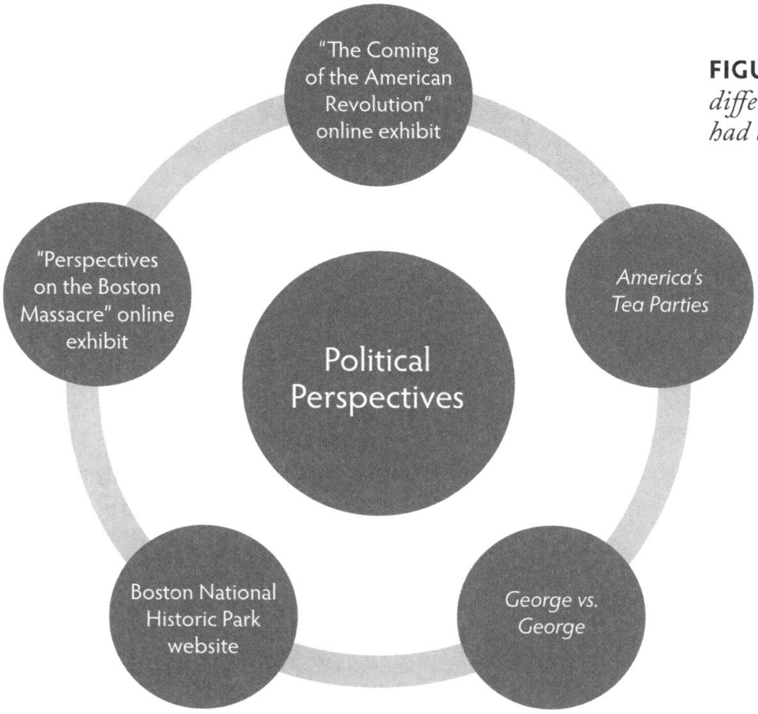

George vs. George
The American Revolution as Seen from Both Sides
George Washington
King George III
by Rosalyn Schanzer

Political Perspectives
"The Coming of the American Revolution" online exhibit
America's Tea Parties
George vs. George
Boston National Historic Park website
"Perspectives on the Boston Massacre" online exhibit

FIGURE 4.12 *This text set focuses on the different political perspectives individuals had during the American Revolution.*

FIGURE 4.13

The Scarlet Stockings Spy
Trinka Hakes Noble
Robert Papp

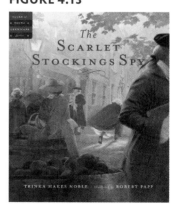

FIGURE 4.14 *This text set focuses on the experiences of children during the American Revolution.*

FIGURE 4.15

FIGURE 4.16 *This text set focuses on the experiences of people who worked behind the scenes to influence the outcome of the American Revolution.*

FIGURE 4.17

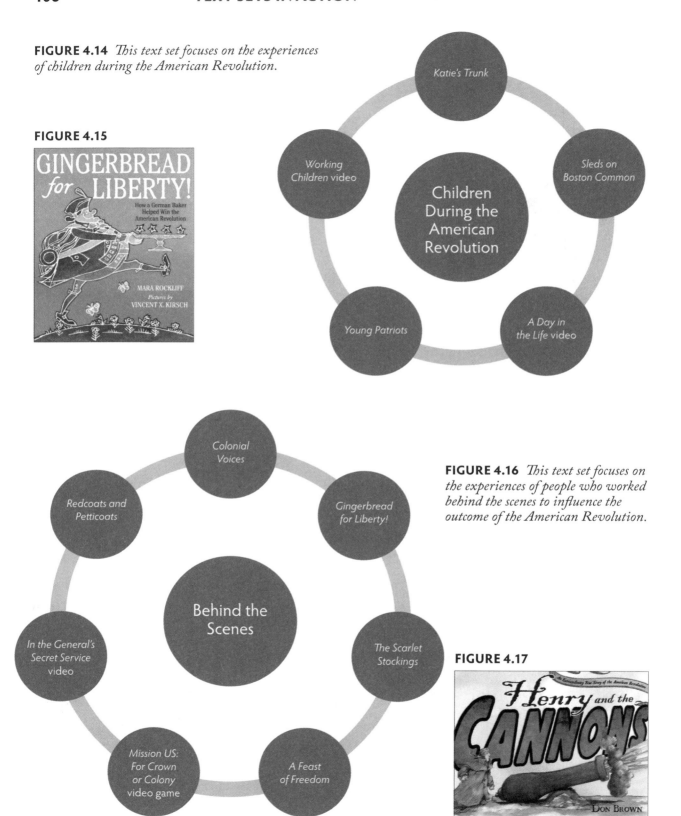

FIGURE 4.18 *This text set focuses on different journeys people took for different purposes during the American Revolution.*

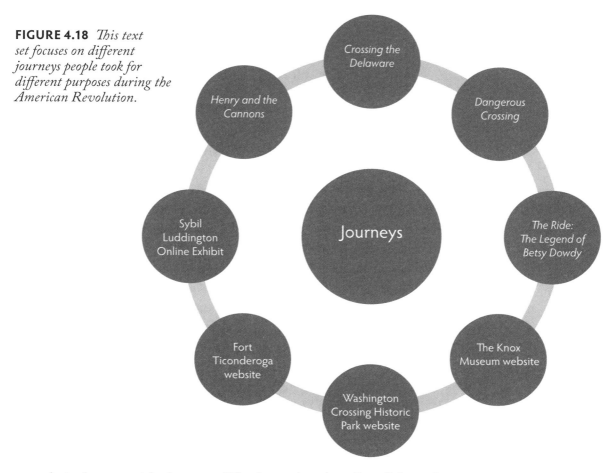

As is the case with classroom life, the students' reading did not always finish exactly when class ended, and both sets of text sets needed more time than was originally allotted. There was no expectation that every student had to read, listen to, or watch every text. However, the students needed enough time to be able to dig in to each perspective, and the varying lengths of texts and the kinds of conversations students would have with one another impacted the timing. This is a challenge that comes with engagement and spotlights the importance of thinking flexibly about the timing of the unit. The students were able to make comparisons and contrasts with the material within each text set, and then as they moved through others, made comparisons and contrasts across the text sets. All the work pointed them toward deeper understanding.

As Haley noticed, "The conversations they have had in small groups, in pairs, or as a class have been a large indicator of their thinking and understanding. I can tell quickly by listening to how they feed and build off of one another that they are learning." Whole-group conversations with both classes combined became an important place to share that thinking. As a result, students were modeling critical thinking for one another regularly. Through these big conversations, Haley and Marie were able to correct misconceptions, offer strategies for working more effectively when students couldn't look at every text in the text set, and pose new questions that students could bring back to the text sets. You'll notice that, in some of the Solar System models, we included primary sources mixed in with secondary sources. Rather than restrict primary sources to an extension text set at the end of the unit, we decided that students could consider these primary sources while immersed in a focused exploration that connected the texts. This gave Haley and Marie the flexibility to differentiate as needed.

Throughout the process, Haley and Marie sat in on small groups to support them as they worked with text sets. Because there was a shared classroom culture, each worked with students from both classes, knowing one another's students as a learners from prior collaborations. Working as a team also gave each of them the flexibility to work more closely with the students from their own classes who needed additional supports as readers, thinkers, and writers. When students' notes or their own observations revealed that students were struggling to identify perspectives because they had to be inferred, they did targeted small-group instruction. When text structures or third-person narration in some books made identifying perspectives and evidence more difficult, the two could anticipate that students would need support, and they jumped in when necessary. When they noticed that one child enthusiastically took many pages of notes but only got through four pages in a text, they turned that into a minilesson for everyone on how to extract important information for notes, rather that copying all information. When some students were hardly taking any notes, they provided minilessons on expanding notes so they could be useful in the future.

NOTE TAKING

An important element of teaching with text sets is the breadth of writing and drawing that students do throughout, often without their even realizing it. As we have mentioned, students responded to texts by taking notes using the same graphic organizer, focused on the essential questions. We know that through reading, writing, speaking, listening, and viewing the same information multiple times, we learn it more deeply because we are using that information. This was our experience watching the note taking unfold, even with students who struggled with using the format of the graphic organizer. Throughout the process, both teachers were far more interested in having students understand the cause and effect of events and the consideration of perspectives than a lockstep understanding of or memorization of the specific dates involved. They felt that this was a

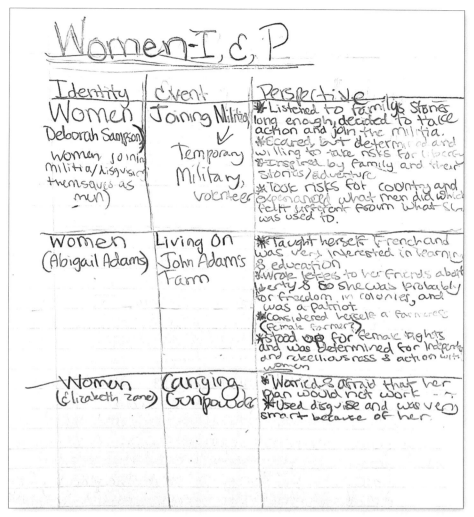

FIGURE 4.19

One student's notes on the roles of women during the American Revolution.

developmentally appropriate way for fifth graders to take notes and build understanding and a foundation for later learning that would stick.

This particular set of notes reveals one student's thinking about the "Women in the American Revolution" text set (see Figure 4.19). We see three women as subjects: Deborah Sampson, Abigail Adams, and Elizabeth Zane. The student clearly identifies an event for two of the three, but struggles to place Abigail Adams within a specific event other that "living on John Adams's farm." Within the notes for each woman, we see a lot of information. Some of this information is more general but then used by the student to give the woman a perspective. For example, Deborah Sampson grew up listening to family stories. Why does that matter with regard to her perspective during the American Revolution? According to this student, she was "inspired by family and their stories" and therefore "took risks for country and experienced what men did, which was different from what she was used to" as a "temporary military volunteer."

Haley and Marie were also careful to make sure that student interests were honored, so that they didn't *only* talk about identity and perspectives. They also knew that these conversations would help students consider what they wanted to research and write about for their writing project, discussed later in this section. In the anchor chart (see Figure 4.20), you can see how much information they absorbed to pose these particular questions.

FIGURE 4.20

A set of questions about the American Revolution generated by students.

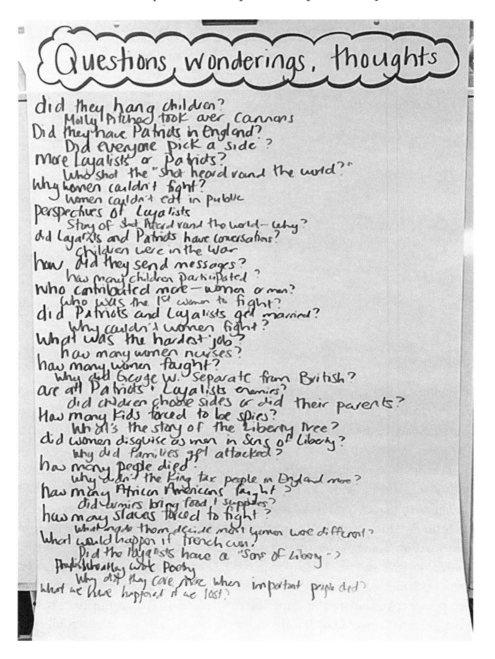

HISTORICAL FICTION LITERATURE CIRCLES

During the language arts block, students were reading self-selected historical novels (see Figure 4.21), using the graphic organizers again to document their thinking about specific events happening. Each of the historical novels took place during a different period of the American Revolution and a different geographical location. Students were able to read more deeply about the colonies beyond New England and to experience an extended exploration of the war through a single character's perspective.

One of the challenges that Marie and Haley faced during this time was the pacing of students' reading and the ability for all students to finish their books during the course of the unit, while they were also consuming so many other texts in varied formats over the course of the day. Students were able to share new perspectives on the war gleaned through their historical novels with other students reading about different experiences.

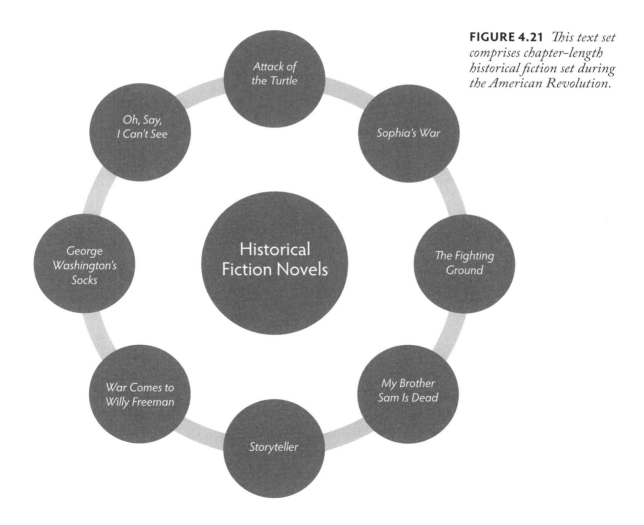

FIGURE 4.21 *This text set comprises chapter–length historical fiction set during the American Revolution.*

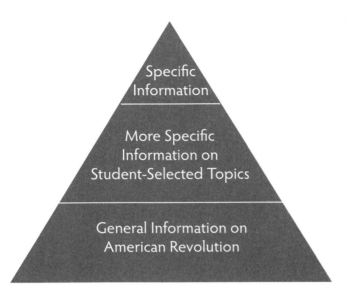

FIGURE 4.22 *Students began with more general reading about the American Revolution, and then selected a specific topic to learn more about, finding ever-increasingly specific texts to research.*

Through these conversations, students deepened their understanding about identity and perspective and the American Revolution as a civil war that impacted everyone differently.

Extension: Conducting Independent Research

For the extension texts, the students used the expanse of digital texts that they were exposed to during the unit and the range of books that Marie and Haley had from previous years to research a topic of interest to them about the American Revolution. This research followed the Mountain model (see Figure 4.22), moving from general information to more specific for each individual student.

Create New Texts: What are the new texts created by students?

In addition to extensive note taking, the students worked collaboratively during the unit to build a timeline of the American Revolution, a set of interview questions for author Steve Sheinkin, and individual newspaper articles.

Building a Collective Timeline

Timelines are effective ways of communicating information visually, and they help learners hold information together. One importance of a timeline emerged early on in our planning conversations, as a way to provide students with that larger "spine" and possibly support students' reading comprehension as they made their way through a range of texts. But rather than have the teachers create a timeline in advance that could end up a mere decoration, they put that power in the students' hands. The timelines in each class emerged organically out of the read-aloud of *King George* (Sheinkin 2015). Students would suggest when an event was important enough to be added to the timeline. Students began to suggest events from the timeline based on their perspectives text sets and historical novels as well (see Figure 4.23). When students were not sure if something was important enough

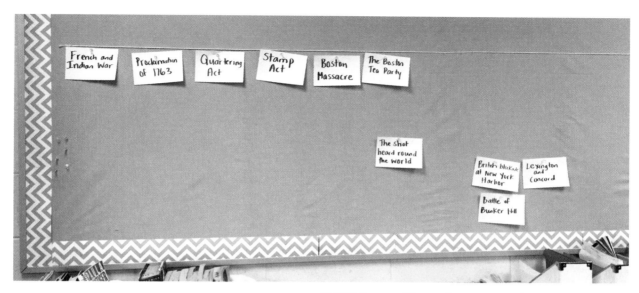

FIGURE 4.23 *The student-suggested timeline during the early stages of the unit.*

to go on the timeline, the teachers placed the information below the timeline, leaving it up to the students to identify when it should either be discarded or included.

Crafting an Interview

We had the opportunity to interview author Steve Sheinkin to better understand how he selected evidence to represent different perspectives in his own writing about the American Revolution. We timed this interview to take place about two-thirds of the way through the unit, when students had completed the perspectives and events text sets and were preparing to do their individual research. It was also right after they spent a day walking the Freedom Trail in Boston. Thus, they had considerable experience at this point learning information, considering perspectives, and doing authentic research through observation on the Freedom Trail.

Like the construction of the timeline, the teachers wanted all of the questions to come from the students organically. Rather than guide the students toward categories of questions, they let them brainstorm the questions and then

FIGURE 4.24 *The student-generated questions in preparation for a Skype interview with author Steve Sheinkin.*

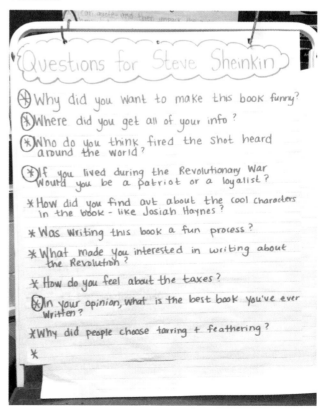

FIGURE 4.25
A student starting off the Skype interview with Steve Sheinkin

determine which ones had the most potential to get quality information. As you can see in the chart in Figure 4.24, students brainstormed questions and then marked the ones selected for the interview. They created an order for the questions so that the interview would be seamless. Student speakers welcomed him and thanked him at the beginning and at the end, and he never saw a teacher throughout the process of the interview (see Figure 4.25).

Student questions reflected their understanding of what they learned as well as their own curiosity about the writing process, which they were about to tackle themselves. In one of the opening questions, a student asked which event of the Revolution Steve would want to witness, a reflection of the critical thinking that they have been doing throughout the process. Sheinkin said that he wanted to witness the "exciting, scary, early days in Boston." Later in the interview, one of the students asked him how he knew that his sources were good. He explained that he read scholars, and then he read the sources those scholars used, since he knew they were reliable. In this way, he moved from secondary sources, like books, to primary sources, like journals and letters. By asking this question, students demonstrated they understood the importance of quality sources. When Steve mentioned primary sources, the students understood him because they had worked with those same materials. Students also revealed their understanding of voice in historical writing, when they asked him why he used so much humor in his writing. Steve shared that he used to write history textbooks. *King George* (2005/2015) was his first trade book, originally published in 2005, and he intentionally wanted to make a shift away from voiceless history writing. The students' final question asked Steve for writing advice. Their trajectory of questions reflected their collective understanding of the writing process, and their understanding of what historical writing demands of the author based on Sheinkin's book as a mentor text.

Writing Colonial Newspapers

The school had recently adopted Lucy Calkins's Units of Study for Writing as its K–5 writing curriculum, and the fifth-grade team planned on integrating the writing curriculum into the unit on the American Revolution. The Units of Study were new to the team, so they did not have previous experience working with the lessons and guidelines. Because of the emphasis on multiple perspectives throughout, the team thought that the students would be able to identify a perspective and write from it as a result of their experience with the curriculum as a whole as well as their individual research. Thus, they would merge the historical study with the research-based argumentative writing.

As the unit played out, several things happened that made the argumentative writing experience challenging. Like so many launches of new curricula, everything took a little longer than we originally planned, and the teachers literally ran out of time. The end of the year in fifth grade is filled with important events and celebrations, all of which impact the daily schedule. The unit bled from May into June, so students and teachers did not have as much time to spend writing as originally hoped.

Because the students had access to so many colonial newspapers, embedding the argumentative writing into a newspaper editorial seemed ideal. Since so many colonial newspapers featured argumentative writing on the front page of the paper, students could use colonial newspapers as mentor texts for voice and style and strive to write their article from an eighteenth-century perspective. We thought it would be fairly easy for students to take on a single identity and write from that perspective. However, because the students had focused *so much* on multiple perspectives, many of them struggled to write from just one person's perspective. Others were so excited about the research they did and the emphasis on multiple perspectives that they began to write from multiple perspectives. Because the team wanted to respect student interest and maximize student enthusiasm during the last few weeks of school, the emphasis on researched argumentative writing was dropped. Some students focused on a range of text types as they created first pages of a colonial newspaper. Like the historical newspapers they were using as mentor texts, students' colonial newspapers blurred the lines between informing and editorializing.

As a result, we can't explore the student writing in alignment to the goals and objectives of contemporary persuasive writing. But we can explore the writing with a consideration of the ways in which it reveals their understanding of the essential questions of the unit. We explore what the student writing tells us about their historical thinking, their consideration of multiple perspectives, and the way they unconsciously used the texts that they were exposed to throughout the unit as mentor texts.

One student's writing on Abigail Adams shows how she makes sense of the colonial world through the language of our contemporary society. Megan's stories (see Figure 4.26), written from Adams's perspective, show her using Adams's voice almost as a tour guide of the American Revolution for contemporary readers.

FIGURE 4.26
Stay home, mom!

Stay Home, Mom

When John is at war, it is my responsibility to make financial decisions, to educate the kids, and to farm. I teach all of my children how to read and write. I have six children: Abigail, John Quincy, Susanna, Elizabeth (born-dead), Charles, and Thomas. I have been used to John making all of the decisions financially so it can be hard at sometimes. I can hear gunshots from wars sometimes. That makes me very nervous as well as the kids too. My kids and I have also tried to help others as much as we can. It is a very busy household as you can see. I teach all of my children to take on a long tradition of public service. I want to surround my children with intelligent people as I was so fortunate to have.

Megan's Abigail Adams explains her various responsibilities on the farm. This reflects Megan's understanding of the different roles that women had during the war, gleaned from the women's text set. We see Adams's worries about nearby fighting, experiences and emotions documented by Adams in her many letters to her husband available on the Massachusetts Historical Society's website. We can note that Megan understood Abigail Adams had an exceptional education for a young woman at the time and that she passed on the value of an education, and the value of public service, to her children, one of whom eventually became president of the United States. We can also see jarringly modern terminology in the title, "Stay home, mom!" Here, too, we see Megan thinking about contemporary and colonial motherhood concurrently, and also adopting the humorous subtitles used by Sheinkin.

Another piece of Megan's writing takes on a more overtly political, rather than informational, tone (see Figure 4.27). The title of this piece is a nod to Adams's famous line in one of her 1776 letters to Adams while he was working on the Declaration of Independence in Philadelphia, in which she urges him to "remember the ladies" (Massachusetts Historical Society, n.d.). **(www.masshist.org/digitaladams/archive/doc?id=L17760331aa)**

FIGURE 4.27
Remember the Women in Your Life

Remember the Women in Your Life

I believe that even women made a difference to getting our freedom and becoming our own government because although we didn't fight we were still essential to the war. I want people to know that I was part of the Lexington and Concord war by letting soldiers get better and to let them train in my yard. Women should also have the same rights as men. We all need to feel equal. This makes me angry when women and slaves as well, don't get the liberty and freedom that I strongly believe we deserve. I will never back down no matter who gets in my way. As I always say in my letters to John, "remember the women!"

In this story, we see editorializing much like the editorializing the students read in the *Boston Gazette* from October 7, 1765. Here, Megan demonstrates her knowledge of Adams's experiences by reinforcing that she allowed soldiers to train on her property. But her Adams makes the claim that "we all need to feel equal." Her comments about equality include both women and enslaved Africans, again showing the ways in which Megan has synthesized information and perspectives from the text sets.

Another student's introductory paragraph for a newspaper (see Figure 4.28) focusing on the Boston Massacre embraces the notion of shared responsibility for the event. Despite the fact that "most people" think it was the fault of British soldiers, Cory is quick to explain that "both sides were to balm [blame]." Cory also reinforces the notion that no two people experience an event the same way: "No one has the same perspective on what happened that horrible night." Cory is able to articulate an understanding of cause and effect, because a "chain of events" occurred that was dependent on every "little thing." Each event matters in that chain, otherwise "if one

FIGURE 4.28
Introduction to Boston Massacre.

The Boston Massacre was a terrible thing, most people think that it was the red coats fault. I'm here to tell you that both sides were to balm [blame]. No one has the same perspective on what happened that horrible night. Whatever happened set of [off] a chain of events. If one little thing was different nothing would be the same. This page will tell you how it started and how it ended. So if you're looking for a little bit of both sides this is the thing you want to read!!!

little thing was different nothing would be the same." Cory then lets readers know that this newspaper is going to focus on how the massacre started and ended, with "a little bit of both sides."

Cory's first story, "The Bad Blood Began," describes the start of the Boston Massacre, instigated by a colonial wigmaker's apprentice. This story has proved to be more legend than truth, and the Massachusetts Historical Society (n.d.) (**www.masshist.org/revolution/massacre.php**) presents a series of primary source documents to reconstruct the events of the week leading up to and including the massacre. But Cory's framing of the story places the blame on the colonists, while traditional narratives for young people often ignore how the event started and focus on the murder of civilians. While Cory has suggested that both sides will be shared, Cory's second piece, written in the first person as a diary entry from the perspective of a female loyalist and Boston resident, is even more sympathetic to the Tories (see Figure 4.29).

FIGURE 4.29
One Unfair Night

One Unfair Night
Tonight was a horrible night where British Soldiers were taunted and beaten almost to death!! When they defend themselves there were called bad names. It's a sad day when the king's subjects turn on each other. No gentleman should ever have to go to trial for a crime they didn't commit!! I guess that the patriots are still sour about our king taxing us. I think the colonists should go to jail for treason. I also think those souls that died that night deserved what came to them, still I mourn their death for anything but that would be unladylike. I was there to witness the event I have to get questioned this evening. I think the rude men of "Sons Of Liberty" should be hung, that would stop this rioting. It would also be great entertainment. I wish that the colonist who started this whole thing would be put on trial. The overworked King will not be pleased about this event.

– Still and always a loyalist Aana Meri

We see that Cory has absorbed some of the language that would have been used by colonists in Boston, when Aana Meri laments that the "king's subjects" have turned on one another. Indeed, they were the king's subjects at the time. Aana Meri suggests that "the colonists should go to jail for treason" and goes on to blame the victims that were killed, as they "deserved what came to them." However, Aana Meri checks herself, reminding herself that she should not be "unladylike" in her disposition. This reveals that Cory has also absorbed some of the social norms and expectations placed upon women during the eighteenth century. But the fictional Aana Meri can't help herself as she suggests that the perpetrators of riots should be hung. Again, we see Cory's absorption of eighteenth-century norms when Aana Meri suggests that a hanging would deter future riots and serve as "great entertainment." Finally, it is important to note that Aana Meri claims to have witnessed the event, and she expects to be questioned that evening. This demonstrates that Cory understood that in the eighteenth century, as today, those who witness a crime provide details to the authorities so that there is evidence for a criminal trial. For illustrations, Cory used two primary sources: a print of Paul Revere's sketch of the Boston Massacre, created in the aftermath of the event, and a photograph of the gravestone at the Granary Burial Ground, where the victims were buried together in March 1770.

Another student also writes about the Boston Massacre from multiple perspectives. The titles of Devon's articles, "I Hear the Church Bells," "I Think You're Guilty," and "A Patriot Turned," are a nod to Sheinkin's pithy section titles in *King George: What Was His Problem?*, such as "Kick Out the French" and "Try, Try Again." Let's take a look at "A Patriot Turned" (see Figure 4.30) written from John Adams's perspective, about his decision to defend the British soldiers put on trial in response.

FIGURE 4.30
A Patriot Turned

A Patriot Turned

I'm John Adams, I'm a Patriot. Since I'm a lawyer I had to defend any side that I thought was right. So in that case I defended the British. I was worried that the trial would lead to more violence. This was the point when I lost a lot of friends (for not taking their side). I think that the British fired for self defense. Plus they had the right to defend against an angry mob. I got elected President for everybody to have Justice. Which includes the British too. I think the British are right in this case. The Patriots that were guilty are really mad that I defended the British and it isn't there fault. People needed to learn what happened and both sides of the story. Then decide who is right when they have a better perspective. I wanted to be respectful about British laws. I'm also happy that most of them were found not guilty for their acts.

In this piece, there are some confusing elements in the context of historical thinking. For example, Devon writes about Adams being elected president—after George Washington's first term—in the middle of the paragraph about the Boston Massacre, which took place *before* the American Revolution began. We also see Devon, like many students, use Patriot/British binary language, despite the fact that all involved were actually British and did not refer to themselves in any other way. However, this is a political nuance that many fifth graders may not be able to absorb. It is far more important to note the critical thinking that Devon did. Devon believes that Adams was willing to defend the soldiers because he thought they fired out of self-defense. Devon recognizes Adams's perspective and recognizes that Adams himself considered the perspectives of the soldiers. Devon acknowledges that Adams took a lot of political heat for his decision to act on behalf of the accused soldiers. And in the end, Devon's John Adams encourages all people to do what all of the fifth graders have been doing in this unit of study, and consider "both sides of the story."

The writing at the end of this unit was rushed, something that you may have experienced when you are rolling out a new unit. When teaching with text sets for the first time, there is much to learn about the process and the pacing. It was so much more important for the teachers to follow the students' lead than to attempt to cover researched argumentative writing. Regardless, the students did not have as much time to revise and edit as we planned. Despite that, we see student work that meets the teachers' goals, as the writing reflects: multiple perspectives, critical thinking, and the integration of language arts and social studies. The writing also reveals a consideration of audience and voice, as gleaned from the colonial newspapers they explored, and an understanding of modern stylistic choices for nonfiction writing, as shaped by their conversation with author Steve Sheinkin and their reading of his work.

Notes for Next Year

In the following year, the team decided to start the unit earlier and to separate the research-based argumentative writing and the study of the American Revolution. By flipping the timing of this unit and their ecology unit from March to May, there would be fewer disruptions during the American Revolution unit, they could take advantage of spring weather for the ecology unit, and they could embed their research-based argumentative writing unit within ecology. This allowed the students to explore ecology through the lens of research, advocacy, and critical literacy. In all, a much better fit for the required writing.

The team felt that reading multiple text sets and historical novels concurrently became burdensome for some of the students. Therefore, they made the historical novels optional for students, choice texts for their ongoing independent reading. Those who wanted to dig deeper could, and those who needed to read self-selected texts of personal interest could have their reading needs met as well. This also simplified planning, which gave the team one less structure to have to work into the day. The team also decided that specific important events during the war should not be concentrated in a separate text set. Some students struggled to make sense of the event text set in isolation. Therefore, the students explore specific events as they were discussed in *King George* (Sheinkin 2005/2015), moving from a separate Solar System text set to a Sunburst model, with *King George* at the center.

Based on the students' experiences writing the newspaper and magazine stories, the team wanted to provide future students with the opportunity to choose the ways in which they showed what they learned. Therefore, the following year, as the unit progressed, they asked the students what they might be interested in creating to demonstrate their learning. The students from both classes decided to collaborate on a ten-act play, featuring the major events of the American Revolution, as told from various perspectives (see Figures 4.31). The students chose to serve as interpreters of information, to transform the timeline on the board into an embodied learning experience, and to give voice to specific people and perspectives.

The essential question asked, "What is the story of the American Revolution?" But what the team found most powerful was how the two subquestions served as vehicles for disciplinary thinking: From whose perspective? What's the evidence? They saw the potential for framing the entire social studies curriculum with these two subquestions, reframing fifth-grade social studies with a disciplinary lens. The team also saw how multimodal, multigenre text sets transformed their students into engaged participants who built their own knowledge and understanding through repeated exposure to texts. Starting with more primary sources and an emphasis on multiple perspectives from the beginning of the school year would allow students to take their thinking and learning to an even deeper level.

To reframe the exploration of colonialism in September, the team spent time over the summer exploring artifacts, art, and documents from

FIGURE 4.31
Time-traveling narrators link the different events of the American Revolution for their audience of parents and community members.

and about various nations in the Americas, Europe, and Africa. Students began fifth grade exploring these different American and African nations as the rich, complex, and fascinating cultures that they were, rather than looking at those nations as mere resources to be conquered, the subtext of the dominant narrative so often used by textbooks, which presents this history only from the perspective of the European colonizers. This reorienting of the curriculum, to center the history of Native nations and those Africans brought to North America by force, is an ongoing effort. Ideally, the publishing industry will provide more well-written books about the experiences of Native nations, to make the study of U.S. history more inclusive and more accurate at the elementary level.

VOICES FROM THE CLASSROOM *Taylor, Fifth-Grade Teacher*

During the first year of our collaboration, Taylor was serving as curriculum coordinator at Haley and Marie's school, and she was an important part of our work. The next year, Taylor joined the fifth-grade team.

The texts sets have certainly changed, grown, and been modified over the past few years. The first year this work was done by Haley and Marie and involved a lot of planning together but teaching separately. The books, digital files, and artwork all worked well but needed to be pared down. When I took over in Marie's absence, Haley and I had already built the idea of perspective with our first unit of "Three Worlds Meet," our unit on the Age of Exploration and the beginnings of colonization. We cotaught our social studies units together so that all students could share and grow together as active citizens in our classroom community. Because of this, students were much more easily able to see the different perspectives and identities as well as understand them at deeper, more empathetic levels.

When we first cotaught this unit together, the students chose to write the play as a group and, boy, was that powerful! The next year, students wanted to also do a play (since they had heard about it from our former students), but they felt they had to put their own indelible mark on it. One student posed the idea of freezing each scene to have a student come forward and share a soliloquy from that person's perspective. This addition brought the play to a new level of understanding for both audience and participants.

As for today, we face a new challenge with Competency Based Education. Social studies will not focus on specific times in history, but competencies. One competency we will use is based on change over time. Some students may choose different events in history to explore, through multimodal experiences, so we may only model with the Revolutionary War. As student voice and choice come into play, we face a new challenge of finding new text sets to cater to the choices of the students currently in front of us. This task seems a bit overwhelming. We would certainly look to our media specialist as well as our reading specialist to help put text sets as fast as possible into our learners' hands. Education is an ever-changing lifestyle but benefits our changing world of learners! It truly puts our students in the driver's seat of their lives!

Comprehensive Text Sets

Figure 4.32 shows a comprehensive listing of the different text sets that the team has used over the past few years, with additional new texts, to help you design your text sets on this topic. Some books were used in multiple text sets, but to save space, we have placed them in just one text set.

FIGURE 4.32 *A comprehensive listing of texts from the unit*

SCAFFOLD TEXT SETS	
Developing Understanding of Vocabulary: Event, Identity, and Perspective	• "Pittsburgh Woman Creates Gender Pay Gap Awareness by Asking Men to Pay More," May 2015, DOGO News **www.dogonews.com/2015/5/2 /pittsburgh-woman-creates-gender-pay-gap-awareness-by-asking -men-to-pay-more** • *The Boston Gazette*, October 7, 1765, Massachusetts Historical Society: **www.masshist.org/dorr/volume/1/sequence/221**

IMMERSION TEXT SETS	
Chronological Overviews of the American Revolution	*Book* • *King George: What Was His Problem? Everything Your Schoolbooks Didn't Tell You About the American Revolution* by Steve Sheinkin (2015) *Multimodal Texts* • Museum of the American Revolution Interactive Timeline, Philadelphia: **www.amrevmuseum.org/timeline/**
Women During the American Revolution	*Books* • *Founding Mothers: Remembering the Ladies* by Cokie Roberts and illustrated by Diane Goode (2014) • *Independent Dames: What You Never Knew About the Women and Girls of the American Revolution* by Laurie Halse Anderson and illustrated by Matt Faulkner (2008) • *They Called Her Molly Pitcher* by Anne Rockwell and illustrated by Cynthia von Buhler (2002) • *Write On, Mercy! The Secret Life of Mercy Otis Warren* by Gretchen Woelfe and illustrated by Alexandra Wallner (2012) *Multimodal Texts* • *Women's Service with the Revolutionary Army*, Colonial Williamsburg: **www.history.org/history/teaching/enewsletter/volume7/nov08/women_ revarmy.cfm** • "Women of the Revolution" video, Colonial Williamsburg: **resourcelibrary. history.org/womenrevolution/video** • Abigail Adams Historical Society: **www.abigailadamsbirthplace.com/**

Women During the American Revolution *continued*	***Multimodal Texts continued*** • Abigail Adams's "Remember the Ladies" letter, Massachusetts Historical Society: **www.masshist.org/digitaladams/archive/doc?id=L17760331aa** • Mercy Otis Warren portrait, Museum of Fine Arts, Boston: **www.mfa.org/collections/object/mrs-james-warren-mercy-otis-32409**
Free and Enslaved African Americans During the American Revolution	***Books*** • *Answering the Cry for Freedom: Stories of African Americans and the American Revolution* by Gretchen Woelfe and illustrated by R. Gregory Christie (2016) • *Prisoner for Liberty* by Marty Rhodes Figley and illustrated by Craig Orback (2008) • *Samuel's Choice* by Richard Berleth and illustrated by James Watling (1990/2012) • *The Untold Story of the Black Regiment Fighting in the Revolutionary War* by Michael Burgen (2015) ***Multimodal Texts*** • *No Master over Me* video, Colonial Williamsburg: **resourcelibrary.history.org/no-master-over-me/video** • Phillis Wheatley portrait, National Portrait Gallery, Smithsonian Institution: **npg.si.edu/object/npg_S_NPG.88.51?destination=node/63231%3Fedan_q%3Dwheatley** • Phillis Wheatley, "America's Story from America's Library," Library of Congress: **www.americaslibrary.gov/jb/revolut/jb_revolut_poetslav_1.html**
Political Perspectives	• *America's Tea Parties: Not One but Four! Boston, Charleston, New York, Philadelphia* by Marissa Moss (2016) • *The Boston Tea Party: Would You Join the Revolution?* by Elaine Landau (2014) • *George vs. George: The American Revolution as Seen from Both Sides* by Rosalyn Schanzer (2004) • *Those Rebels, John and Tom* by Barbara Kerley and illustrated by Ed Fotheringham (2012) • *An Indigenous Peoples' History of the United States for Young People* by Roxanne Dunbar-Ortiz, adapted by Jean Mendoza and Debbie Reese—Chapter 4 (2019) ***Multimodal Texts*** • "The Six Nations Confederacy During the American Revolution." Fort Stanwix National Monument, National Park Service: **www.nps.gov/fost/learn/historyculture/the-six-nations-confederacy-during-the-american-revolution.htm**. • "Joseph Brant and Native Americans." PBS: **www.pbs.org/ktca/liberty/popup_brant.html**

Political Perspectives *continued*	*Multimodal Texts continued* • "The Coming of the American Revolution, 1764–1776," Massachusett's Historical Society: **www.masshist.org/revolution/massacre.phpl** • "Perspectives on the Boston Massacre," Massachusetts Historical Society: **www.masshist.org/features/massacre** Boston National Historic Park, National Park Service: **www.nps.gov/bost/index.htm** Paul Revere portrait, Museum of Fine Arts, Boston: **www.mfa.org/collections/object/paul-revere-32401** John Warren portrait, Museum of Fine Arts, Boston: **www.mfa.org/collections/object/joseph-warren-31064** Adams National Historic Park, National Park Service: **www.nps.gov/adam/index.htm** George Washington's Mount Vernon: **www.mountvernon.org/**
Children in the American Revolution	*Books* • *Katie's Trunk* by Ann Warren Turner and illustrated by Donald Himler (1992/1997) • *Sleds on Boston Common* by Louise Borden and illustrated by Robert Andrew Parker (2013) • *Young Patriots: Inspiring Stories of the American Revolution* by Marcella Fisher Anderson and Eilzabeth Weiss Vollstadt (2004) *Multimodal Texts* • *Working Children* video, Colonial Williamsburg: **resourcelibrary.history .org/node/83** • *A Day in the Life* video, Colonial Williamsburg: **resourcelibrary.history.org /node/217**
Behind the Scenes	*Books* • *A Feast of Freedom: Tasty Tidbits from City Tavern* by Walter Staib and Jennifer Fox and illustrated by Fernando Juarez (2010) • *Colonial Voices: Hear Them Speak* by Kay Winter and illustrated by Larry Day (2008/2015) • *Gingerbread for Liberty! How a German Baker Helped Win the American Revolution* by Mara Rockliff and illustrated by Vincent X. Kirsch (2015) • *Redcoats and Petticoats* by Katherine Kirkpatrick and illustrated by Donald Himler (1999/2018) • *The Scarlet Stockings Spy* by Trinka Hakings Noble and illustrated by Robert Papp (2004) *Multimodal Texts* • *For Crown or Colony?*, Mission US WNET, New York: **www.mission-us.org/**

Behind the Scenes *contined*	***Multimodal Texts continued*** • "American Spies During the Revolution," George Washington's Mt. Vernon: **www.mountvernon.org/george-washington/the-revolutionary-war/spying-and-espionage/american-spies-of-the-revolution/** • *In the General's Secret Service* video, Colonial Williamsburg: **resourcelibrary.history.org/node/240**
Journeys	***Books*** • *Crossing the Delaware: A History in Many Voices* by Louise Peacock and illustrated by Walter Krudop (1998/2007) • *Dangerous Crossing: The Revolutionary Voyage of John Quincy Adams* by Stephen Krensky and illustrated by Greg Harlin (2004) • *Henry and the Cannons: An Extraordinary True Story of the American Revolution* by Don Brown (2013) • *The Ride: The Legend of Betsy Dowdy* by Kitty Griffin and illustrated by Marjorie Priceman (2010) ***Multimodal Texts*** • Washington Crossing Historic Park: **www.washingtoncrossingpark.org/history/** • Fort Ticonderoga: **www.fortticonderoga.org/** • Sybil Luddington, National Women's History Museum: **www.womenshistory.org/education-resources/biographies/sybil-ludington** • The Knox Museum: **knoxmuseum.org/**
Historical Fiction Text Set	***Books*** • *Attack of the Turtle* by Drew Carlson (2006) • *The Fighting Ground* by Avi (2009) • *George Washington's Socks* by Elvira Woodruff (2012) • *My Brother Sam Is Dead* by James Lincoln Collier (2005) • *Oh, Say, I Can't See: The Time Warp Trio* by Jon Scieszka (2007) • *Sophia's War: A Tale of the Revolution* by Avi (2012) • *Storyteller* by Patricia Reilly Giff (2010) • *War Comes to Willy Freeman* by Christopher Collier and James Lincoln Collier (1987)

EXTENSION TEXTS

	• *Give Me Liberty! The Story of the Declaration of Independence* by Russell Freedman (2000) • *The Journey of the One and Only Declaration of Independence* by Judith St. George (2014)

Evidence and Inquiry in Science
Adaptations and Biological Evolution

We were invited by prolific nonfiction trade book author Melissa Stewart to collaborate with third-grade teachers in a suburban district as they worked to implement a new district-wide science curriculum that included a unit on adaptation. Melissa, the coauthor of *Perfect Pairs* (2014b), and an award-winning author with background in both biology and science writing, is familiar with and an advocate of our approach to teaching with text sets. We were excited about this opportunity to explore how well-written science texts could be combined with experiential learning to facilitate students' understandings of the abstract and complex concepts of adaptation and biological evolution.

In this chapter, we describe how texts can be layered to develop student understanding of science concepts and processes. Using the example of birds in their local region, teachers and students examined heredity, survival, and biological adaptation. In planning this unit, we selected texts that model the inquiry process of science, emphasizing changes in knowledge over time. The unit included experiential learning through direct observation of birds, via nature walks and online bird cameras. Students were asked to document observations in text and pictures, offering evidence for their evolving understandings about adaptation. As a culminating project, students composed expository texts describing local birds, using multiple mentor texts as writing resources, including Melissa Stewart's science books. Melissa also visited the class to talk about her research and writing processes.

Establish Goals: What do you want for your students?

Lucy and Sabina, experienced third-grade teachers, teach in a diverse public school in a suburban setting. We were invited to participate in the process of implementing a revised science curriculum by infusing text sets into a new unit on evolution and adaptation. Our initial planning meeting was attended by the two teachers, the district science and language arts coordinators, author Melissa Stewart, and the two of us. To guide our initial conversations, we had a district science curriculum, the Next Generation Science Standards (NGSS), and an array of children's books that the teachers had used in the past as well as those that we had brought to suggest as new possibilities.

In past years, the teachers had taught a unit that focused on the life cycles of plants and animals and the concepts of survival and heredity—new this year was an additional focus on biological adaptation. The unit would be structured around the following questions from the district curriculum guide:

- How are the life cycles of birds and flowering plants alike and different?
- What characteristics help some living things survive better than others in an environment?
- How are plants and animals similar to their parents?
- How have living things changed over time?

As we talked, we wrestled with the question of how third graders could be supported to understand biological evolution, a process that typically occurs over long stretches of time and thus is not directly observable. We spent the majority of our initial meeting talking through the unit questions to see how we could create a narrative arc across these ideas. We discussed definitions and how to find kid-friendly language to connect these concepts. We also mapped out approximate sections of time that would be devoted to each question, ultimately dividing the unit into three sections: (1) comparing plant and animal life cycles; (2) survival and heredity: traits and adaptations; and (3) survival over time: investigating biological evolution. The chart in Figure 5.1, created during this planning session, captures our thinking on how to best sequence the content of the unit.

FIGURE 5.1
An overview of the content for this unit on adaptation and biological evolution.

	1.Comparing Plant and Animal Life Cycles (1 week)	2. Survival and Heredity: Traits and Adaptations (4 weeks)	3. Survival over Time: Investigating Biological Evolution (2 weeks)
Essential Questions	How are the life cycles of birds and flowering plants alike and different?	What characteristics help some living things survive better than others in an environment? How are plants and animals similar to their parents?	How have living things changed over time?
Concepts/ Big Ideas Über-concept—all plants and animals have life cycles and experience adaptation Variation— adaptation— evolution Looking back and looking forward— birds / dinosaurs / climate change and bird habitats (students predict)	**Scaffold** Understanding life cycle and life activity: birth, growth, reproduction, and death. A life cycle has a beginning and an endpoint for individuals. Individual dies, but the species continues through reproduction. Life cycles of plants and animals are more alike than different.	**Immersion** Animals and plant inherit traits of the species through reproduction. Mutations occur within individuals (they are a natural phenomenon)—a mutation is a change in an individual's DNA that leads to a different physical characteristic for it. Different physical characteristics afford greater or lesser chances of survival. These physical characteristics are carried on through the life cycle (reproduction) if they are favorable. They become a characteristic of the species. This process is called *adaptation.* The characteristics are biological adaptations.	**Extension** Link to the idea of life cycle—reproduction creates ongoing survival of species. Biological adaptations lead to evolution over time. New discoveries—some evolutionary processes are fast! Fossils as evidence of changes in traits over time. From dinosaurs to birds—this is evidence of adaptation over time. Focus on the scientific process—how do we know what we know about changes over long periods of time? What have we theorized?

Reading across the chart in Figure 5.1, you can see how each section of the unit of study builds upon the previous one. The first week, with a focus on life cycle, would serve as a scaffold to the more complex concepts of heredity, survival, and adaptation. The concept of life cycles has been previewed for the students in grades 1 and 2—reviewing this content serves to introduce the focus on survival and heredity, which will be the immersion focus of the unit. Students would spend four weeks thinking about physical characteristics (traits) and how they are related to species survival. They would also be introduced to the concept of a mutation and the idea that mutations can be favorable or detrimental to survival. Linking back to the concept of life cycles, students learn that favorable mutations can become a characteristic of the species over time. This sets up the concept of biological adaptation, which is the focus of the final two weeks and an extension of the content students have reviewed in the first two phases of the unit.

Lucy and Sabina were interested in exploring how birds could be a focal point for the unit, which would extend logically into a look at evolution and adaptation. When students think of animals from long ago, dinosaurs are the first creatures that come to mind. The dinosaur–bird connection is now a well-established theory of evolution, a theory that we knew students would find fascinating. The focus on birds with firsthand observation of bird characteristics and behavior was also well matched to the disciplinary literacies of science that we hoped to emphasize—inquiry and evidence. It provided an excellent opportunity to discuss how scientific theories evolve over time, exemplified by the dinosaur-bird connection.

An additional hope that we held for the unit was that we would raise students' awareness around conservation. When we talked together, we discussed the crises faced by many species due to climate change—the idea that evolution occurs very slowly over generations so that rapid evolution to meet changing habitat conditions is simply not possible for most species. Although we wanted to avoid a doom and gloom perspective for students, we wanted to be sure that we emphasized the connection between a specific adaptation and the species' habitat.

Find Texts: What are the best texts to help you meet your goals?
A Balance of Experiences and Texts

Once we had established a narrative arc for the unit, our conversation turned to texts and activities. We knew that we wanted experiential learning to play a strong role in this unit of study. As we said in Chapter 2, we believe that you learn about science by doing science, not just by reading about it. Past iterations of the unit had included field trips to a local arboretum to find observable evidence of the life cycle of birds, insects, and amphibians. We knew we wanted to keep these nature walks as an integral part of the unit. Additionally, past units had incorporated a visit from Wingmasters, visiting educators who would provide students with the opportunity to observe raptors up close and to learn about the history of human interaction with these fascinating species. We knew that this experience would further students' understandings of the concept of adaptation as they learned how specialized the beaks, wings, and talons are for these birds of prey. New to the unit would be a visit from Melissa Stewart, who would share her research and writing processes for *Feathers: Not Just for Flying* (2014a), her award-winning book on the functions of feathers. We also spent time brainstorming options for the third part of our unit, dinosaurs. It was lucky that the school is within driving distance from the Beneski Museum of Natural History (**www.amherst.edu/museums/naturalhistory**) at Amherst College where students would have the chance to observe actual dinosaur footprint fossils and to experience the museum's exhibits.

Books

We sought out texts that were well matched to the content across the three phases of the unit. Since the life cycle is a commonly taught topic in K–3, we had many choices there and the teachers had books that they had used in the past. In considering books that addressed adaptations, we used some favorites, but we also sought out new texts. Since we were focusing on birds throughout the unit, we were happy to locate texts that specifically addressed bird characteristics. It was most challenging to find texts that were well suited to introduce the relationship between adaptation and evolution. We hoped that texts could support student understanding of the passage of long periods of time—quite an abstract concept for third graders. Books about dinosaurs abound, but we wanted texts that emphasized the nature of science and how our understandings about dinosaurs have changed over time. We looked for texts that emphasize the connection between dinosaurs and modern-day birds. We were fortunate in this process to have the consultation of Melissa Stewart, who is tremendously knowledgeable about science nonfiction published for the elementary grades. Additionally, we drew on our tried and true resources: Titlewave searches for well-reviewed titles and the National Science Teaching Association lists of outstanding trade books for science.

Digital Texts

We sought digital texts that would play a variety of roles in the unit. Although students would have firsthand observation opportunities on nature walks and with feeders attached to the classroom windows, we knew we could provide additional observational activities with the many online bird cameras available on the Internet. We looked, too, for additional content on bird adaptations that could be used in Solar System text sets. We knew digital texts could provide additional content to support students' understanding of evolution and dinosaurs and we were looking for museums and institutions that had rich online resources. Finally, we gathered a collection of links to websites that would support students as they researched Massachusetts birds.

Mentor Texts for Writing

Our initial planning sessions also included a discussion of what kinds of texts we hoped that students would produce during the unit. We liked the idea of incorporating some poetry writing—offering students examples of poetry as mentor texts. We also considered using Melissa Stewart's books in her A Place For . . . series as models for student writing about animals found in the arboretum. Finally, though, we settled on having students select a bird species to focus on—using a variety of mentor texts as models, including Melissa's (2014a) *Feathers: Not Just for Flying*, they would create a piece of writing that demonstrated their understandings of how the species they had chosen was ideally adapted to its environment.

Organize Texts for Instruction: How can we arrange the texts for critical thinking?

With a sequence of content in place, an outline of the unit that included three phases, texts selected, and a rough idea of the kinds of texts we would like the students to create to demonstrate their new knowledge, it was time to decide how we would organize the texts to support student learning. We were deliberate in our sequencing of the texts, hoping to layer students' understandings, beginning with the more familiar and observable concept of life cycles and parent–offspring relationships and moving toward the more abstract concepts of adaptations and evolution. In the sections that follow, we'll describe the text sets used in each phase of the unit. We also provide some samples of the graphic organizers used by the students for note taking and photographs of anchor charts and students' science notebook entries. A complete listing of the text sets used in this unit can be found at the end of the chapter.

Scaffold: Comparing Plant and Animal Life Cycles

The key question in the first phase of this unit of study was: *How are the life cycles of birds and flowering plants alike and different?* We knew that the concept of life cycles would be familiar to students as this content was included in science instruction in the primary grades. We employed texts that would reinforce the continuity of life cycles—the idea that species are born, develop, reproduce, and die, but the species carries on. This idea serves as a scaffold for the concept of adaptation, the focus of the next phase.

The NGSS standard addressed in this phase of the unit is:

- 3-LS1-1 Use simple graphical representations to show that different types of organisms have unique and diverse life cycles. Describe that all organisms have birth, growth, reproduction, and death in common, but there are a variety of ways in which these happen.

To launch the unit, we chose a single book, Molly Bang and Penny Chisholm's (2009) *Living Sunlight: How Plants Bring the Earth to Light* (see Figure 5.2). This book, cocomposed by the acclaimed picture book author and a Massachusetts Institute of Technology professor, describes the process of photosynthesis, situating this process within a description of the interconnectedness of plant and animal life cycles. We viewed this text as an opportunity to revisit the concept of plant and animal life cycles while deepening student understanding of relationships in nature (see Figure 5.3).

FIGURE 5.2

FIGURE 5.3 *An anchor chart records key takeaway ideas from Living Sunlight.*

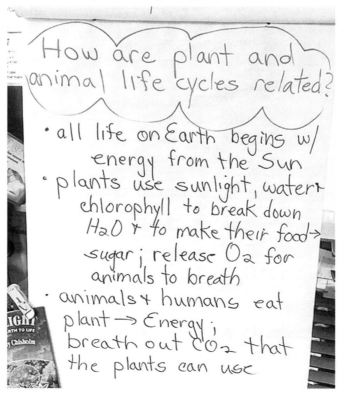

FIGURE 5.4 *In this Duet model, students compare two nonfiction picture books about seeds and plant life cycles.*

As it turned out, the teachers were not able to obtain this book in time and used it later in the unit, but our original intent was to use this title to launch the unit.

PLANT LIFE CYCLES

Following an introductory read-aloud experience, we planned a specific focus on plant life cycles. Students experienced a Duet model read-aloud experience (Figure 5.4), including *A Seed Is Sleepy* by Dianna Aston (2007) (see Figure 5.6) and *A Seed Is the Start* by Melissa Stewart (2018) (see Figure 5.7). These texts are ideal for use in a duet model because they offer an opportunity to compare how two authors present similar content (see Figure 5.5).

FIGURE 5.5

Comparing the text and illustration of A Seed Is Sleepy *and* A Seed Is the Start.

A SEED IS SLEEPY	A SEED IS THE START
• Text is an illustrated nonfiction picture book. • Primary text describes seeds using adjectives (sleepy, secretive, fruitful . . .). • Secondary text offers explanation for the primary statement; includes description of the functions of seeds. • Content includes characteristics, functions, behaviors (locomotion and germination), life cycle, and conditions for growth. • Front pages include illustrations of a variety of single seeds. • End pages include images of plants with their seeds.	• Text is a nonfiction picture book illustrated with photographs. • Primary text introduces a plant life cycle and seed locomotion, then follows with verb statements indicating how seeds travel (e.g., "Seeds fly."). • Secondary text offers additional description of how seeds travel; includes question and answer text structure. • Content includes life cycle, characteristics, locomotion. • Back matter includes an index, selected sources, and resources for more information.

When reading these aloud, the teachers focused the conversation on what they were learning about seeds from these two texts, creating an anchor chart (see Figure 5.8).

FIGURE 5.6   **FIGURE 5.7**

Throughout the unit, students recorded their learning in science notebooks. Reading through students' journal entries, it is evident that they were quite fascinated by the characteristics and behaviors of seeds. One student's entry reads: "I noticed that all seeds have a way to travel. One way I did not know but I learned is that some seeds travel inside some animals bods [*sic*], then when the scat comes out of the animal body, the seed can have a place to grow, I also learned some new seeds like the Japanese Maple and the hopseed, Seeds have a lot of ways to get to place or to grow. Some plants start from a seed and even take <u>100</u> years to grow."

The next text set in phase one extended students' understanding of the plant life cycle. Consisting of a range of multimodal digital texts (see the comprehensive text set in Figure 5.53 at the conclusion of this chapter for a listing of the digital texts that we used), this Solar System model was available to students to explore independently. A graphic organizer required them to select and describe the content of two of the texts. We asked students to draw in response to one text of their choice and then to use explanatory language to reflect the content of a second text (see Figure 5.9).

To transition to a look at animal life cycles, we next introduced a text set model that focused on the interaction between plants and habitat.

FIGURE 5.8 *An anchor chart capturing the information students noted in the seeds Duet model comparison.*

What seeds do	What seed are like
spins	
traveling	sleepy (dorman
explode	adventurous
produce	
burst	inventive
sways	secretive
float	
creep	ancient
choose	naked
rides inside	fruitful
grow outside	generous
sprout	silky
fly	

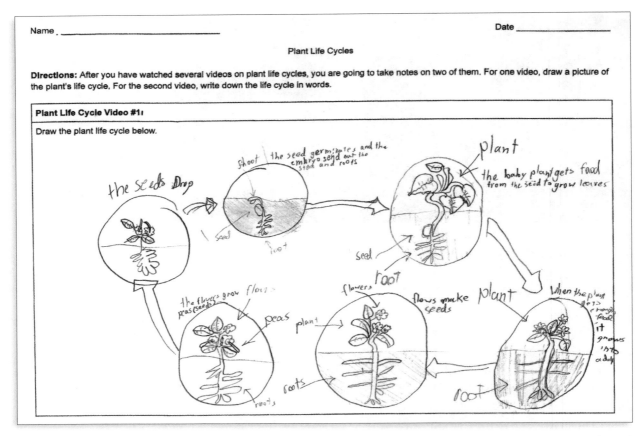

Name _____   Date _____

Plant Life Cycles

Directions: After you have watched several videos on plant life cycles, you are going to take notes on two of them. For one video, draw a picture of the plant's life cycle. For the second video, write down the life cycle in words.

Plant Life Cycle Video #1:

Draw the plant life cycle below.

FIGURE 5.9 *A graphic organizer representing plant life cycles.*

FIGURE 5.10 *In this Duet model of tree books, students learn about interdependencies in plant and animal life cycles.*

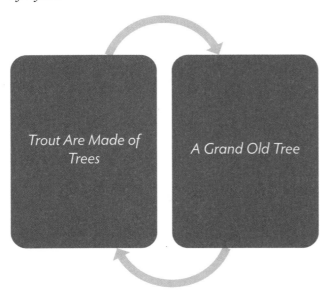

Using a Duet model comparison, we selected two texts that considered both plants in a habitat and the idea of plants as a habitat. We used two picture books: *Trout Are Made of Trees* by April Pulley Sayre (2008) and *A Grand Old Tree* by Mary Newell DePalma (2005) (see Figure 5.10).

Both are illustrated picture books. *Trout Are Made of Trees* is one of our favorite texts for the concept of interdependence in nature. With lyrical and playful language, Sayre unpacks how trout reproduction and growth is facilitated by the trees that line a stream. In *A Grand Old Tree*, DePalma details the life cycle of a "grand old tree" and the many animals that live in the tree or benefit from its fruits. Even when the tree has died, its trunk and branches create habitats for many creatures, while the offspring from its scattered seeds host animals as well. Students used a graphic organizer to compare the two books, listing the plants and animals that live in each habitat and comparing the life cycles featured in each book.

ANIMAL LIFE CYCLES

We began our look at animal life cycles with a single introductory text, Dianna Aston's (2006) *An Egg Is Quiet* (see Figure 5.11). This choice was driven by several reasons: many animals begin their life cycle as an egg; students would be studying the adaptations and evolution of birds; the book includes mention of fossilized dinosaur eggs; and having read *A Seed Is Sleepy* (2007), students were familiar with the text structure employed within the book. Both *A Seed Is Sleepy* (2007) and *An Egg Is Quiet* (2006) are books that encourage observation and inquiry, by inviting young readers to consider the many different characteristics of seeds and eggs. During the read-aloud, students noted in their science notebooks the adjectives used by Aston to describe the characteristics of eggs (see Figure 5.12). Following the read-aloud, teachers created an anchor chart recording their connections (see Figure 5.13).

FIGURE 5.11

FIGURE 5.12 *Students make notes while listening to* An Egg Is Quiet.

FIGURE 5.13 *An anchor chart created to record egg characteristics described in* An Egg Is Quiet.

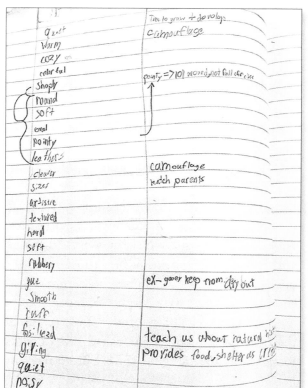

Sabina described this process in the daily feedback journal: We created an anchor chart for *An Egg Is Quiet*: What are eggs like [adj] and How it helps. The students did the same in their scientist notebooks. They made insightful connections to the texts from the previous day. For example, noticing how a seed is generous and an egg is giving both had to do with how both provide everything that is needed for the embryo. We were able to head outside for a nature walk and noticed so many seeds. The students found and sketched the seed heads of the cattails, goldenrod, etc. We also encountered dog pooh and Eastern Cottontail skat and discussed why seeds may be in one, but not the other.

Following this single text introduction, we employed a Solar System text set (see Figure 5.14) that included time lapse videos of eggs hatching, a slideshow of egg images, and two books that incorporate bird life cycles: *Hatching Chicks in Room 6* by Caroline Arnold (2017) (see Figure 5.15), and *City Chickens* by Christine Heppermann (2012) (Figure 5.16). Using a similar graphic organizer to that used with the plant life cycle Solar System of texts, students recorded notes about animal life cycles using both images and text (see Figure 5.17).

Students also took a nature walk to observe evidence of animal and plant life cycles firsthand. They collected a variety of seeds, giving them the opportunity to examine a variety of shapes and characteristics and to speculate how the characteristics of a seed might be related to its ability to reproduce (see Figures 5.18 and 5.19). During the walk, students looked for and recorded any animal activity they encountered (see Figure 5.20). During this activity, we introduced another kind of text—field guides. Sabina and Lucy shared a variety of field guides with their students, including a locally developed guide that features plant and animal species of which they were certain to find evidence.

At the conclusion of this first phase in the unit, Lucy and Sabina asked the students to respond to the guiding question for this

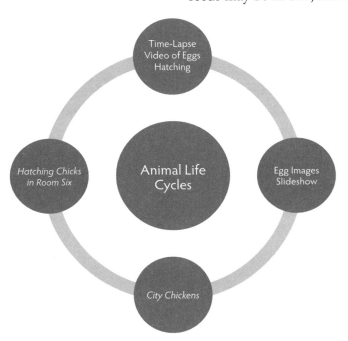

FIGURE 5.14 *This Solar System model of texts focuses on animal life cycles.*

FIGURE 5.15

FIGURE 5.16

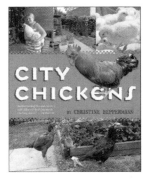

Name _____   Date _____

Animal Life Cycles

Directions: After you have watched several videos on animal life cycles, you are going to take notes on two of them. For one video, draw a picture of the animal's life cycle. For the second video, write down the life cycle in words.

Animal Life Cycle Video #1:
Draw the animal life cycle below.

Robins life Cycle   The Robin can die at any time

egg

hatchling

Adult

Chick

Fledgling

Death

FIGURE 5.17 (above)
A graphic organizer to record learning about animal life cycles.

FIGURE 5.18 (far left)
Observing the seed of trees on a nature walk.

FIGURE 5.19 (left)
A close examination of pine cones.

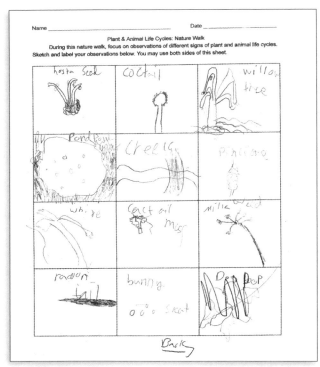

FIGURE 5.20 *Recording observations from the nature walk on a graphic organizer.*

Name

Date

Compare/Contrast Animal & Plant Life Cycles

Now that you have investigated the life cycles of some plants and animals, write a reflection describing how they are both alike and different You may use your science recording sheets and the class chart, as well, to plan your response.

The life cycles of plants and birds are similar and different, But the plants life cycle starts with a seed, Although an animalslife cycle starts with an egg but they both have an embryo. In the plant the seeds sprout and become a young plant, but a bird emerge from an egg to become a hatchling and a plant makes its own food but an animal is fed by its mother. but they both need food. When new flowers die, they release the seeds and animals do not give birth upon death.

FIGURE 5.21 *Students compare the life cycles of plants and animals.*

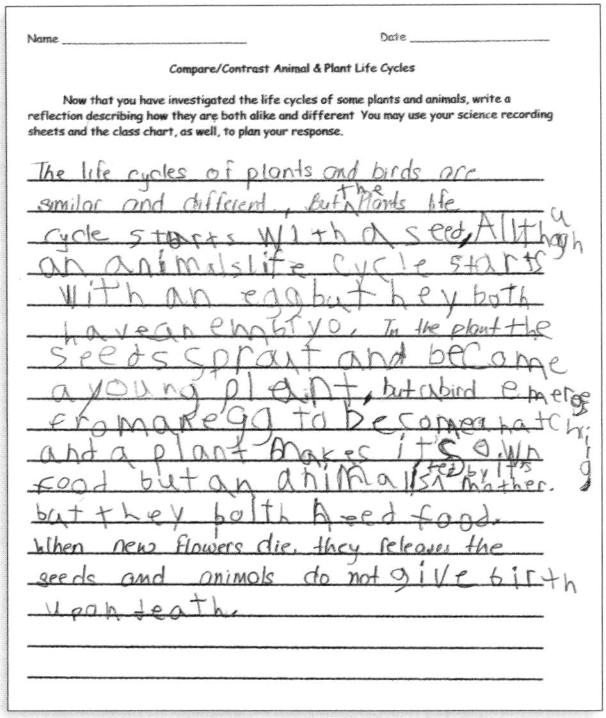

FIGURE 5.22 *Students compare the life cycles of plants and animals.*

Name

Date

Compare/Contrast Animal & Plant Life Cycles

Now that you have investigated the life cycles of some plants and animals, write a reflection describing how they are both alike and different You may use your science recording sheets and the class chart, as well, to plan your response.

There are similar and different ways in a Animal and Plant Life Cycle, For example, a Animal lays a egg, but for the Plant, The life cycle starts with a seed, Another way is when the seed turns into a seeling, the egg turns out to be a hatchling when it hatches, Both of them can have their own life cycle interrupted when a predator comes between them and of course they all have a point where they reproduce and in addition the life cycle starts again the plant makes it's own food which the plant uses sunlight, nutrients and water but the chick gets Fed from it's momma, The plant and animal have many similarities and differences between them.

phase in writing, prompting them to compare and contrast animal and plant life cycles. Student responses indicated that most of them understood life cycles as a series of stages, which includes reproduction (see Figures 5.21 and 5.22).

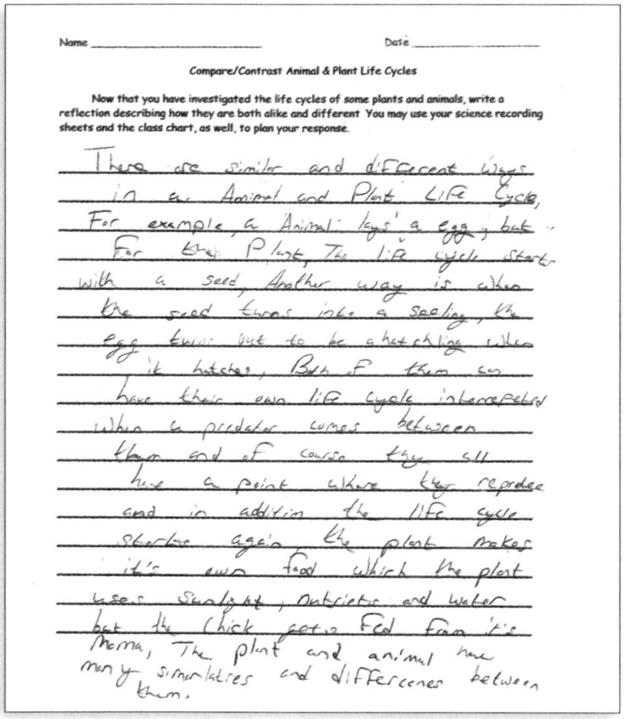

Immersion: Survival and Heredity—Traits and Adaptations

The key questions in the second phase of this unit of study were: How are plants and animals similar to their parents? and What characteristics help some living things survive better than others in an environment? We had planned to spend about four weeks on this portion of the unit, hoping that immersion in texts and hands-on investigations would lead students to understand the following:

- Animals and plants inherit traits of the species through reproduction.
- Mutations occur within individuals (they are a natural phenomenon)—a mutation is a change in your DNA that leads to a different physical characteristic for the individual.
- Different physical characteristics afford greater or lesser chances of survival.
- These physical characteristics are carried on through the life cycle (reproduction) if they are favorable. They become a characteristic of the species. This process is called adaptation, and the resulting changes are biological adaptations.

The NGSS standards addressed in this phase of the unit are:

3-LS3-1	Provide evidence, including through the analysis of data, that plants and animals have traits inherited from parents and that variation of these traits exist in a group of similar organisms.
3-LS3-2	Distinguish between inherited characteristics and those characteristics that result from a direct interaction with the environment. Give examples of characteristics of living organisms that are influenced by both inheritance and the environment.
3-LS3-2	Use evidence to construct an explanation for how the variations in characteristics among individuals within the same species may provide advantages to these individuals in their survival and reproduction.
3-LS4-3	Construct an argument with evidence that in a particular environment some organisms can survive well, some survive less well, and some cannot survive.
3-LS4-4	Analyze and interpret data about changes in a habitat and describe how the changes may affect the ability of organisms that live in that habitat to survive and reproduce.
3-LS4-5	Provide evidence to support a claim that the survival of a population is dependent upon reproduction.

PARENT–OFFSPRING RELATIONSHIPS

Following the pattern established in the first week, we used a single picture book as a scaffold to launch this new content exploration—the relationships between parents and their offspring. *What Bluebirds Do* by Pamela Kirby (2009) is a striking photo essay that depicts the courtship, nesting, hatching, and nurturing of a bluebird pair and their offspring. The back matter includes expository text describing a dip in the bluebird population in the 1970s and subsequent conservation efforts. The text encourages young readers to develop nesting boxes in their own yards. Students created a comparison chart noting what adult bluebirds do, what baby bluebirds do, and what both adult and babies do.

CHARACTERISTICS TO HELP SOME LIVING THINGS SURVIVE BETTER THAN OTHERS IN AN ENVIRONMENT

After this introductory look at parents and offspring, we moved through a series of text sets designed to help students understand how certain characteristics support survival in a particular environment. We began with a Duet model (see Figure 5.23) using *What Do You Do When Something Wants to Eat You?* by Steve Jenkins (2001) (see Figure 5.24) and *Creature Features* by Steve Jenkins and Robin Page (2014) (see Figure 5.25).

FIGURE 5.23 *The two texts in this Duet model describe specific animal adaptations and how they support survival.*

Both books feature Jenkins's collage-style illustrations and emphasize animal adaptations. In *What Do You Do When Something Wants to Eat You?*, Jenkins emphasizes animal defenses. The text structure employs a page turn and ellipses: "When an octopus is threatened . . . [page turn] it squirts a thick cloud of black ink into the water, confusing its attacker." Strategies for escaping a predator include using camouflage, speed, body alterations, and poisons. In *Creature Features*, Jenkins and Page give voice to a variety of animals with unusual appearances, using a question and answer format: "Dear mandrill: Why is your nose so colorful? My bright red and blue nose tells other mandrills that I'm a full grown monkey, so they'd better not mess with me. My rear end is pretty colorful too, but I'd rather not talk about that" (n.p.). Together these two texts offer students an array of examples of animal characteristics and how they facilitate survival. The teachers used these two texts as read-alouds, creating anchor texts on which they recorded animal characteristics and how these characteristics support animals in their environment.

FIGURE 5.24

FIGURE 5.25

BIRD ADAPTATIONS

Following this general look at adaptations, the teachers moved students into a specific look at bird species. After having an opportunity to observe birds on a nature walk and using bird cams (see the listing of text sets in Figure 5.53 at the end of this chapter for suggested bird cams), students experienced a sequence of multimodal Solar System text sets models about birds' feathers, beaks, and feet (see Figures 5.26–5.28). Each of these text sets included a book specifically about the bird feature along with more general resources including bird guides, digital texts including video, and Annette LeBlanc Cate's (2013) engaging book, *Look Up! Bird-Watching in Your Backyard* (see Figures 5.29–5.32). For each text set, students completed a graphic organizer, noting the source, the type of bird, and information about feathers, beaks, or feet.

These reading experiences were accompanied by hands-on activities that teachers had used in the past; these involved simulations

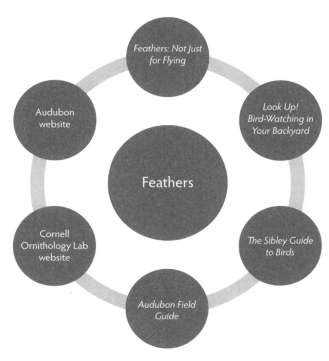

FIGURE 5.26 *This Solar System model provides a look at bird feathers as adaptations.*

FIGURE 5.27 *This Solar System model provides a look at bird beaks as adaptations.*

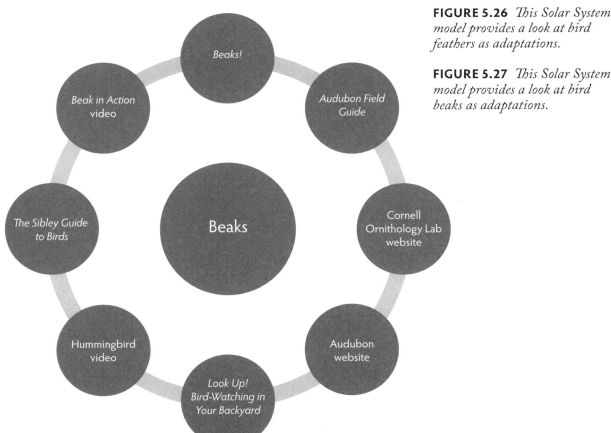

FIGURE 5.28 *This Solar System model provides a look at bird feet as adaptations.*

FIGURE 5.29

FIGURE 5.30

FIGURE 5.31

FIGURE 5.32

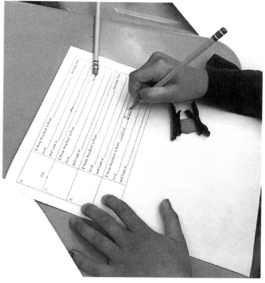

FIGURE 5.33 *Investigating how bird beaks function.*

FIGURE 5.34 *Investigating how bird feet function.*

and/or observation activities that demonstrated the functions of beaks (see Figure 5.33) and feet (see Figure 5.34).

During this time, students also experienced a visit from Wingmasters, giving them the opportunity to observe raptors up close. Students recorded notes about the adaptations of falcons, hawks, and owls (see Figures 5.35 and 5.36). Additionally, Melissa Stewart visited the classes, sharing her books and talking about how she carried out her research for *Feathers: Not Just for Flying* (2014a) and her series, A Place For . . . (see Figures 5.37 and 5.38). These simulations and visits afforded lots of opportunity for talk about the concept of adaptation. Students examined similarities and differences across bird species and found that they had new questions. These questions were recorded by Sabina in the Daily Feedback Journal:

> On Friday we read *Feathers: Not Just for Flying* with the document camera. While the students took notes on the organizer, the grade-level assistant wrote notes on an

FIGURE 5.35 *Recording adaptation notes during the Wingmasters' visit.*

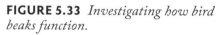

Wingmasters Adaptations

Think about the birds that visited us here at Conant. Record some of the adaptations you learned about and tell what the adaptation helps the bird do. Use the owl example to help you.

	Falcons	Hawks	Owls
Feathers	Sharp strong pointy Like plastic → speed	flash Red tail to show territory	Soft feathers- they can fly silently and their prey won't hear them
Beaks	curved sharp and pointed → tear meat	curved sharp strong → tear meat	strong curved → tear meat
Feet	Long thin toes → Not powerful	strong muscular toes sharp talons	muscular strong sharp talents feathered legs
Other adaptation?	black markings absorb sun hunt in air eyes high near brow	bird call is a warning	ear hole slightly higher than the other facial brings in soundwave.

FIGURE 5.36
During Melissa's visit, students compare their arm span to a bird's wingspan.

FIGURE 5.37

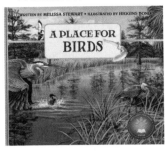

FIGURE 5.38 *Students use the language of claims and evidence to consider adaptations.*

anchor chart. The students requested revisits to particular pages to add to their notes. We used the related questions to foster a whole-class conversation. I built a Venn diagram to record their thinking. They realized that although birds may have methods to attract mates, those methods may be different: the manakin may make a whistling noise with its wings while the showy peacock displays its feathers. In addition they noted that birds have different ways to avoid predators, such as the "trickster" junco and camouflaged female cardinal. Students wondered what the female sandgrouse may be doing while the male brings water to the chicks. Do birds other than the red-tailed hawk use feathers as sunscreen?

The teachers guided the students to use the language of "claim and evidence" as they framed their questions and ideas about how adaptations support survival (see Figure 5.38). This disciplinary literacy was reinforced through work with additional non-bird-related digital texts, including a look at an online video about the adaptations of rock pocket mice and an online game focusing on adaptation and survival.

The final text set of this phase of the unit focused on bird communication. This Solar System model of texts (see Figure 5.39) included Lita Judge's (2012) *Bird Talk: What Birds Are Saying and Why* (see Figure 5.40) along with digital texts and revisiting *Look Up! Bird-Watching in Your Backyard* by Annette LeBlanc Cate (2013). Students watched bird cams and made notes about the vocalizations and accompanying behaviors that they observed.

FIGURE 5.39 *This Solar System model of texts focuses on how birds communicate.*

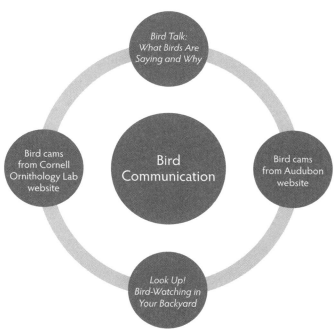

Extension: Survival over Time—Investigating Biological Evolution

We knew that the third phase of our unit would hold the most challenging science content for our students. The linkage between adaptation and biological evolution would be abstract for most students. We hoped to support students to make connections between their new understandings about the link between adaptations and survival in a particular environment and the biological evolution of new species over time. In our initial planning, we mapped out these ideas on the following page as a series of connections:

FIGURE 5.40

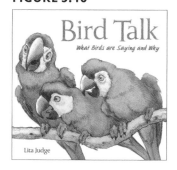

- In a life cycle, reproduction creates ongoing survival of species.
- Biological adaptations are passed on through adaptation.
- Over time biological adaptations lead to evolution of new species.
- Fossils are evidence of changes in physical traits over time.
- From dinosaurs to birds—this is evidence of biological adaptation over time.

The NGSS standards that we hoped to meet through the text sets in this phase of the unit were:

3-LS4-1	Use fossils to describe types of organisms and their environments that existed long ago and compare those to living organisms and their environments. Recognize that most kinds of plants and animals that once lived on Earth are no longer found anywhere.
3-LS4-4	Analyze and interpret data about changes in a habitat and describe how the changes may affect the ability of organisms that live in that habitat to survive and reproduce.

To build disciplinary literacies and critical thinking, we intended to focus heavily on the scientific process in this phase of the unit, considering questions such as: How do we know what we know about changes over long periods of time? What have we theorized?

CHANGE OVER TIME IN THE SAME GEOLOGICAL PLACE

FIGURE 5.41 *The two texts in this Duet model address change over time in a geographic location.*

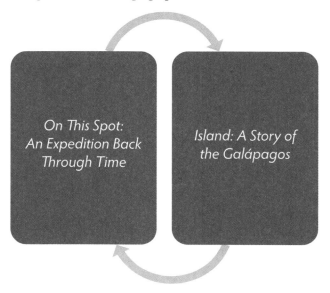

The first text set that we used was a Duet model of nonfiction picture books that presented change in an environment over time (see Figure 5.41). In this text set model, Susan Goodman's (2004) *On This Spot: An Expedition Back Through Time* serves as a scaffold to the more complex look at change over time and natural selection that are explored in Jason Chin's (2012) *Island: A Story of the Galápagos* (see Figure 5.42).

Both books focus on change over long time spans—*Island*: from six million years ago to Darwin's arrival in 1835; *On This Spot*: from the present to 540 million years ago. *On This Spot* offers a more general overview of change over time, while *Island* is more specific to adaptation. After reading *On This Spot*, Sabina and

Lucy created a two-column chart to record (1) changes over time depicted in the book and (2) questions inspired by the book. Teachers also used a document camera to project the timeline in the back matter and invited students to read and interpret this infographic.

Next, the teachers read aloud *Island*. Distributing sticky notes to the students, they invited them to write down the connections that they were making and the questions that they had. This book is organized into sections—the teachers paused between sections so that students had time to write. On the following day, Sabina and Lucy divided their classes into small groups. Using multiple copies of the book, the small groups worked on two tasks: (1) sorting, comparing, and discussing the connections and questions that they had written on their post its and (2) representing an assigned time period covered in the book: birth, childhood, adulthood, and old age of the island. Each group constructed a visual image on large chart paper that illustrated and explained the changes during that time period.

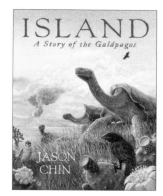

FIGURE 5.42

THE DINOSAUR–BIRD CONNECTION

Next, it was time to introduce students to the dinosaur–bird connection, emphasizing how scientists have come to understand this connection over time. To explore these ideas, we once again employed a Duet model of nonfiction picture books (see Figure 5.43). Kathleen Kudlinski's (2005) *Boy, Were We Wrong About Dinosaurs!* (see Figure 5.44) introduces the ideas that our understanding of dinosaurs, based on their fossilized remains, has changed over time. Next, a read-aloud of Lita Judge's (2010) *Born to Be Giants: How Baby Dinosaurs Grew to Rule the World* (see Figure 5.45) demonstrated the ways our thinking about dinosaurs has changed based on new evidence. Additionally, this book has the added benefit of connecting to prior topics explored in the first two phases of the unit (eggs, heredity, and parent–child relationships). Furthermore, it reinforces the idea of the dinosaur–bird connection introduced in *Boy ,We Were Wrong About Dinosaurs!* Both mention the dinosaur to bird evolution over time.

As the teachers read aloud these texts, they made charts recording key foundational

FIGURE 5.43 *The two texts in this Duet model explore the theory that today's birds are the ancestors of dinosaurs.*

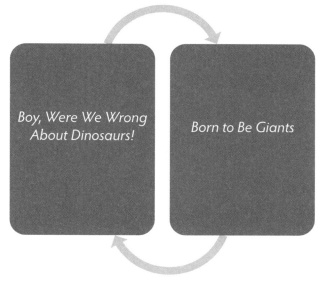

FIGURE 5.44

FIGURE 5.45

concepts about dinosaur–bird evolution. The anchor chart for *Boy ,Were We Wrong About Dinosaurs!* had the following four columns: (1) "Body Part"; (2) "What Scientists Thought"; (3) "Fossil Evidence"; and (4) "What Scientists Think Now." Sabina and Lucy were careful to emphasize that thinking about dinosaurs has changed even since the publication of this book! For *Born to Be Giants*, the anchor chart was a two-column one, prompting students to note "Dinosaur Activity" and "Connection to Birds."

Both *Born to Be Giants* and *Boy, Were We Wrong About Dinosaurs!* include timelines, offering an opportunity to connect with the concepts about change over time explored in the previous Duet model with *On This Spot* (Goodman 2005) and *Island* (Chin 2012). The teachers used a document camera to project the two visual timelines. Students compared how the timelines depicted dinosaurs evolving into birds. In keeping with our focus on body parts and adaptations, they invited students to describe what they noticed in the illustrations about feet, legs, arms, wings, mouths, and beaks.

Our next Solar System model (see Figure 5.46) focused students even more specifically on the characteristics of dinosaurs and their evolutionary connection to birds. Brenda Guiberson's (2016) picture book *Feathered Dinosaurs* (see Figure 5.47) describes thirteen dinosaur species and their characteristics that relate to modern-day birds. Opening and concluding segments describe the ongoing discoveries that strengthen scientists' theories about the evolution of dinosaurs to birds. Guiberson's text is accompanied by William Low's immersive oil and acrylic illustrations.

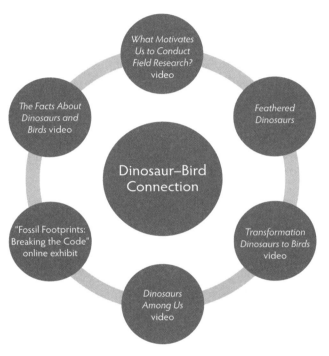

FIGURE 5.46 *This Solar System model consists of a collection of digital texts and a nonfiction picture book exploring the connection between birds and dinosaurs.*

FIGURE 5.47

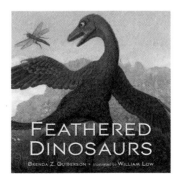

Along with *Feathered Dinosaurs*, the two classes explored an array of digital resources, making notes about their discoveries on a graphic organizer. This book and the other two illustrated books about dinosaurs that students had read previously provided an important opportunity to remind students that scientists only have some ideas about what dinosaurs looked like, based on fossilized evidence. If time had allowed, the teachers and students could have explored the idea of paleo-art and the work of paleo-artists.

FIGURE 5.48
Students are guided through the Beneski Museum in Amherst, Massachusetts.

As the culmination of our focus on biological evolution, Lucy and Sabina planned a field trip to Amherst, Massachusetts, to visit the Beneski Museum of Natural Science. There, students had the opportunity to observe dinosaur footprints firsthand. The museum contains the largest collection of dinosaur prints in the world. The third president of Amherst, Edward Hitchcock, a scientist, was the first to discover these, before the term *dinosaur* was even coined. He also completed a chemical analysis of fossilized dinosaur dung and recognized that it was chemically related to

FIGURE 5.49
Students stand alongside dinosaur footprints.

birds, not mammals, reptiles, and so on. He was the first to recognize this evolutionary step and wrote of it to Charles Darwin. The college has Darwin's reply letter among its manuscripts and it is accessible digitally online. The students were fascinated by the large slab fossils at the museum that clearly displayed footprints from 150 million years ago (see Figure 5.48). As they browsed the museum collection, students had an opportunity to observe, sketch, and record their questions. They also had a chance to view dinosaur prints outside, even to place their own feet next to these fossils (see Figure 5.49).

This phase of the unit occurred during a very busy time of year for the teachers. Interruptions created by snow days and state testing days made this extension phase less focused and less convenient to document. Additionally, the student writing projects required time and attention to bring to completion during this time period.

Create New Texts: What are the new texts created by students?

From the start, we knew that we hoped to engage students in the creation of new texts that would demonstrate their understanding of the key science content of the unit. We had discussed several possibilities, but ultimately, because time was limited and because the content felt new and complex, Lucy and Sabina decided that it would make sense to have students work collaboratively to create a class book. They would focus specifically on Massachusetts birds, with students having a choice of which bird they would like to research and write about. Students would be asked to feature special characteristics about each bird that make it uniquely adapted to its environment. Knowing that this was the content we wished to highlight, we then turned to a consideration of which mentor texts we could use to support student writing.

As we were discussing how to best scaffold the students' research and writing processes, Melissa offered us a title suggestion that held immediate appeal. Maria Gianferrari's (2018) picture book *Terrific Tongues* is structured by a patterned text, incorporating a text frame that we thought would appeal to students and that they would readily be able to model their own writing after. The book uses similes to explain the various functions that animal tongues can serve. The book opens with a metaphorical hook that provokes curiosity and engagement: "It's a sword. It's a straw. It's a nose. It's a mop. It's a . . . TONGUE. STICK OUT YOUR TONGUE" (n.p.). Next begins the pattern that will be repeated throughout the text: "If you had a tongue like a sword, you might be a . . . [page turn] WOODPECKER!" Accompanying an illustration of the featured animal, a secondary text explains how the tongue functions like a sword: "The red-bellied woodpecker's tongue is three times as long as its beak and as sharp as a sword. It uses its barbed tongue to stab beetle larvae and other insects that burrow beneath the tree bark."

We were confident that students would be able to imitate this structure in their own writing. Although we typically like to give students more choice in how they demonstrate their learning, for this unit, we decided to compromise a bit. We knew that the time available for a writing project was limited and that the content of the unit was complex and new to both the teachers and the students. This patterned text seemed a good option—one that would allow students to produce a piece of writing fairly quickly but also be a concrete format in which students could clearly demonstrate their understanding of adaptation.

The students would work together to create a single writing product—a Google Slide presentation that explained significant adaptations of Massachusetts birds. Each student would be responsible for composing:

1. Simile statement (primary text)

2. Expository text that explains the adaptation (secondary text)

3. Fun fact: additional information they want to include about their bird

The fun fact was included to offer space for additional choice of content for students. *Terrific Tongues* includes a page in the back matter that offers additional information about each of the animal tongues featured in the book. We left the "Fun Fact" section open so that students could include any additional information they wished about the bird they selected.

Student Research

Students began work on their Massachusetts bird writing during phase two of the unit. They selected a bird that interested them and began to identify resources to learn more about their bird. Sabina and Lucy curated a collection of websites that students could browse to make their selection and to begin to gather information.

After looking closely at the characteristics and functions of beaks, feathers, and feet, students were well prepared to find and consider information about the feathers, beaks, and feet of the Massachusetts bird they had chosen. They were ready, too, to consider additional characteristics of their bird and how these characteristics supported survival and represented adaptation. As they read through the multimodal texts they were using as sources, students recorded notes on a graphic organizer (see Figure 5.50). We found that they needed time and some coaching to identify characteristics as an adaptation. In the daily feedback journal, Sabina noted: "The students are working on their research, and are coming to understand that figuring out the important adaptations of their selection may require some inferences. We talked about *Feathers* and posed the question, Do you think when Melissa Stewart was researching for this book she found an article that said that the feathers of the red tail hawk are like sunscreen? They are starting to figure this out, but need research blocks."

Name:
Bird:

Research Bird Trait Adaptation Graphic Organizer

Directions: Using books, bird cameras, websites, and guide books, write down information that you learn about how the bird you have selected to research uses its feathers, feet, beaks and other traits that help it to survive in the wild.

Source	What do the Feathers Do and Why?	What do the Beaks do and Why?	What do the Feet Do and Why?	Other Traits & How They Help

FIGURE 5.50
Graphic organizer for recording bird research notes.

Once students completed their graphic organizers, having explored several sources, they met with a small group of classmates. Together, they considered each other's organizers, discussed the information they had learned about their bird, and worked toward selecting one particular adaptation to feature in their writing (and on their slide). This peer support proved to be critical to the process as was some additional coaching for some students. Sabina noted in the daily feedback journal:

> It seems that some of the students are struggling to identify what is important. One of my students chose the blue jay. I had a collective source for him with a few paragraphs about the blue jay. He came to me and said he read it and that there really wasn't anything to record. I read the passage aloud to him; it was fascinating. We learned that the blue jay is part of the crow family and was once a forest dweller, but adapted to diminishing habitat by living in suburban parks, backyards, etc. On his own, he didn't see that this was significant information. The students need support with this process; I'm grateful that they are working in pairs and triplets.

Composing New Texts: Organizers, Models, and Mentor Texts

During the composing process, we supported students toward their finished texts in a variety of ways, including the use of a graphic organizer for drafting their text, providing a model of the text structure they were striving toward, and revisiting texts from the unit as mentor texts for the students' own writing.

Lucy and Sabina created an organizer for student writing that was specific to this project, but that also included an organizer for paragraph writing that was familiar to the students. The instructions at the top of the organizer read: "Using your graphic organizer for your research, decide which trait best serves your bird helping it to survive in the wild." Next was a text frame drawn from the patterned text of *Terrific Tongues* (Gianferrari 2018): "If you had a/an _____ like a _____ you'd be _____." The remainder of the page offered a space for paragraph drafting. Spaces were provided for students to record a topic sentence, several important details, and an ending.

The teachers also created samples for students to view, discuss, and use as models. They chose the peregrine falcon as their focus and created research notes, the writing organizer, and a finished slide to share with the students as they worked on each of these steps (see Figure 5.51).

FIGURE 5.51
Lucy and Sabina created this exemplar slide as a model for students' writing.

Peregrine Falcon Exemplar

If you had feathers that were sharp and strong like a plastic comb, you'd be the peregrine falcon, built for speed and hunting your prey while in flight.

Strong, sharp feathers aren't the only trait that make this raptor an expert at daylight hunting. However, these feathers make up the long, pointed wings of the peregrine falcon that are built to cut through the sky at the greatest speeds of any creature on this planet. Diving speeds can range from 100 to 200 miles per hour! In addition to speed, the wings allow this raptor to change direction quickly, making it nearly impossible for a songbird or pigeon to avoid this master at flight.

Like football players who need to look up into the sky during their sport, the peregrine falcon has dark markings beneath its eyes called a mustache. These absorb the sunlight during their daylight hunting. Their eyes are also placed high in their skulls near the brow arch. This placement also provides keen vision for daylight hunting.

The peregrine falcon is the master of the diurnal hunt with its long, sharp feathers, unlike the nocturnal owl with soft, fringed feathers who surprise their prey with their silent flight.

Thumbnail: Interesting Fact

The peregrine falcon could be described as "the comeback kid." This species was nearly wiped out because of the chemical DDT, which was used in pesticides beginning in the 1950s. Once the pesticide was banned in the US, and with the work of scientists who bred the species, the peregrine falcon was removed from the federal endangered species list in 1999.

Using texts that we had previously explored for content learning, we also planned a series of minilessons during which we would revisit these texts to look at specific writing techniques—these texts served double duty in this unit of study as resources for science learning and for writing instruction. We mapped out minilessons that went from "whole to part": we first focused on structure, then on style and illustration. Finally, we returned to structure with a minilesson on back matter. For each of these minilessons, we looked at several examples from the unit texts, unpacked what was happening in text and illustration through whole-class discussion, and then sent students back to their own writing to try out the craft techniques they had learned. Figure 5.52 provides an overview of these minilessons.

FIGURE 5.52 *A series of minilessons using mentor texts to support students' writing about bird adaptations.*

FOCUS OF MINILESSON	TEXTS USED	DESCRIPTION
Structure: Similes in Patterned Text	*Terrific Tongues* (Gianferrari 2018) *Feathers: Not Just for Flying* (Stewart 2014a) *Paddle Perch Climb: Bird Feet Are Neat* (Angus 2018)	Examining variations in the use of similes within the patterned texts of these books
Style: Writing Similes	*Terrific Tongues* *Feathers: Not Just for Flying*	Discussing the quality of the similes used—what they say and how they convey information
Style: Writing Short Expository Paragraphs	*Bird Talk* (Judge 2012) *Feathers: Not Just for Flying* *Beaks!* (Collard 2002)	Close reading of the expository paragraphs that comprise the secondary text: How do you write short expository paragraphs focused on one trait/strength?

Style: Descriptive Vivid Verbs and Specific Adjectives	*Terrific Tongues* *Feathers: Not Just for Flying* *Paddle Perch Climb: Bird Feet Are Neat* *Bird Talk*	Examining authors' word choices: How do the authors of these texts use language to create images in the minds of their readers? How does the author's word choice help a reader to visualize how the featured bird looks? How does the author's word choice help a reader to visualize how they move/behave?
FOCUS OF MINILESSON	**TEXTS USED**	**DESCRIPTION**
Illustration: Illustrations vs. Photographs	Paper collage in *Beaks* and *Paddle Perch Climb* Watercolor in *Feathers: Not Just for Flying* and *Bird Talk* Photographs in *What Bluebirds Do* (Kirby 2009)	Comparing and contrasting medium, space and context, and content and ideas within the illustrations: How does the illustrator use image to enhance the reader's understandings of the adaptation that is being described?
Structure: Back Matter	*Feathers: Not Just for Flying* *Paddle Perch Climb: Bird Feet Are Neat* *Bird Talk*	Examining the back matter: What kinds of information are included? How does this information enhance and expand the reading experience?

The two teachers approached the final writing product in different ways. Sabina had her students work in teams, and she asked them to consider the feather, beaks, and feet of their selected bird. The teams wrote longer entries than Lucy's students, who worked individually and focused on one trait for their main text, including other interesting facts as secondary text.

The following writing was produced by a group of students in Sabina's class. Each segment of text was presented on a slide and illustrated with photos that students had curated from the web (providing a citation for each).

If you had eyes that were ten times sharper than a human's eyes, like binoculars . . .

you'd be a Bald Eagle.

Eyesight.
The American Bald Eagle's eyesight is very sharp and made for detecting fish in the river or lake. It flies very high in the air and dives at the fish.

Range and Habitat.
It is a very powerful bird and is the symbol of the United States of America. It likes to live near water and on cliffs, and has a wide range across the United States from the east coast to the west coast. It is common in winter along the Mississippi and Missouri Rivers and near large lakes and reservoirs. Here in Massachusetts, Bald Eagles are found near the Quabbin Reservoir.

Feathers and Wings.
Bald eagles have about 7000 feathers, and they are layered to trap air and protect it from the cold and rain. The strong wings of the eagle beat slowly; it can fly up to 30 miles per hour and dive at 100 miles per hour.

Feet.
It uses its talons to kill prey. The powerful feet are made for snatching prey from the water or sometimes to steal fish from osprey's feet. The Bald Eagle's toes have spicules to hold on to slippery fish.

Beak.
The beak has a hook at the tip that is used for tearing meat and fish. When necessary, the Bald Eagle will switch to devouring rabbits, rodents and other small animals. This adaptation ensures that the Bald Eagle will never go hungry.

Thermals.
To soar, Bald Eagles use thermals, which are rising currents of warm air and updrafts, generated by terrain at valley edges or mountain slopes. The tail is used for flight maneuvering; in flight the tail feathers are spread to get the largest surface area to increase the effect of thermal updrafts.

Interesting Facts.
1. Their nest may be up to 6 feet across.
2. The founding fathers chose the Bald Eagle to be the symbol of the USA because with its head and tail feathers it presents a noble image that

reflects our ideals and beliefs. The birds' strength and hunting ability tells other nations that we are ready to defend ourselves.
3. Their wingspan is 7 feet wide.
4. The Bald Eagle is at the top of the food chain.

Sources.
www.baldeagleinfo.com
Cornell Lab of Ornithology
Birds of Prey from Falcons to Vultures, 2001 by Sarah Miller
Birds of Prey, 2005 by Andrew Solway
Birds of Prey, A Look at Daytime Raptors, 1999 by Sneed B. Collard III

Reading through this sample, you will notice a clear focus on adaptation. Each characteristic of the bald eagle described by the students is directly linked to a description of how this feature helps the eagle to thrive in its environment. Notice that this group was able to follow the pattern established by the mentor text, *Terrific Tongues* (Gianferrari 2018) and that they created an effective simile to describe the eagle's eyesight. We can also read the opening as a claim and evidence statement. The claim is that the eagle's eyes are as powerful as binoculars and the evidence is that the eagle enters a dive high in the air—it is able to spot its prey and target it accurately from far away. This evidence backs up the claim that the eagle has remarkable eyesight.

We can also see evidence of an understanding of adaptation in this writing sample composed by a student in Lucy's class:

If you had a voice like a fire alarm . . .

You'd be the Purple Finch, ready to alarm your flock that a predator is near.

A Beautiful Voice.
A Purple Finch's beautiful voice can sometimes be as alarming as a giant fire alarm. It uses its amazing beak full of singing to tell the flock to take cover! A furious predator is near! The finch can make some peaceful sounds or songs too. A male can sing a rich song that is slurred, and it contains 6-23 notes. The sounds go from rising to falling. You would often hear this song when a Purple finch is calling to its family. A different song that a male can recite is usually sung alone. It starts with a few of the same notes in the same tone, then ends with a loud high-pitched note. Chirp!

Crazy Good Feet.
The awesome Purple Finch can use its strong feet to hold onto branches, even in a terrifying storm! The feet will wrap around a branch, and then . . . take cover! There's one amazing hold, after another. The Finch sure does have a lot of glorious adaptations to stay alive.

Interesting Facts.
• Purple Finches have great seed-cracking beaks.
• Purple Finches favorite seed is black oil sunflower seeds.
• Male Purple Finches are actually a rose color.
• Females are usually a tan color to camouflage.
• Purple finches are related to house finches.
• House finches may have drove Purple Finches back into the woods.

Resources
www.audubon.org/field-guide/bird/purple-finch
www.allaboutbirds.org/guide/Purple_Finch/overview
www.biokids.umich.edu/critters/Carpodacus_purpureus/

In addition to clearly describing the adaptation and its role in survival, we see this student playing with description and voice, perhaps inspired by the humorous tone of Lita Judge's (2012) *Bird Talk*.

Notes for Next Year

Any unit of study is a work in progress, and we found in this unit that we were challenged to fit in all the elements that we had planned. Snow days and state testing slowed our progress through the content, and the emphasis on writing in the latter half of the unit took more time than we might have anticipated. Moving forward, the whole third-grade team will be using the text set approach to teach the unit. The unit will start in spring, rather than winter, to minimize interruption and maximize opportunities for nature walks in the nearby arboretum. The district science coordinator is continuing to develop experiential learning aspects of the unit.

In this overview of a third-grade science unit on adaptation and evolution, we have emphasized the role that texts can play in scaffolding students' understanding of complex content. The text sets presented here illustrate the potential that carefully selected and deliberately organized texts have for making scientific ideas accessible. The texts that we selected for this unit were also chosen because they model the disciplinary literacies of science, either by describing or reflecting the processes of inquiry or by including clear examples of claims and evidence. We carefully organized and sequenced the texts so that students could move from an understanding of life cycles and reproduction to an understanding of how successful adaptations are passed on, leading to evolution.

VOICES FROM THE CLASSROOM *Lucy, Third Grade Teacher*

Working on integrating literacy into an inquiry-based science investigation initially interested me for a number of reasons. First, I absolutely love rich picture books, and I try to incorporate them into my lessons as much as possible. Third graders truly enjoy being read aloud to, and there is so much value to be found in it. The life science standards at the time of embarking on this collaborative project were fairly new, and implementing some of the more complex concepts was proving to be challenging. We already had several wonderful resources we were using, such as videos and hands-on activities that would contribute to student understanding, but we knew we needed more.

As teachers, our thinking and planning primarily live in a day-to-day structure, and we look very closely at what lessons will look like in the classroom. We ask ourselves questions such as "What will teachers and students be doing, saying, reading, writing, and demonstrating?" It was important to think about and see the larger picture from Mary Ann and Erika's viewpoint, and they were pivotal in helping us create the larger narrative arc of the unit. We were then able to create more explicit day-by-day plans with their support. In both the small scale and larger scale, we always kept student learning as the drive for each decision made.

Separating the unit into three stages and giving time frames for each was one of the first and most helpful steps in designing the architecture of the curriculum. Another hugely important aspect was including our K–6 district science specialist and author and scientist Melissa Stewart in the project. Their science background was imperative to increasing all of our knowledge surrounding the science concepts that needed to be well understood in order to teach the content clearly and accurately to our students.

The picture books that were recommended by Erika, Mary Ann, and Melissa were successfully implemented into our lesson plans, and the texts were the most valuable takeaway for me. They served two important purposes: building student understanding of the more complex science concepts and serving as high-quality mentor texts for student expository writing. Students were exposed to the same ideas through a variety of texts, and the concept became easily accessible after repeated exposure. The more complicated concept of adaptation changing over time was aided by a few websites and videos as well as the texts that we chose for this more complex science concept.

The collaborative project on bird adaptation was a major success, and we incorporated technology using Google Slides, which made it even more engaging for students. The minilessons made it possible for students to feel confident in composing their own piece of expository writing. Particularly helpful was the lesson on zooming in on paragraphs within the mentor texts and analyzing the different features that these authors used in their writing. The mentor texts helped students feel empowered and capable when it came time to try out their own writing styles on their first attempts at rough drafts.

The most difficult part of the project was the initial research that students were asked to do in order to gain more knowledge about a Massachusetts bird of their choice. They were asked to choose and focus on one trait that they believed to be critical to the bird's survival. Since we had read so many texts that had explicitly described certain traits of birds and how exactly they help the bird survive, students were looking for research online that would spoon-feed them the specific information they were looking for. I was met with many frustrated student comments such as "I can't find anything," "It doesn't tell which is the most important trait," or "It doesn't tell how the beaks or feet help." I facilitated quite a few discussions about the challenges and time commitment of research, as well as modeling how to infer from the information we found. This year, in order to make the research piece more accessible to students, I created a more open-ended organizer that did not specifically ask about traits such as the beak, feathers, or feet, but rather asked students to wonder about how the bird hunts or finds food, how it hides from predators, and what traits help it survive. In an effort to utilize time more efficiently, I also had students begin the project during phase two rather than waiting until later in the unit.

Overall, the texts we have implemented and the literacy activities embedded within the science investigation have built such a rich curriculum for third-grade life science. The repeated exposure to adaptation and survival and change over time through such a variety of materials has increased student understanding and helped them build a solid foundation of the concepts. Working with so many invested and knowledgeable professionals was an incredibly valuable experience that has impacted my teaching immensely.

From the PK–6 STEM Science Curriculum Coordinator:

When thinking about how to teach third graders the new NGSS standards focused on heredity and biological evolution, many district science curriculum leaders were at a loss. These were completely new topics and few resources were available, especially for elementary students. Thus, I was thrilled to be a part of this collaboration to develop an integrated science and literacy unit, and then to watch it play out in the classrooms.

This unit represents a true integration of science and literacy. Too often, "integrated" units are either literacy units that touch upon a science topic or science units that incorporate some reading or writing. Here, each text was carefully evaluated and chosen specifically because it was effective for both science and literacy lessons. The teachers viewed and structured their days a bit differently: instead of a literacy block in the morning and a science lesson in the afternoon, they were able to incorporate reading, writing, and science instruction throughout much of their day. Hands-on, digital, and field experiences were supported by what the students were reading and writing about, and vice versa. Everything connected for the students. Witnessing the level of student engagement and depth of student understanding that developed was incredibly rewarding.

Comprehensive Text Sets

In Figure 5.53, you will find an outline of all the texts that were used in this third-grade unit on adaptation and biological evolution.

FIGURE 5.53 *A listing of the texts used in this unit on adaptation and biological evolution.*

PHASE ONE: COMPARING PLANT AND ANIMAL LIFE CYCLES

SCAFFOLD TEXT	
Introductory Text: Animal-Plant-Habitat Interdependence	*Living Sunlight: How Plants Bring the Earth to Light* by Molly Bang and Penny Chisholm (2009)
IMMERSION TEXTS	
Duet Model Text Set: Plant Life Cycles	*A Seed Is the Start* by Melissa Stewart and illustrated by Sylvia Long (2018)
	A Seed Is Sleepy by Dianna Aston (2007)
	Additional
	BrainPop Jr. video plant life cycles
	Lima bean time lapse video: **www.youtube.com /watch?v=iZMjBO6A7AE**
	White House garden: three sisters planting video: **www.youtube.com/watch?v=69wKN1JRilc**
	Cape Abilities Farm: Wampanoag three sisters planting video: **www.youtube.com/watch?v=ZbiVR8PFdp8**
Duet Model Text Set: Plants in Habitats, Plants as Habitat	*Trout Are Made of Trees* by April Pulley Sayre and illustrated by Kate Endle (2008)
	A Grand Old Tree by Mary Newell DePalma (2005)
Introductory Text: Animal Life Cycles	*An Egg Is Quiet* by Dianna Aston (2006)
Solar System Text Sets: Bird Life Cycles	*Hatching Chicks in Room 6* by Caroline Arnold (2017)
	City Chickens by Christine Heppermann and illustrated by Christian Robinson (2012)
	The Dead Bird by Margaret Wise Brown (2016)
	Slideshow of egg images hatching provided by the district
	Baby Robins: Eggs to Flight in 14 Days **www.youtube.com/watch?v=q64QV0rV6lo**

Solar System Text Sets: Bird Life Cycles *continued*	Rockin Robin: The Life Cycle www.youtube.com/watch?v=tfDSnT9nCdg Chicken Embryo Development www.youtube.com/watch?v=PedajVADLGw
Duet Model: Looking Locally	Bird field guides Local arboretum guide

EXTENSION TEXTS

Duet Model: Looking Further, Introduction to Bird Cams	Cornell Lab of Ornithology: All About Birds cams.allaboutbirds.org/all-cams/ Audubon Bird Cams www.audubon.org/birdcams

PHASE TWO: SURVIVAL AND HEREDITY: TRAITS AND ADAPTATIONS

SCAFFOLD TEXT

Introductory Text: Parent Offspring Relationships	*What Bluebirds Do* by Pamela F. Kirby (2009)

IMMERSION TEXTS

Duet Model: Characteristics to Help Some Living Things Survive Better Than Others in an Environment	*What Do You Do When Something Wants to Eat You?* by Steve Jenkins (2001) *Creature Features* by Steve Jenkins and Robin Page (2014)
Solar System Text Sets: Bird Characteristics	*Feathers:* *Feathers: Not Just for Flying* by Melissa Stewart and illustrated by Sarah S. Brannen (2014) *Look Up! Bird-Watching in Your Backyard* by Annette LeBlanc Cate (2013) Bird guides *Beaks:* *Beaks!* by Sneed Collard and illustrated by Robin Brickman (2002) *Look Up! Bird-Watching in Your Backyard* by Annette LeBlanc Cate Macaulay Library: My Media Bin: Beaks! by Sneed B. Collard III www.macaulaylibrary.org/the-internet-bird-collection-the-macaulay-library/ National Geographic: See Hummingbirds Fly, Shake, Drink in Amazing Slow Motion www.youtube.com/watch?v=RtUQ_pz5wlo&feature=youtu.bem

Solar System Text Sets: Bird Characteristics *continued*	***Beaks (continued):*** Utah Education Network: Bird Buffet **www.uen.org/lessonplan/view/2715** Bird guides ***Feet:*** *Paddle Perch: Climb Bird Feet Are Neat* by Laurie Ellen Angus (2018) *Look Up! Bird-Watching in Your Backyard* by Annette LeBlanc Cate Bird guides Simulated bird feet exploration
Solar System Model: Bird Communications	*Bird Talk: What Birds Are Saying and Why* by Lita Judge (2012) *Look Up! Bird-Watching in Your Backyard* by Annette LeBlanc Cate
Solar System Model of Digital Text: Adaptations	Bird Feeding Adaptations: How Beaks Are Adapted to What Birds Eat **www.youtube.com/watch?v=lFZ8NMBDCJw** Galápagos Finch Evolution—HHMI BioInteractive Video **youtu.be/mcM23M-CCog** Brain Pop: Natural Selection **www.brainpop.com/science/cellularlifeandgenetics/naturalselection/** Brainpop: Charles Darwin **www.brainpop.com/science/famousscientists/charlesdarwin/** Animal Planet Top 10 Adaptations Slideshow **www.animalplanet.com/wild-animals/animal-adaptations/** Natural Selection and the Rock Pocket Mouse—HHMI BioInteractive Video **www.youtube.com/watch?v=sjeSEngKGrg&feature=youtu.be**

PHASE THREE: SURVIVAL OVER TIME: INVESTIGATING EVOLUTION

SCAFFOLD TEXTS	
Duet Model: Change over Time in Same Geological Place	*Island: A Story of the Galápagos* by Jason Chin (2012) *On This Spot: An Expedition Back Through Time* by Susan Goodman and illustrated by Lee Christiansen (2004)
Duet Model: Change over Time, Dinosaur–Bird Connection	*Boy, Were We Wrong About Dinosaurs!* by Kathleen Kudlinski and illustrated by S. D. Schindler (2008) *Born to Be Giants: How Baby Dinosaurs Grew to Rule the World* by Lita Judge (2010)

A Solar System Model of Multimodal, Multigenre Resources: The Bird–Dinosaur Connection	*Feathered Dinosaurs* by Brenda Guiberson and illustrated by William Low (2016)
	Smithsonian: What Motivates Us to Conduct Field Research? **cdnapisec.kaltura.com/index.php/extwidget/preview/partner_id/347381/uiconf_id/27644131/entry_id/1_0997j3bz/embed/dynamic**
	American Museum of Natural History: Dinosaurs Among Us **www.amnh.org/exhibitions/dinosaurs-among-us** (Although the exhibition is closed, this website includes several informative videos and articles.)
	PBS: *Eons: The Facts About Dinosaurs and Feathers* **www.pbs.org/video/the-facts-about-dinosaurs-feathers-dterdr/**
	The Pocumtuck Valley Memorial Association: Fossil Footprints: Breaking the Code **dinotracksdiscovery.org/special/feature/**
Mentor Texts for Student Writing	*Terrific Tongues* by Maria Gianferrari and illustrated by Jia Liu (2018)
	Bird Talk: What Birds Are Saying and Why by Lita Judge (2012)
	A Place for Birds by Melissa Stewart and illustrated by Higgins Bond (2009/2015)
	Feathers: Not Just for Flying by Melissa Stewart and illustrated by Sarah Brannen (2014)
	Paddle Perch Climb: Bird Feet Are Neat by Laurie Ellen Angus (2018)
Websites for Student Bird Research Massachusetts Birds	Wingmasters **www.wingmasters.net/aboutus.htm**
	MassAudubon: Common Bird Species in Massachusetts **www.massaudubon.org/learn/nature-wildlife/birds**
	Massachusetts Avian Records Committee: Official State List **maavianrecords.com/official-state-list/**
	World Institute for Conservation and Environment: Birds of Massachusetts **www.birdlist.org/checklists_of_the_birds_of_the_united_states/birds_of_massachusetts.htm**
	Audubon Guide to North American Birds **www.audubon.org/bird-guide**
	The Cornell Lab of Ornithology: All About Birds **www.allaboutbirds.org/?__hstc=161696355.9515bd04093c514dfcb2ab5a3d1be8d0.1521386187196.1521386187196.1521386187196.1&__hssc=161696355.1.1521386187199&_hsfp=2883220800#/_ga=2.49244710.1808302667.1521386185-550240122.1521386185**

| **Websites for Student Bird Research**

Massachusetts Birds
continued | Arboretum: University of Wisconsin–Madison: Journey North for Kids
journeynorth.org/KidsJourneyNorth.html

Washington Nature Mapping Program: Bird Facts for Kids
naturemappingfoundation.org/natmap/facts/birds-k6.html

The Nature Conservancy: Animals We Protect
www.nature.org/en-us/explore/animals-we-protect/ |

Problem Solving and Visualizing Data in Mathematics
Representation in Multiplication and Nonfiction

> *The kids were challenged to use the information in their own books*
> *to create multiplication problems, which made them slow down*
> *and analyze the information in their books in a deeper way.*
>
> —BROOKE, Third-Grade Teacher

I n her first year at a new grade level, despite adjusting to new content and curriculum in every subject, Brooke was eager to collaborate with us and explore the role of text sets in math. We'd previously worked with Brooke on text sets about the regions of the United States in fourth grade. Impressed with her intuitive student-centeredness, we were grateful that she was up for an additional challenge!

From the start of our conversation, it was clear that we should focus our mathematics text set collaboration on her initial multiplication unit, as we knew that would be the first time that students were really grappling with the concept—a perennial third-grade challenge. As Brooke further mapped out her fall units, she mentioned that her third graders would be exploring nonfiction in language arts. We were excited about the opportunity to cocreate a nonfiction language arts unit out of the sheer joy of collaboration on a topic near and dear to our hearts. The more we talked, the more we considered connecting the two units. Could we harness student learning about and from nonfiction to support their emerging understanding of multiplication? Could we harness their emerging understanding of multiplication to help them think differently about their research and the original nonfiction they were writing?

Because it was Brooke's first year in third grade and she had no predetermined "musts" in terms of district curriculum mandates, other than to teach with the standards, we had the ability to build our ideas from scratch.

Establish Goals: What do you want for your students?

When teaching fourth grade, Brooke had students coming to her with exposure to and practice with multiplication and division. As a third-grade teacher, she would be responsible for establishing that foundation. In fourth-grade language arts, students did nonfiction reading and writing, but Brooke felt that there was an opportunity in third grade to give students a deeper exploration of nonfiction, which could serve as a foundation for fourth- and fifth-grade reading and writing.

In Figure 6.1, you will see that the New Hampshire K–12 Mathematics Curriculum Frameworks, the Common Core Standards, guided the content and skills we focused on for math; these can easily be mapped back to the National Council of Teachers of Mathematics Standards for Grades 3–5. The New Hampshire K–12 Language Arts Curriculum Frameworks, the Common Core Standards, also guided our thinking for language arts.

FIGURE 6.1 *This chart documents the standards this unit was designed to meet.*

NEW HAMPSHIRE COMMON CORE MATHEMATICS CURRICULUM FRAMEWORK: GRADE THREE	
M.3.OA.1	Interpret products of whole numbers, e.g., interpret 5 × 7 as the total number of objects in 5 groups of 7 objects each. For example, describe a context in which a total number of objects can be expressed as 5 × 7.
M.3.OA.3	Use multiplication and division within 100 to solve word problems in situations involving equal groups, arrays, and measurement quantities, e.g., by using drawings and equations with a symbol for the unknown number to represent the problem.
NATIONAL COUNCIL OF TEACHERS OF MATHEMATICS STANDARDS GRADES THREE TO FIVE	
Number and Operations Grades 3–5, Operations:	Understand various meanings of multiplication and division.
Number and Operations Grades 3–5, Computation:	Develop fluency in adding, subtracting, multiplying, and dividing whole numbers.
Data and Probability Grades 3–5:	Compare different representations of the same data and evaluate how well each representation shows important aspects of the data.

NEW HAMPSHIRE COMMON CORE LITERACY STANDARDS GRADE THREE	
CCSS.ELA-LITERACY. RI.3.1	Ask and answer questions to demonstrate understanding of a text, referring explicitly to the text as the basis for the answers.
CCSS.ELA-LITERACY. RI.3.7	Use information gained from illustrations (e.g., maps, photographs) and the words in a text to demonstrate understanding of the text (e.g., where, when, why, and how key events occur).
CCSS.ELA-LITERACY. RI.3.8	Describe the logical connection between particular sentences and paragraphs in a text (e.g., comparison, cause/effect, first/second/third in a sequence).
CCSS.ELA-LITERACY.W.3.4	With guidance and support from adults, produce writing in which the development and organization are appropriate to task and purpose.
CCSS.ELA-LITERACY.W.3.6	With guidance and support from adults, use technology to produce and publish writing (using keyboarding skills) as well as to interact and collaborate with others.
CCSS.ELA-LITERACY.W.3.7	Conduct short research projects that build knowledge about a topic.

As we have written in previous chapters, these standards were again more of the floor than the ceiling. For math, Brooke's students' critical thinking was foremost in her mind. Brooke shared that she wanted her students "to have an understanding that multiplication means 'groups of,' and to be able to represent multiplication problems with models and equations." At the heart of this experience was not that students "solve problems quickly in their heads or memorize facts," but rather, that they "have a conceptual understanding of what it means to multiply two numbers." Supporting this conceptual understanding of multiplication and its function and application is at the heart of our work with text sets in mathematics, not just in how we asked students to use information in texts to consider the process of multiplication, but also in the texts that they would create to demonstrate their understandings of multiplication.

The goals for nonfiction reading and writing were more fluid, and the standards were even more of a floor, as some of the work that we did with students flowed into the fourth-grade standards for reading and writing nonfiction and informational text. All of us were eager to see if students were able to write more than the basic survey books, often known as "all about books," and how we could intentionally broaden their understanding of different categories of nonfiction.

Over the years we have written about different ways of categorizing nonfiction. Most recently, in 2018, Mary Ann and nonfiction children's author Melissa Stewart published an article in *School Library Connection* about the four "traditional" categories of nonfiction books for children: survey books, concept books, life stories, and specialized nonfiction. This set of categories left out field guides as well as how-to books, such as experiment and activity books and cookbooks. Since then, Melissa has created a new set of nonfiction categories, which focuses on a combination of the author's intentions and the reader's uses of nonfiction. But we were curious to see if students would be able to understand the differences between the more traditional categories, named for the type of information they convey, and how an exposure to these different types of nonfiction books might influence students' nonfiction writing. We describe those categories in more detail later in this chapter. We were also hoping that exposing students to the rich language and sophisticated illustrations of today's high-quality nonfiction would enhance students' ability to write and illustrate original nonfiction.

Ultimately, our conversations about multiplication and illustrated nonfiction led us to the concept of exploring infographics in both language arts and mathematics. First, students could explore the visual representation of information in illustrated nonfiction picture books. In math, we could introduce infographics as a genre that can serve as a model for representing multiplication. After the exposure to infographics, we could have students use infographics as way to reveal their understanding of multiplication, using information from their research in language arts as the content. Infographics that demonstrate multiplication served as conceptual models of multiplication and mentor texts for students as they created infographics to demonstrate their understanding of multiplication and their research *using* infographics.

In Figure 6.2, you will see the goals that Brooke articulated and the outcomes that demonstrate those goals.

FIGURE 6.2 *This chart documents the goals and outcomes for this integrated unit.*

GOALS	OUTCOMES
To integrate language arts and mathematics	Students will use their familiarity with certain nonfiction texts to better understand the concept of multiplication.
To emphasize the process of multiplication	Students will understand that in multiplication there are groups of something.

To emphasize critical thinking	Students will create word problems to demonstrate their understanding of what is being multiplied within an equation and model.
To expose students to reading and creating infographics	Students will create infographics that reflect their understanding of functions and applications of multiplication. Students may choose to also include infographics in the back matter of their original nonfiction picture books.
To expose students to the four traditional categories of nonfiction for children	Students will write original nonfiction picture books in one of the four categories.

Find Texts: What are the best texts to help you meet your goals?

Books

Because Brooke was new to the grade level and did not have an extensive collection of nonfiction picture books to use in whole-class minilessons, we drew upon some of our favorite nonfiction books from popular award lists, such as the National Council of Teachers of English's Orbis Pictus Award, the Sibert Medal from the American Library Association, and books on the National Council of Teachers of Social Studies/Children's Book Council's Notable Social Studies Trade Books for Young People and National Science Teachers Association/Children's Book Council's Outstanding Science Trade Books annual lists. Additionally, we brought in recently published nonfiction books that we and the teachers in our graduate courses, and their students, found to be particularly interesting. We also looked for high-quality books that included infographics. Although we were tempted to look for books about multiplication to include, those books are usually fictional, and we wanted to stay focused on nonfiction.

Digital Texts

Our search for digital texts stayed focused on finding age-appropriate infographics that we could use as mentor texts for the students when creating their own. We were grateful that both National Geographic Kids and Kids Discover, two kid-friendly websites, had a range of simple infographics easy for third graders to access and understand. We knew from the start that we wanted to use Piktochart, a website that allows you to design your own infographic, as the platform for student infographic creation.

Organize Texts for Instruction: How can we arrange the texts for critical thinking?

Unlike our specific focus on adaptation in the previous chapter, we were not using the texts to reveal specific content information in either language arts or math. Instead, we focused on understanding the genre of infographics and nonfiction and the ability to express mathematical understanding of multiplication in those genres. As a result, there were many ways that we could have considered the roles that the different texts would play.

We spent more time considering the roles of the nonfiction texts in language arts, because there were so many choices to make. We decided that we would first have an open-ended exploration of nonfiction texts, and then focus on a single scaffold text that would surprise the students in some way, serving as a foundation for the unit as a whole. The immersion books would be books that fell under one of the specific categories of nonfiction (survey, concept, life story). The extension texts would be the books and digital texts that the students used to research topics of choice to write original nonfiction.

In math, we decided that it made the most sense to have the scaffold texts be nonfiction books that they were already exposed to in language arts and that could offer content to be turned into multiplication problems. We knew the students would have already had a lot of experience with those engaging texts. The immersion texts would be infographics that revealed multiplication concepts, some in books, some digital. The extension texts for math were the very same extension texts as language arts: the texts used for research for the original nonfiction books the students were creating.

Exploring Nonfiction in Language Arts

The language arts unit began well before the mathematics unit, so that we could harness what students had learned about and with nonfiction to support their conceptual understanding of multiplication. In Figure 6.3, you can see an overview of how we organized the various text sets. Following that, you'll read about the use of these texts more in-depth.

FIGURE 6.3 *This chart provides an overview of the nonfiction genre study in language arts.*

SCAFFOLD TEXTS	
Big ideas about nonfiction	Solar System model: • Fiction and nonfiction texts • Range of nonfiction texts *Giant Squid* by Candace Fleming (2016), illustrated by Eric Rohmann

IMMERSION TEXTS	
Exploring survey books, concept books, and life stories	Duet models of survey books • Paired readings of survey books on the same topic Solar System model: concept books Duet models of life stories • Paired readings of biographies about the same person Solar System model: nonfiction books with different text structures
EXTENSION TEXTS	
Researching topics using nonfiction	Mountain model: print and digital texts for student-based research on topics of interest

SCAFFOLD: BIG IDEAS ABOUT NONFICTION

To know what the third graders knew and did not know about the differences between fiction and nonfiction, we began with a preassessment survey, which revealed a lot of confusion about what nonfiction is. But at the end of the survey, when the students were asked what they might want to research to write nonfiction, all responded with appropriate real-world topics.

Next, we had Brooke do a focused minilesson. She collected a group of fiction and nonfiction picture books, and as she held each one up, she had students identify the book as fiction or nonfiction, and why. Doing this helped the students to refresh their memories on the similarities and

FIGURE 6.4
Brooke's students cocreated an anchor chart detailing the differences between fiction and nonfiction.

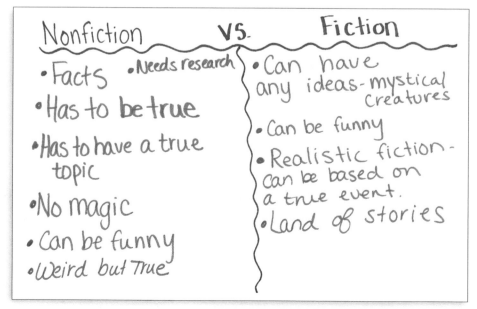

differences between the two genres, which they documented in an anchor chart (see Figure 6.4).

Next, the students spent some time exploring a wide array of non-fiction books that Brooke made available. Using a graphic organizer, each student was asked to first explore different nonfiction books at different tables. Next, they were asked to identify five different topics explored in the books. Most students struggled to determine the difference between the topic of the book and its title. The students were then asked to do a picture walk through three books. This took more time than we anticipated, because the students were excited about many of the books and wanted to linger. They were then asked to synthesize similarities and differences between the three books and then read one book of their choosing from cover to cover.

Two samples reveal the different ways that students responded to the task and to the nonfiction books in front of them. One student (see Figure 6.5) focused on the illustration styles and what was similar and different, and the goals of the books: "making people want to read it." Another student was able to demonstrate synthesis of the qualities of nonfiction in their listing of similarities and noted different stylistic choices and text features

FIGURE 6.5 *One student's synthesis of nonfiction book topics, similarities, and differences.*

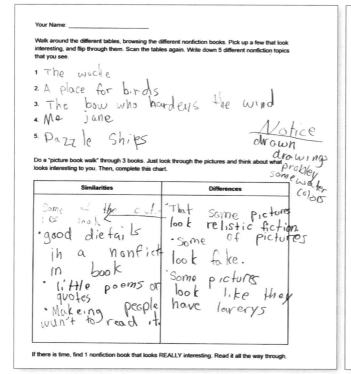

FIGURE 6.6
Another student's synthesis of nonfiction book topics, similarities, and differences.

FIGURE 6.7

Your Name: _____

Walk around the different tables, browsing the different nonfiction books. Pick up a few that look interesting, and flip through them. Scan the tables again. Write down 5 different nonfiction topics that you see.

1. Giant squids
2. Stealing home
3. Rivers
4. Bees
5. Sharks

Do a "picture book walk" through 3 books. Just look through the pictures and think about what looks interesting to you. Then, complete this chart.

Similarities	Differences
• all show true information • all stay focused on the topic	• Stealing home has tex Boxes and giant squds has photographs • rivers has maps of rivers and giant squids has paintings.

If there is time, find 1 nonfiction book that looks REALLY interesting. Read it all the way through.

(see Figure 6.6). Again, the students came together to share what they had noticed about the similarities and differences across those texts, and the resulting class discussion was captured in a second anchor chart on the qualities of nonfiction.

Using this open-ended exploration as a foundation, the next day, Brooke read aloud the surprising and engaging concept book *Giant Squid* (see Figure 6.7) written by Candace Fleming (2016) and illustrated by Eric Rohmann. Prior to our work with Brooke, we developed a visual literacy protocol to analyze nonfiction picture books. Brooke transformed the protocol into an interactive graphic organizer, which she projected on her whiteboard (see Figure 6.8) to help students unpack how the words and pictures convey information and shape meaning.

FIGURE 6.8 *The interactive graphic organizer Brooke used to document student thinking about the text and the images in* Giant Squid.

TITLE OF BOOK: *Giant Squid*

Previewing the Book

Scan the book and notice the pictures, titles, end pages, and back matter. • What images stand out to you? • Do any images repeat throughout the book? • What information can you learn by previewing the pictures? • What questions do you have before reading?	"Why is their ink when they squirt it out black?" "Where does the ink come from?" "I noticed most of the pictures were very similar." "At the end there was a picture that showed all the pieces—a diagram?" "By looking at the picture I could tell it's really big and it has a lot of defenses. It has hooks and ink and a big beak." "I noticed it kept going down and down the body." "Why did they make the pictures so big?" "I learned before reading that the pictures gave me information about squid." "The tentacles repeated throughout the book."

During Reading

What images stand out to you? Use sticky notes to write what you are noticing.	Student responses were recorded on sticky notes.

After Reading

• How do the pictures help you understand the subject of the book? • How do the pictures match the words on the pages? • How do the pictures help you understand the setting of the book? • What information can we learn from the pictures? • What images, colors, or shapes are repeated in the book? What did the illustrator want you to notice? • What creatures or objects are really big in the illustrations? Why? • What did the illustrator want you to think about by zooming in? • What creatures or objects are far back in the pictures? Why? What did the illustrator want you to think about by zooming out?	"It helps me understand the subject because the picture goes with the words and shows the squid and what it looks like." "They are zoomed in because they are talking about the parts of the squid's body." "I had no idea that they had pockets full of ink." "I learned all about the squid's body?" "I could tell it was in the ocean because the background was blue." "It looked realistic." "I didn't know they had spikes on their tongues." "How did they get more ink?" "When he zoomed in on the picture of the eye and the body it make it look more real."

FIGURE 6.9
One student's graphic organizer to document thinking about the text and images in Stealing Home *by Robert Burleigh (2007).*

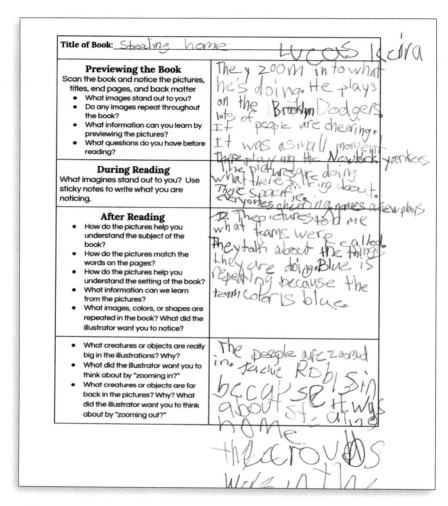

By exploring *Giant Squid* as part of a whole-class lesson, guided by specific questions that asked them to examine the book's format and illustrations, Brooke's students were able to name important questions about giant squid and to consider the important role illustrations can play in conveying information in nonfiction. This focus on illustrations set the stage for their work throughout the rest of the unit. Students had the opportunity to complete the graphic organizer in pairs on a book of their choosing (see Figure 6.9), to further practice a focused exploration of reading illustrations as representation of information.

IMMERSION: EXPLORING SURVEY BOOKS, CONCEPT BOOKS, AND LIFE STORIES

During the immersion phase, Brooke and her students focused on an exploration of different nonfiction categories and text structures. Originally, we planned to focus on four types of categories: survey books, concept books, life stories, and specialized nonfiction (see Figure 6.10).

FIGURE 6.10 *Nonfiction categories chart (adapted from Cappiello and Stewart [2018])*

NONFICTION CATEGORY	NONFICTION CATEGORY DESCRIPTION
Survey Books	Survey books provide a broad overview of a topic. We sometimes think of survey books as traditional nonfiction.
Concept Books	Concept books focus on an abstract idea or a system of classification. Whereas survey books cover an overview of something often concrete, concept books focus on abstract concepts (think adaptation or photosynthesis or life cycle). Concept books most often appear in picture book form.
Life Stories	Life stories include biography, autobiography, and memoir. Biographies don't have to cover the entirety of someone's life, such as the cradle-to-grave biographies often written as part of series. Partial picture book biographies are an exciting addition to life stories.
Specialized Nonfiction	Specialized nonfiction is typically an in-depth exploration of an event or topic. Specialized books are more likely to be longer and to be written for an older audience. The difference between a survey book and a specialized nonfiction book can be difficult for adults and children alike who are new to thinking about nonfiction categories.

After exploring the first three categories with the third graders, it was evident that they were unlikely to understand the differences between a survey book and a specialized book. So, we dropped the fourth category, knowing that students would have ample opportunity to learn about specialized nonfiction as they read more of it in the years ahead.

Brooke introduced the three types of nonfiction categories in separate minilessons, often reading aloud an example of the nonfiction category and then providing time for students to explore examples of those books in pairs and take notes together. Survey books are hard to read aloud, and so Brooke instead held up a bunch of titles and asked students to think about what those titles had in common (they all had just a word or two as a title). Next, the students explored two survey books on the same topic in a Duet model. We believed the similarities and differences across the two texts would allow the students to see and understand what the category "does." Throughout this book, we have highlighted high-quality nonfiction titles. But this is an activity that you can do with any survey books to which you have access. For our exploration of multiple Duet models of survey books on the same topic, we gathered books from our bookshelves and Brooke's.

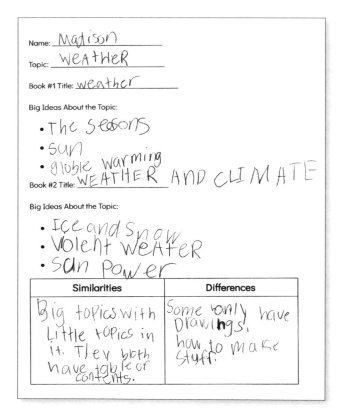

Name: Madison

Topic: WEATHER

Book #1 Title: weather

Big Ideas About the Topic:

- The Seasons
- sun
- globle warming

Book #2 Title: WEATHER AND CLIMATE

Big Ideas About the Topic:

- Ice and Snow
- Volent WEAtER
- Sun Power

Similarities	Differences
Big topics with little topics in it. They both have table of contents.	Some only have Drawings. how to make stuff.

FIGURE 6.11 *One student's graphic organizer about two weather survey books.*

Students looked at survey books in a Duet model; topics included sharks, Ellis Island, the weather. In some cases, as one example demonstrates (see Figure 6.11), students were able to identify some meaningful differences between the books. But many tended to copy headings in the books instead of synthesizing the big ideas of the book. One challenge was that survey books are packed with information, so the task of surveying the book to compare and contrast using headings was overwhelming for some third graders.

Students came back together to synthesize their observations and cocreate another anchor chart (see Figure 6.12). Survey books were the category of nonfiction with which the students were most familiar from exposure in the primary grades in their independent reading and library selections. In this anchor chart, we see that students understand that you often don't have to read these books cover to cover and that a table of contents and headings help readers navigate the different topics.

FIGURE 6.12
Brooke's students' ideas about attributes of survey books and concept books.

FIGURE 6.13

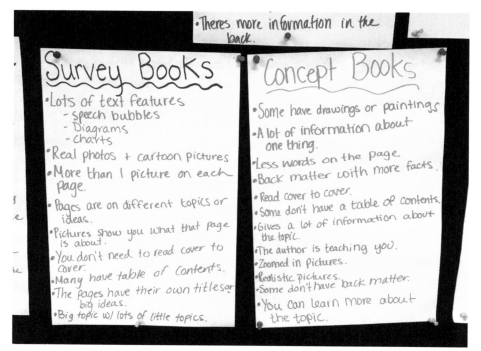

- Theres more information in the back.

Survey Books
- Lots of text features
  - speech bubbles
  - Diagrams
  - charts
- Real photos + cartoon pictures
- More than 1 picture on each page.
- Pages are on different topics or ideas.
- Pictures show you what that page is about.
- You don't need to read cover to cover.
- Many have table of Contents.
- The pages have their own titles or big ideas.
- Big topic w/ lots of little topics.

Concept Books
- Some have drawings or paintings
- A lot of information about one thing.
- Less words on the page
- Back matter with more facts.
- Read cover to cover.
- Some don't have a table of contents.
- Gives a lot of information about the topic.
- The author is teaching you.
- Zoomed in pictures.
- Realistic pictures.
- Some don't have back matter.
- You can learn more about the topic.

FIGURE 6.14 *The concept books Brooke's students explored in depth.*

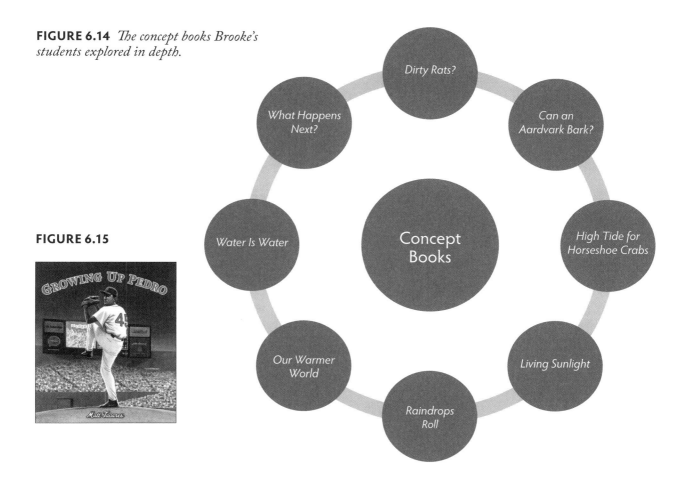

FIGURE 6.15

The next day, we did the same activity but with a Solar System model of carefully curated concept books (Figure 6.14). First, Brooke read aloud *Dirty Rats?* by Darrin Lunde (2015) (see Figure 6.13), a fascinating and engaging look at the beneficial role rats play in different ecosystems around the world. The students explored single books in pairs and reported back their thoughts to the group (see again Figure 6.12). The concept books really surprised the students with their versatility and uniqueness.

Finally, students explored life stories. To begin, Brooke read aloud *Growing Up Pedro* by Matt Tavares (2015) (see Figure 6.15). In this exploration, we had students once again reading pairs of books in the Duet model. Again, we thought they might understand the ranges of

FIGURE 6.16 *Paired biographies of researcher and animal rights activist Jane Goodall.*

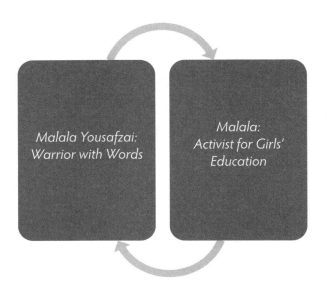

FIGURE 6.17 *Paired biographies of Nobel Prize–winning education and girls' rights activist Malala Yousafzai.*

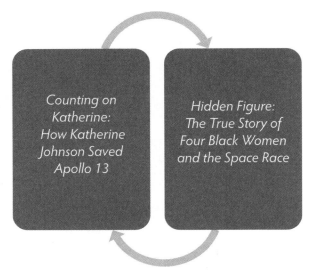

FIGURE 6.18 *Paired biographies of African American mathematician Katherine Johnson.*

FIGURE 6.19 *Paired biographies of environmentalist and author Rachel Carson.*

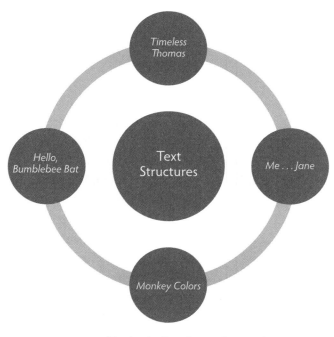

FIGURE 6.20 *The books Brooke used to explore different text structures with her students.*

styles and structures used in biography if they could compare and contrast different picture book biographies of the same person. Students looked at biographies of Jane Goodall, Malala Yousafzai, Katherine Johnson, and Rachel Carson, among others. (See Figures 6.16–6.19 for some Duet models.)

Brooke followed up the explorations of the categories of nonfiction with a Solar System text set (Figure 6.20) of the different kinds of text structures used in nonfiction books, using the following texts: *Timeless Thomas: How Thomas Edison Changed Our Lives* by Gene Barretta (2012) for comparison and contrast; *Me . . . Jane* by Patrick McDonnell (2011) for chronological narrative; *Hello, Bumblebee Bat* by Darrin Lunde (2007), illustrated by Patricia Wynne, for question and answer; and *Monkey Colors* by Darrin Lunde (2012), illustrated by Patricia Wynne, for description.

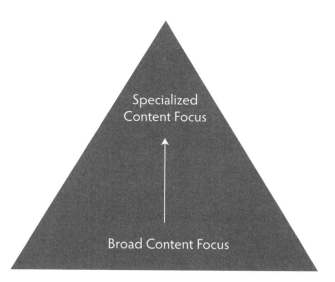

FIGURE 6.21 *Students began with more general reading about their topic, and then, with the support of Brooke, narrowed down their reading to ever-increasingly specific texts.*

EXTENSION: RESEARCHING TOPICS USING NONFICTION

After the first two weeks of learning about nonfiction, students transitioned into the individual research on topics of their choice. Brooke provided students with opportunities to brainstorm topics they were interested in learning more about, from sports teams to civil rights activists to endangered animals. Using the Mountain model (see Figure 6.21), students read, viewed, and listened to print and digital texts curated by Brooke and the school librarian. Specifics on this stage appear later in the chapter.

Exploring the Function and Application of Multiplication in Mathematics

As we shared earlier, our goal was to use visual literacy to support students' understanding of multiplication and their expressions of their understanding through the use of infographics. In the chart in Figure 6.22, you can see an overview of how we organized the various text sets in this aspect of the unit. After that, you'll read about the use of these texts in greater depth.

FIGURE 6.22 *This chart provides an overview of the exploration of multiplication in mathematics.*

SCAFFOLD TEXTS	
Word problems based on information in popular nonfiction picture books	Solar System model: popular books from the nonfiction unit
IMMERSION TEXTS	
Representations of multiplication in infographics	Solar System model: books with infographics and digital infographics
EXTENSION TEXTS	
Print and digital texts for student-based research on topics of interest	Mountain model: using infographics to apply student understanding of research and multiplication

SCAFFOLD: WORD PROBLEMS BASED ON INFORMATION IN POPULAR NONFICTION PICTURE BOOKS

As mentioned earlier in this chapter, Brooke's primary goal was for students to be able to understand that "multiplication means groups of, that they would be able to represent multiplication problems with models and equations, and that they would finish this initial exploration of multiplication with a conceptual understanding of what it means to multiply two numbers." In other words, the emphasis was on why you might use multiplication, its function and application.

Brooke started off the unit by observing how students responded to discussion and demonstration of some basic tasks that involved groupings of numbers. Working with small groups, she asked students to draw models, such as "Show me three groups of two." After students showed her that representation, she asked them to turn the model into an equation. Most students were able to do this through the give-and-take of conversation and hands-on drawing. However, when she followed the small-group work with independent practice problems, students struggled. Word problems were a challenge.

Brooke considered that "this may have been in part because I was not using similar language in the small groups. I was simply having them build models in isolation from context." The next day, Brooke again worked with small groups and used more specific language in her verbal tasks, asking students to draw pictures that were models of multiple pens, cookies, and apples. She noted that "it was clear that the students were able to visualize the problems with this small change, because they were able to successfully draw pictures to represent the problems during their independent work time." On the third day, Brooke shared original word problems that we cocreated, drawing from the nonfiction picture books we explored in language arts. The books we utilized in the Solar System model (Figure 6.23) were popular with the students, and they contained information we could easily turn into simple multiplication word problems.

The first day, we focused on multiplication problems from two life stories that we read: *Whoosh! Lonnie Johnson's Super-Soaking Stream of Inventions* by Chris Barton (2016), illustrated by Don Tate, and Meghan McCarthy's (2015) *Earmuffs for Everyone! How Chester Greenwood Became Known as the Inventor of the Ear Muff.* In the student example (see Figure 6.24), you can see how models and arrays were drawn and equations written based on scenarios drawn off of the information in these books. This student shows an accurate representation of earmuffs. In her equation for Lonnie Johnson's pitches at the Toy Fair, she has her groups mixed up. It should read two interviews a day times three days. Drawing made student learning visible and revealed to Brooke which students needed help with different methods of representing the problem.

On the fourth day, Brooke shared another set of problems with the class. All three problems came from information gleaned in Darrin Lunde's (2015) concept book *Dirty Rats?* Again, students explored ways to represent the information in the word problem through a model, an array, and an equation. The problems for this exploration involved higher numbers to compute, as you can see in Figure 6.25.

On the fifth day, Brooke shared a set of problems coming from *Giant Squid* (Fleming 2016), the book that launched the nonfiction exploration. The numbers in these problems are higher, requiring more attention to accuracy

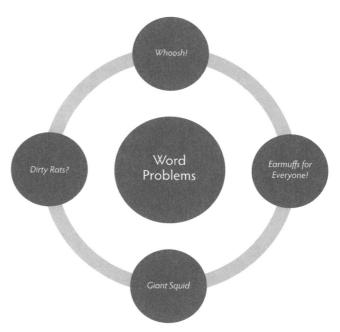

FIGURE 6.23 *We used nonfiction books popular in language arts to create multiplication word problems.*

FIGURE 6.24 *One student's response to multiplication word problems from the popular nonfiction books.*

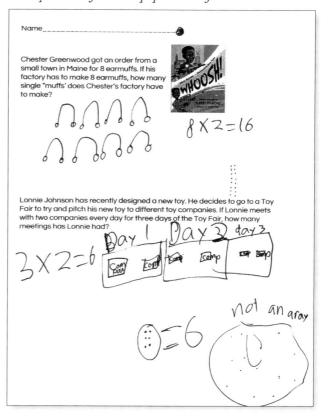

and representation in the model. There are instances, such as the sample in Figure 6.26, where students have a correct model and array, with some fabulous squid drawings, but the computation for the answer is wrong. Conceptually, the student has demonstrated an accurate understanding of what is being multiplied, by how many times, and what the final total is. Brooke was able to consider how this happened. Was the student rushed? Was the student distracted during the computation? Again, with the drawings making conceptual understanding visible, she used flexible groups to follow up with students strategically.

On the back of the *Giant Squid* problem set, students were asked to develop their own word problem involving multiplication, drawing on the knowledge they were learning in their nonfiction research. In Figure 6.27, you see one student's example of multiplying baby elephants in a herd. In the immersion stage of this text set, you'll see how students expand these original problems into infographics.

FIGURE 6.25 *One student's response to word problems based on* Dirty Rats?

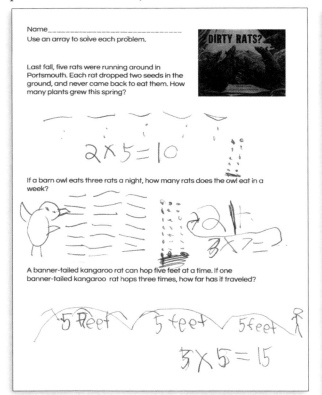

FIGURE 6.26 *One student's response to more complex word problems based on* Giant Squid.

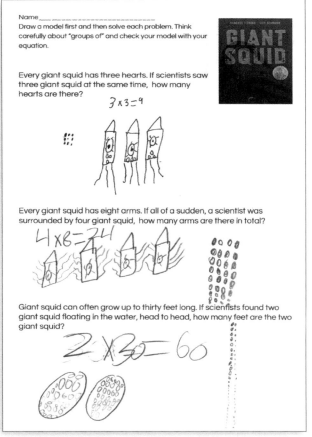

Challenge: Think of a story problem that is related to the nonfiction research you are doing. Write and solve the story problem below using a model and equation.

there are 5 elephants with 8 baby elephants behiend them. How many baby elephants are there in all

FIGURE 6.27
One student's original multiplication word problem, based on her research on elephants.

FIGURE 6.28

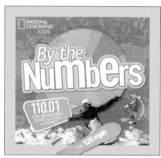

As Brooke noted,

The kids were challenged to use the information in their own books to create multiplication problems. It required them to think deeply about the information in their books. One student who was reading about wolves created the following problem: *There are 7 packs of wolves. Each pack has 3 wolves. How many wolves are there in all?* This student was using vocabulary specific to the topic they were studying (packs), and also demonstrating their understanding that multiplication means "groups of."

IMMERSION: REPRESENTATIONS OF MULTIPLICATION IN INFOGRAPHICS

Knowing that we wanted the students to ultimately use infographics to demonstrate their understanding of multiplication, we showed them examples of a variety of infographics (see Figure 6.28), both print and digital, in a Solar System model (Figure 6.29).

FIGURE 6.29 *Texts used to introduce students to infographics.*

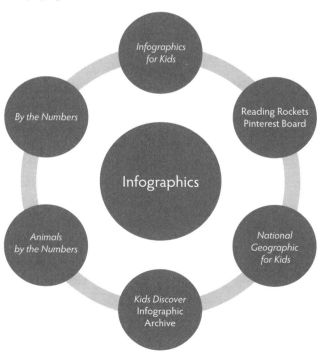

Infographics for Kids: Putting Information in the Picture, by Susan Martineau (2016), illustrated by Vicky Barker, was an ideal way to ground students in infographics as a form of graphical/visual literacy. Since we began the nonfiction exploration focusing on how the illustrations shape the information in ways that are often equal to the text in picture books (and sometimes beyond the text), this book takes students' visual literacy skills to an even deeper level, zooming in on an understanding of graphs, charts, diagrams, and more. The first two-page spread is a great primer on the different ways that infographics can function to convey understanding and models different types of graphics and their purposes.

Graphics have the potential to be much more complex than text features, which are often simple and relatively obvious and don't change much from book to book. Graphics are everywhere, in print, online, and in our world (the doctor's office, the grocery store, etc.). It is important that students know how to read them, and the best way to gain that understanding is by immersing them in infographics and reading them as designers. Brooke also shared examples of infographics available through the open-access Kids Discover Infographic Archive, the Reading Rockets Pinterest Board of kid-friendly infographics, and the National Geographic for Kids Animals website that includes a very simple infographic for each animal displayed.

FIGURE 6.30

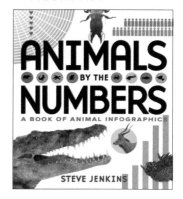

Probably the strongest example of infographics in this text set is award-winning author-illustrator Steve Jenkins's (2016) *Animals by the Numbers: A Book of Animal Infographics*) (Figure 6.30). Jenkins's work is thorough, child-friendly, and colorful, set against his signature white background. Several infographics within the book show multiplication and can serve as really great mentor texts for infographics that demonstrate multiplication, as detailed in our discussion of one of those spreads back in Chapter 2. Some of these infographics work well with third graders, and some are more ideal for slightly older students.

EXTENSION: USING INFOGRAPHICS TO APPLY STUDENT UNDERSTANDING OF RESEARCH AND MULTIPLICATION

The extension texts for this introductory unit on multiplication were the Mountain model text sets individual students were using to research topics for their original nonfiction writing. These extension texts not only helped students become nonfiction authors and illustrators, but also gave students the information to build their own original word problems and their own original infographics to explain the answers to these word problems. You'll find more on these in the next section.

Create New Texts: What are the new texts created by students?

FIGURE 6.31

Students created several products over the course of these two interconnected units. In language arts, they researched, wrote, and illustrated an original nonfiction book. In math, they created an original word problem from their nonfiction research and then created an infographic to demonstrate their understanding of the content they were researching and the concept of multiplication.

Creating Texts in Language Arts

NOTE TAKING

Brooke told us that in previous years her fourth graders would "essentially copy word for word and their nonfiction texts become a regurgitation of the texts they've read." To avoid that happening with her third graders, she had students take notes on sticky notes, one fact on each sticky. Brooke felt that this decision was a good idea. "Their note taking was much better than in years past because taking smaller notes required them to synthesize and add style to their writing later on."

FIGURE 6.32

As students were researching, Brooke put together a Solar System model of author interviews (Figure 6.33), which included interviews with Chris Barton (2016), author of *Whoosh!* (see Figure 6.31), and Jason Chin (2017), author of *Grand Canyon* (see Figure 6.32).

Brooke also had students read an interview with veteran nonfiction author and former teacher Sandra Markle. Together, the group determined some key processes for doing research (see Figure 6.34) on an anchor chart. Throughout the unit, students also had the opportunity to explore the back matter in the various books they were reading to learn more about authors' and illustrators' processes.

FIGURE 6.33 *Author–illustrator interviews were helpful ways for students to consider their own writing and illustrating processes.*

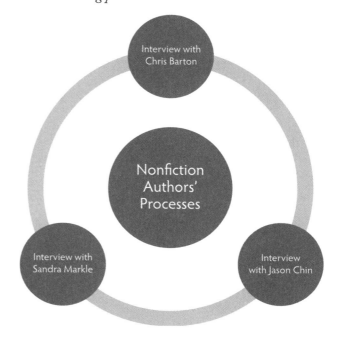

WRITING AND ILLUSTRATING NONFICTION BOOKS

Students spent several days researching their self-selected topics of interest, and then they selected which category of nonfiction was best for their topic. Obviously, those researching people wrote life stories. Everyone else wrote a

FIGURE 6.34
Students synthesized the different ways that authors approach their nonfiction research process.

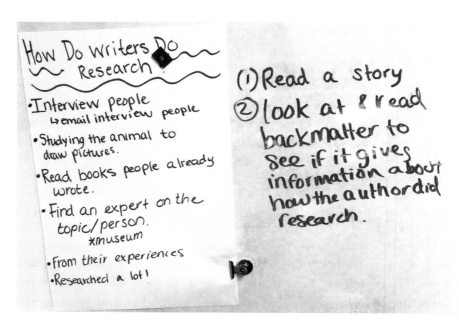

survey book. Given that the concept books received some of the strongest reactions from students, we were very surprised that no one tried to create one. Students were ready to read concept books, but the task of creating one may have been too daunting for individual third graders to write independently.

Students selected a text structure from one of the four explored: narrative, compare and contrast, question and answer, and topic/subtopic (description). We created graphic organizers for each to support students as they organized their sticky notes into an appropriate text structure (see Figures 6.35–6.38).

FIGURE 6.35 *Students interested in writing narratives could use this graphic organizer to outline their sticky notes. (When reproducing these graphic organizers, allow space for your students to write on the organizer.)*

Introduction to People, Places, and Things

Introduction to Conflict/Problem

Ways That the People or Animals Try to Solve the Problem/Conflict

Ending the Problem/Conflict

FIGURE 6.36 *Students interested in writing with the comparison-and-contrast text structure could use this graphic organizer to outline their sticky notes. (When reproducing these graphic organizers, allow space for your students to write on the organizer.)*

Introduction Details

Compare and Contrast #1

Fact About One Topic	Fact About the Other Topic

Compare and Contrast #2

Fact About One Topic	Fact About the Other Topic

Compare and Contrast #3

Fact About One Topic	Fact About the Other Topic

Compare and Contrast #4

Fact About One Topic	Fact About the Other Topic

Conclusion Details

FIGURE 6.37 *Students interested in writing with the question–and–answer text structure could use this graphic organizer to outline their sticky notes. (When reproducing these graphic organizers, allow space for your students to write on the organizer.)*

Introduction Details

Question and Answer Topic #1

Question:
Answer:

Question and Answer Topic #2

Question:
Answer:

Question and Answer Topic #3

Question:
Answer:

Question and Answer Topic #4

Question:
Answer:

Conclusion Details

FIGURE 6.38
Students interested in writing with the topic/subtopic text structure could use this graphic organizer to outline their sticky notes. (When reproducing these graphic organizers, allow space for your students to write on the organizer.)

Introduction Details

Subtopic #1 = _____

Subtopic #2 = _____

Subtopic #3 = _____

Subtopic #4 = _____

Conclusion Details

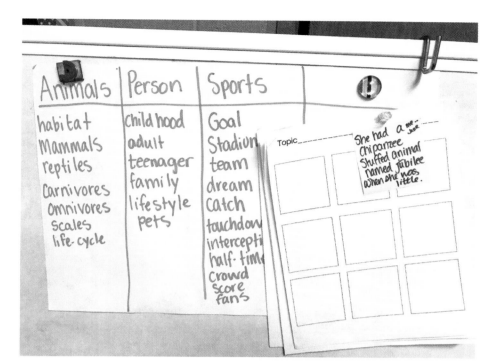

FIGURE 6.39
Brooke and her students cocreated a chart with words that might be useful in their nonfiction writing.

For many students, the graphic organizers were a helpful place to start in providing a concrete structure. As Brooke noted, "Most students chose to write an all-about book, which leads easily to a topic/subtopic description structure and is much more concrete for third grades than a narrative structure. The students who decided to write a narrative book had mostly studied people. Providing students with a story arc graphic organizer would have shown students that narrative stories have a beginning, middle, and end." The graphic organizer we created for narrative helped students to group their notes in ways that gathered pertinent information for rising action, turning point, and resolution, but that did not reflect the traditional narrative story arc diagram with which they are familiar. They needed both.

Throughout the writing process, Brooke conducted minilessons on voice and leads and met with flexible groups of students to support them as they faced challenges such as struggling with organizing information, outlining their work using the graphic organizers, thinking of content-specific vocabulary to use in their books (see Figure 6.39), or transitioning into different phases of the writing process.

While students were drafting their nonfiction books, Brooke offered them the opportunity to start working on their watercolor illustrations. Brooke made this decision because she knew that some students need to

There are 8 planets in are solar system. they are Mars,Jupiter,Mercury,Saturn,Uranus,Neptune,Venus,Earth. the hot side of Mercury is 800*F. The shady side is 280*F. Colder than snow hotter than summer Many planets have a layer that acts like a blanket to keep heat in I can't imagine how hot they are. The blazing hot sun can fit one million earths inside itself. Isn't that a lot of earth's don't you think. The sun is about 100 times hotter than summer and I thought summer was hot.

FIGURE 6.40

The page from one student's nonfiction book reveals a specific use of figurative language, as well as a visible author's perspective.

draw to write, to get past certain writing blocks or hurdles. She noticed, "For some of the struggling writers this was highly motivating because they were able to visualize their final product and base their writing off of their illustrations." Brooke also noticed how beneficial it was for the students to illustrate their own nonfiction, instead of relying on images from the Internet as her fourth graders had previously. She shared, "When students create their own pictures, it requires them to make connections between the words on the page and their illustrations." By utilizing a different modality, and switching from words to images, students were able to move forward with their sequencing more fluidly.

When we looked across the student work, we saw some wonderful examples of student voice in the writing. One student demonstrates her command of figurative language (see Figure 6.40): "Colder than snow hotter than summer." In addition to these comparisons, we see a simile: "Many planets have a layer that acts like a blanket to keep heat in." We also see signs of the visible author, as the writer lets us know her feelings on some of the content. In Figure 6.41, a student inspired by *Giant Squid* (Fleming 2016) reveals their own ability to write descriptively, with varied sentence structure and the use of onomatopoeia: "Grind crunch grind crunch."

FIGURE 6.41
One student's nonfiction reveals varied sentence structure and onomatopoeia.

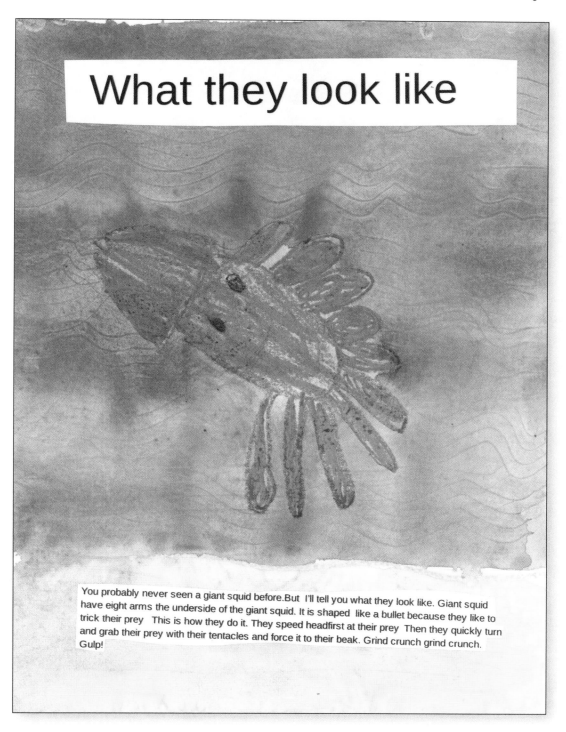

What they look like

You probably never seen a giant squid before. But I'll tell you what they look like. Giant squid have eight arms the underside of the giant squid. It is shaped like a bullet because they like to trick their prey This is how they do it. They speed headfirst at their prey Then they quickly turn and grab their prey with their tentacles and force it to their beak. Grind crunch grind crunch. Gulp!

As Figure 6.42 demonstrates, we see that one student chose a fictional snapshot to introduce what is otherwise a traditional survey book about foxes. Figure 6.43 reveals a classic example of a traditional survey book, with the heading "What Foxes Look Like" to guide our attention to the specific information that will be conveyed. In writing about the appearance

What Foxes Look Like

There are several colors of a foxes fur. There are red foxes, white foxes, brown foxes and grey foxes, and orange foxes. They have very sharp teeth so that they can bite into their prey. On their legs they have black fur. They have white around their eyes. Arctic foxes have fur around their paws so they don't slip on the ice. Foxes have large ears and really good hearing. Foxes more fur than it looks like. Their fluffy tails are for keeping them warm when they are sleeping.

Fun facts:
A Fennec fox is the smallest fox. Foxes are all over the world.

FIGURE 6.43
This page represents the traditional topic/subtopic focus of a survey book.

of foxes, the student went beyond merely listing information about foxes. They described the adaptation that caused the feature: "They have very sharp teeth so that they can bite into their prey."

One student's life story of surfer Bethany Hamilton uses the narrative structure. Bethany is introduced with descriptive language and varied sentence structure in Figure 6.44. In Figure 6.45, we see that the student has absorbed elements of visual literacy, in particular nonrepresentational art as a means of conveying action and mood. Once Bethany has been bitten by a shark, the page turns, and the reader sees a splatter of red, blue, and green to represent the attack and the chaos that ensued. This student understands that the page turn in narrative nonfiction can be as dramatic as the page turn in fictional narratives.

To celebrate the students' nonfiction writing, families were invited to school for a writer's café. Students came up with questions in advance that they could ask one another, such as:

- "What did you learn about writing a nonfiction text?"
- "How did you find your information?"
- "What was the hardest part of writing your book?"

Students shared their stories in small groups of four and invited parents and peers to ask questions when they finished reading. Making their

FIGURE 6.44
One student introduces their subject with rich description and sentence variation.

She jumped on her surfboard and paddled out to the ocean. The surf erased everything that came to mind. The first wave was approaching. She did it. She caught her first wave and instantly knew she was a surfer

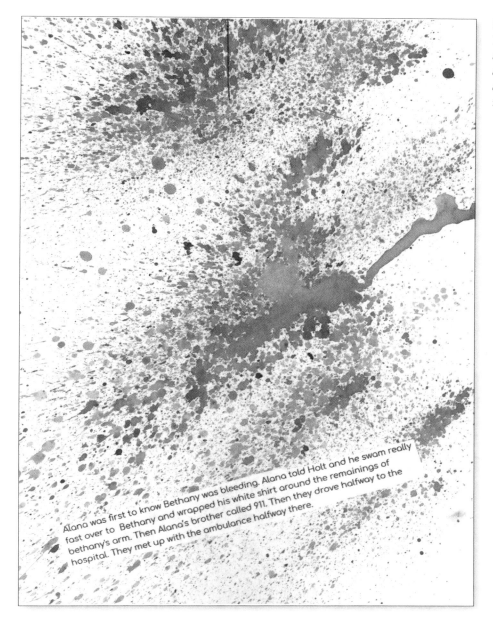

FIGURE 6.45
The student also reveals an understanding of how abstract illustrations can convey meaning in nonfiction.

writing public was an ideal way to honor their hard work, and a final affirmation that writers publish their work to share their ideas with the world.

Creating Texts in Math

In math, students wrote their own multiplication word problem based on their nonfiction research and created an infographic to represent a model of the problem as well as the numeric solution. Having students demonstrate that they can create an infographic that matches the information they would like to share is a helpful way for them to grow their visual literacy as it relates to nonfiction reading and writing. It's also an authentic, real-world way to demonstrate their understanding of multiplication.

INFOGRAPHICS

For these third graders, in addition to demonstrating their synthesis of reading and their understanding of multiplication, creating infographics also required learning how to use a new digital platform. Piktochart is a free website that provides users with a limited number of free infographics each year; individuals and organizations can pay a subscription for more options.

Any mentor text can feel intimidating when students only look at the final polished product. It's why we think it is so important to highlight mentor processes. After exploring infographics as a genre, Brooke modeled mentor processes and created mentor texts by turning the word problems we created based on *Giant Squid* (Fleming 2016) into original

FIGURE 6.46 *The first of two word problem infographics that Brooke created as a model for her students.*

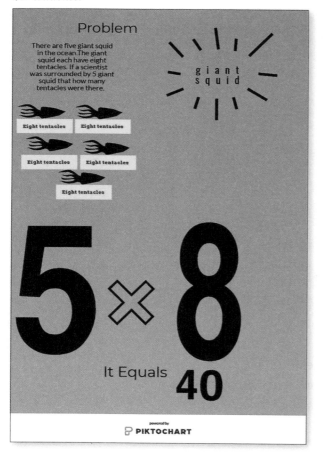

FIGURE 6.47 *The second of two word problem infographics that Brooke created as a model for her students.*

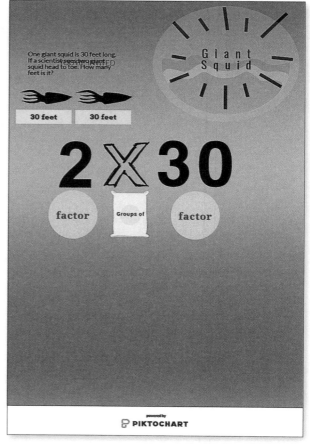

infographics (see Figures 6.46 and 6.47). In this way, she could introduce Piktochart as a tool and work with information that all the students had already experienced.

Students then went on to work independently, transforming their original word problem into an infographic. Most students were able to create an infographic that had visual clarity. To create the infographic, students navigated multiple systems at once: specific information about their topic, conceptual information about multiplication, and concepts of design and visual literacy. To manage all of these at once is a challenge!

It is important to note that Brooke did not consider the creation of the infographic as a summative assessment on students' understanding of multiplication. Because Brooke's school is embracing a competency-based model of learning, she did not expect all of her students to demonstrate complete understanding of their research and multiplication in this one task. Infographics are an ideal teaching tool *and* formative assessment. For some students, their understanding came together in the application of the multiplication rooted in a topic they were deeply interested in. For others, it facilitated their learning of multiplication and helped Brooke to see where she needed to continue to work with them. Brooke's class would be working with multiplication and division on an ongoing basis for the next few months, and she supported her students in flexible groups.

As seen in Figure 6.48, some students were able to convey accurate information about their research topic but confused the order of factors in their model and equation. Some had flawed information about their research but created a mathematical problem that made sense and represented it accurately. For example, in

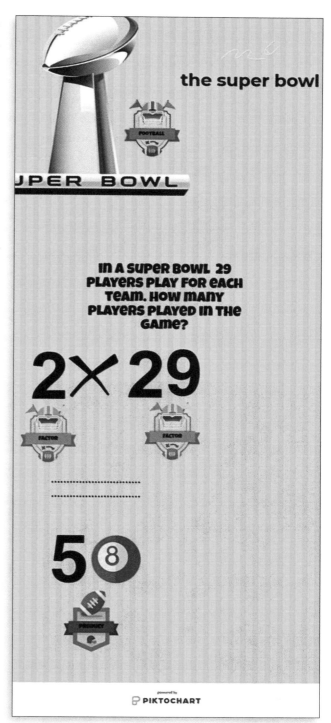

FIGURE 6.48 *One student's infographic revealed an error in the order of factors.*

Figure 6.49, individual planets don't have multiple stars. Stars have planets that revolve around them, and planets have moons that orbit them. But the student got the multiplication correct and understood what was being multiplied, even if it did not make sense scientifically. Still others had accurate information in all aspects of the infographic, except they still somehow arrived at the wrong answer in their equation (see Figure 6.50).

Some students were so excited about creating infographics that they created two. Comparing one student's first infographic (see Figure 6.51) to the second (see Figure 6.52), you can note that the student took ownership over the genre, and she worked to build in more information about her research topic in the second.

A colleague of Brooke's, when looking at the infographics, noted that they "really level the playing field for all kids to be successful." Brooke realized that a benefit of using the online platform was that an outsider

FIGURE 6.49 *Another student misunderstood research about the universe but revealed correct mathematical understanding.*

FIGURE 6.50 *Another student revealed correct under-standing of researched information and the multiplication process but arrived at an incorrect answer.*

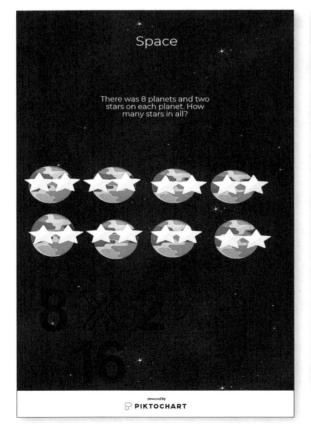

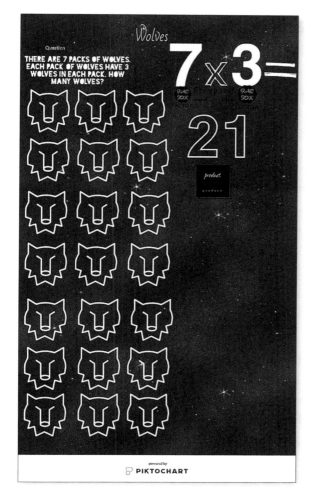

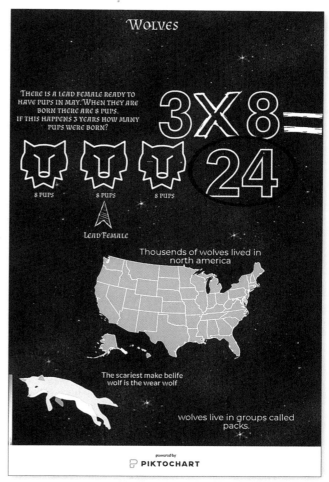

FIGURE 6.51 *This student's first infographic revealed basic information about wolves.*

FIGURE 6.52 *This student's second infographic revealed more complex information about wolves.*

"could not tell if students struggled with reading, or handwriting," since it was all about the digital templates and the students' conceptual understanding of multiplication. Brooke felt that infographics are an important genre to explore and "a new way of representing and learning information. We see infographics everywhere so creating their own allowed them to have firsthand experience with how infographics can be a powerful tool for communicating information."

Notes for Next Year

As Brooke worked on the nonfiction unit in language arts, she shared the process with her colleagues. We had shared thirty-forty books with Brooke, which she in turn shared with some of her colleagues, so that they would have a sense of how we built the unit. This led to a conversation about revising and replicating the unit next year for the whole third-grade team. Brooke has more to say in the next section about her own thoughts for fine-tuning writing minilessons while students are drafting and revising next year. We know that some of the students were challenged by the different nonfiction categories and text structures, so we are now thinking through how to scaffold nonfiction writing across the categories vertically K–5.

Another conversation that surfaced is the progression of visual and graphical literacy within third grade and the school as a whole. *Graphical literacy* refers to students' ability to read and understand graphical devices, such as diagrams, flowcharts, graphs, tables, timelines (Roberts et al. 2013). What elements of visual and graphical literacy need to be introduced when? When are children ready to put multiple pieces of information together in an infographic? How can infographics be used at other grade levels?

Finally, we wonder if students may benefit from more specific use of manipulatives before moving on to multiplication word problems and, ultimately, multiplication infographics. There are students who can do the equations in their head and get the right answer. But how can we further ground them in a concrete path that allows them to be cognizant of what groups are being multiplied?

Throughout the language arts nonfiction genre study and exploration of multiplication in mathematics, students were focused on critical thinking. In language arts, they were constantly considering genre, voice, and theme as they examined author's and illustrator's craft in works of nonfiction, author's and illustrator's notes, and author interviews. The study of visual representation in nonfiction dovetailed with students' efforts to visually represent information conveyed in multiplication word problems, those written by others as well as self-created problems. By hand, students created original illustrations, both drawing and painting with watercolors, but they also composed digital infographics. Students were given multiple opportunities to make their own choices about topics and formats. Their experiences with text sets in language arts informed their math learning, and vice versa.

VOICES FROM THE CLASSROOM *Brooke, Third–Grade Teacher*

The nonfiction writing that the kids produced during this unit was the best work I have seen kids do. I think this was due to the vast exposure to nonfiction texts. I ended up sharing several of the books with another teacher in our school who told me daily how engaged her students were. She said one struggling reader said, "This is the BEST nonfiction book I have ever read," after reading *Growing Up Pedro*. It forced me to look closely at the nonfiction books I have in my library and realize that we need to offer kids more time to read different types of nonfiction texts. I think the kids' excitement and engagement in writing nonfiction directly correlated to their excitement they had in reading new, high interest picture books.

It was so interesting to see how when we teach kids that nonfiction books have "real" photos, a table of contents, text features, etc., it narrows their understanding of nonfiction texts. In the beginning of the unit, any nonfiction book that wasn't a survey book the kids said was fiction. Through exploration, they discovered that not all nonfiction books have a table of contents or real photos as they were taught in years past. I think using a variety of nonfiction texts is so important and a shift all teachers need to make. Nonfiction has traditionally been taught through the lens of survey books, but the kids are much more engaged in the narrative picture books that read like a story.

At the end of the year, we gave the kids the opportunity to choose between doing another nonfiction book or a fairy tale adaptation. We followed a very similar structure for researching; however, one change that we made was for students to come up with subtopics first. For example, if they were researching an animal, they brainstormed subtopics such as habitat, food, etc., first and then researched. In the unit in this chapter, we had students take notes on sticky notes and then categorize their notes in subtopics from there. This second nonfiction unit gave us an opportunity to try it another way. It turns out that having the kids pick the subtopic first narrowed their reading and thinking far too much. They became too focused on finding facts that only fit into their subtopics that they stopped reading to learn all about their topic. Also, looking back, the skill of categorizing their facts after researching really encourages the students to synthesize and make connections between the information they learned. I was glad we were able to try it both ways with the kids and see the benefit of how we did it in the nonfiction unit in this chapter!

Having the students watercolor the pictures for their books was another change I made this year, and I will never go back to having kids use pictures from the Internet as I had done in the past. It encouraged the kids to have a deeper understanding of the connection between words on a page and illustrations. Also, so many of the narrative nonfiction books that were used as mentor texts used paintings or pictures that weren't "real photographs" as we so often tell students nonfiction texts have.

It is worth adding that the infographics allow all students, whether artistic or not, to showcase their work in an attractive, easy-to-understand way. You couldn't tell the difference between the kids who always produce neat work and are more artistic from those that struggle with producing quality work. The infographics allowed students to be creative while also creating a more visually similar product than most platforms.

Comprehensive Text Sets

To help you design your own text sets, Figure 6.53 shows a comprehensive listing of the different text sets used in both the nonfiction genre study as well as the exploration of multiplication.

FIGURE 6.53 *A comprehensive listing of texts from the unit.*

LANGUAGE ARTS

SCAFFOLD TEXT
Giant Squid by Candace Fleming (2016), illustrated by Eric Rohmann

IMMERSION TEXTS	
Duet models of survey books	• You can do this with any survey books you have in your school or classroom library.
Solar System model: concept books	• *Can an Aardvark Bark?* by Melissa Stewart, illustrated by Steve Jenkins (2017) • *Dirty Rats?* by Darrin Lunde, illustrated by Adam Gustavson (2015) • *High Tide for Horseshoe Crabs* by Lisa Kahn Schnell, illustrated by Adam Marks (2015) • *Living Sunlight* by Molly Bang and Penny Chisholm, illustrated by Molly Bang (2009) • *Raindrops Roll* by April Pulley Sayre (2015) • *A Warmer World* by Caroline Arnold, illustrated by Jamie Hogan (2012) • *Water Is Water* by Miranda Paul, illustrated by Jason Chin (2015) • *What Happens Next?* Flip the Flap & Find Out by Nicola Davies, illustrated by Mark Boutavant (2012)
Duet models of life stories	• Can be done with any paired readings of biographies about the same person (some suggested pairings can be found on pages 183 and 184)
Solar System model: nonfiction books with different text structures	• Compare and Contrast: *Timeless Thomas: How Thomas Edison Changed Our Lives* by Gene Barretta (2012) • Narrative: *Me . . . Jane* by Patrick McDonnell (2011) • Question and Answer: *Hello, Bumblebee Bat* by Darrin Lunde, illustrated by Patricia Wynne (2007) • Topic/Subtopic: *Monkey Colors* by Darrin Lunde, illustrated by Patricia Wynne (2012)

Solar System model: interviews and conversations with nonfiction authors	The Nonfiction Minute **www.nonfictionminute.org/** Reading Rockets—video interviews of authors and illustrators **www.readingrockets.org/books/interviews** Ed Puzzle **edpuzzle.com/** Sandra Markle interview—**writersrumpus.com/2016/07/08/meet -sandra-markle-author-of-more-than-200-nonfiction-books-for -children/**

MATH

SCAFFOLD TEXT	
Solar System model of nonfiction books ideal for math problems	• *Dirty Rats?* by Darrin Lunde, illustrated by Adam Gustavson (2015) • *Earmuffs for Everyone! How Chester Greenwood Became Known as the Inventor of Earmuffs* by Meghan McCarthy (2015) • *Giant Squid* by Candace Fleming, illustrated by Eric Rohmann (2016) • *Whoosh! Lonnie Johnson's Super-Soaking Stream of Inventions* by Chris Barton, illustrated by Don Tate (2016)
IMMERSION TEXTS	
	Books • *Animals by the Numbers: A Book of Infographics* by Steve Jenkins (2016) • *By the Numbers 3.14: 110.01 Cool Infographics Packed with Stats and Figures* by National Geographic Kids (2017) • *Infographics for Kids: Putting Information into the Picture* by Susan Martineau, illustrated by Vicky Barker (2016) *Digital* • Piktochart: **www.piktochart.com** • Kids Discover Infographic Archive: **www.kidsdiscover.com /infographics/** • National Geographic Kids Animals: **kids.nationalgeographic.com /animals/** • Reading Rockets Pinterest Board of Kid-Friendly Infographics: **www.pinterest.com/readingrockets/infographics/**

PART III

INVITATIONS
How To Read Part Three

We did not want to end this book having shared the experiences of various classrooms without providing you with a clear path to trying out text sets in *your* classroom. In Part 2, you read about in-depth examples of the planning processes, decision making, and student learning in four units of study cocreated with teachers. Although Part 3 is similarly organized to Part 2, in this section you will read about sample text sets that serve as invitations for you and your intermediate-grade students. They aren't examples of classroom practice but models for you to follow on your own.

You will find four invitational text sets, one for each of the core content areas: language arts, social studies, science, and math. As in our previous chapters, the text sets in this chapter use high-quality children's literature combined with texts of other genres and modalities. Although we have created outlines for substantial units, you don't have to try everything we outline lockstep. These units are written so that you can choose to use all or just some of the text sets that we share.

Starting small is a great way to transition to a text set approach to curriculum design, so feel free to customize these text sets and use them in the ways that work best for your classroom. Although we built the text sets as scaffolds, immersions, and extensions within a comprehensive curriculum unit, we strove to shape text sets that can be used independent of one another. You may choose to follow a full unit from one chapter, but you may choose to try out just one or two text sets from another. It's up to you!

Language Arts Invitations
How Does Figurative Language Shape Our Reading and Writing?

Introduction

In this text set exploration, you and your students can explore the possibilities that figurative language provides in genres of all kinds: fiction, nonfiction, memoir, and poetry. Often, figurative language is considered "fancy" or ornamental, but not really necessary, something kind of la-di-da. We know it's more than that. In selecting the texts for this chapter, our goal is to provide you and your students with a way of seeing figurative language as an important tool to convey just about anything you want to convey in your writing: mood, characterization, persuasion, and even scientific facts. Figurative language is all around us, all the time.

The following text sets focus on National Council of Teachers of English-International Literacy Association (NCTE-ILA) Standard 6 (see Figure 7.1).

FIGURE 7.1 *This chart documents the standards this unit was designed to meet.*

NATIONAL COUNCIL OF TEACHERS OF ENGLISH–INTERNATIONAL LITERACY ASSOCIATION (NCTE-ILA) **Standards for the English Language Arts**	
Standard 6:	Students apply knowledge of language structure, language conventions (e.g., spelling and punctuation), media techniques, figurative language, and genre to create, critique, and discuss print and non-print texts.

So, here's our invitation: try out some, or all, of the text sets. You can use them all, in combination with one another, or you can choose to use just one of the text sets to explore. It's up to you and how much time you have to devote to figurative language. We created a logical progression of experiences, from broad to narrow. But we know that you may see other ways to use these text sets in a different order. You might explore this exclusively in language arts, or you might seize this opportunity to combine some science and language arts learning. It's up to you.

Scaffold: Introducing Figurative Language
Duet Model: Figurative Language in Fiction and Nonfiction

You can read these two texts in either order (see Figure 7.4). The sharp contrast of the mood in each of the two books demonstrates the potential of the Duet model for the comparison and contrast of texts. *Big Blue Whale* (Davies 1997) (see Figure 7.2), a nonfiction picture book, is a thoughtful and informative text that evokes wonder about the world around us as it describes the attributes of the blue whale. In sharp contrast, anyone who has spent time with toddlers will find *Finn Throws a Fit!* (Elliott 2009), a work of fiction (see Figure 7.3), hysterical. Your students are old enough to look at Finn's antics with their own mature sense of humor.

Create an anchor chart to help students document their thinking about the language in each book, with "Language in *Finn Throws a Fit!*" on one side and "Language in *Big Blue Whale*" on the other. Depending on your students, you might want to start off with *Finn Throws a Fit!* because it's an easier book. However, the concept of metaphor that it reveals is a more sophisticated concept than that of the simile, which is used extensively in *Big Blue Whale*. In that context, you might find *Big Blue Whale* a better starting point.

In *Finn Throws a Fit!*, author Elliott uses metaphor to describe the actions Finn takes while having a fit. For example, when Finn screams and yells there is "lightning in the kitchen!" (n.p.). When Finn kicks, "an earthquake shakes the world." Everyday actions of small children are revealed through the use of

FIGURE 7.2

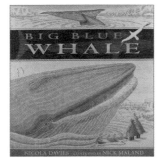

FIGURE 7.3

FIGURE 7.4 *This Duet model compares and contrasts figurative language in fiction and nonfiction.*

Fiction:
Finn Throws a Fit!
by David Elliott

Nonfiction:
Big Blue Whale
by Nicola Davies

metaphor, complemented by concrete illustrations that convey the metaphor. Through the words and illustrations, the reader is asked to make meaning, to understand that there isn't really lightning in the kitchen, just Finn's inexplicable anger.

The similes in Nicola Davies's *Big Blue Whale* are used to convey specific information about blue whales. For example, Davies writes that the blue whale's skin is "springy and smooth like a hard-boiled egg, and it's as slippery as wet soap" (9). On the very same page Davies writes that the eye of a blue whale is "as big as a teacup and as dark as the deep sea" (9) and that "just behind the eye is a hole as small as the end of a pencil." Throughout this text, similes allow the reader to better understand the attributes of the blue whale, through the use of similes that compare the blue whale's features to objects with which children are familiar.

Regardless of which order seems best for your students, read aloud one book one day and one the next. After reading each book, ask students the following questions: How do the words set the mood in the book? How do the illustrations set the mood? Next, introduce or reintroduce the definition of metaphor or simile. Ask students to identify the similes or metaphors in the book and document them on the anchor chart. On the third day, introduce alliteration, and reread both books, since they are brief read-alouds. Ask students to identify any alliteration they see within each text. When you preview the text, you will see that there is far more alliteration in *Big Blue Whale* than in *Finn Throws a Fit!*, in part because there is far more language in *Big Blue Whale*.

Ask students to consider how figurative language impacts the reader of each book. What is the point of the metaphors in *Finn Throws a Fit!*? The similes in *Big Blue Whale*? The alliteration in each? Why do writers of fiction and nonfiction use figurative language? Document your students' thinking on another anchor chart.

Duet Model: Figurative Language in Fiction and Nonfiction About the Natural World

FIGURE 7.5

This second Duet model (see Figure 7.6) moves into a focus on figurative language and the natural world, through a work of lyrical fiction, *Over in the Wetlands* (Rose 2015), and a work of lyrical nonfiction, *Seashells: More Than a Home* (Stewart 2019) (see Figure 7.5). What makes writing lyrical? Melissa Stewart (2019), author of *Seashells*, has written on her blog that "repetition and opposition" and "longer sentences with more dependent clauses (and commas) make writing more lyrical" (**celebratescience .blogspot.com/2019/03/what-is-voice.html**).

FIGURE 7.6 *This Duet model compares and contrasts figurative language in fiction and nonfiction about the natural world.*

Read these texts aloud to your students, and again, ask them what they notice about the language. What similes, metaphors, and/or alliteration do they notice? How do they impact the reader? Track student responses on another anchor chart, with "Language in *Over in the Wetlands*" on one side and "Language in *Seashells*" on the other.

In both books, the writers use similes to establish mood and to convey information. For example, in *Over in the Wetlands*, Rose writes: "Gentle as a whisper too soft to hear, / a faint breeze hints that a storm draws near" (n.p.). On the next page, she writes that "wind stirs moss like silent bells." Melissa Stewart follows the same format she used in *Feathers: Not Just for Flying* (2014), which we discussed back in Chapter 5. In this case, similes are used to convey conceptual understanding of mollusks. For example, Stewart starts the book with: "Seashells can rise and sink like a submarine" (n.p.). Illustrator Sarah Brannen includes a small drawing of a submarine on the same page, so readers can see the object to which the shell is being compared. This pattern extends throughout the book. Stewart also uses comparison and contrast with her similes quite effectively. For example: "Seashells can let in light like a window . . . or belch out waste like a ship's smokestack." You can hear the alliteration in this sentence as well, with the repetition of *l* in the first clause, and *s* in the second.

Immersion: Going Deeper with Figurative Language
Solar System Model: Figurative Language in Multiple Genres and Modalities

It's important for students to realize that figurative language is not something that just pops up in books that you read in school. Figurative language is everywhere! You might want to photograph signs and advertisements in your community in advance of this unit to show students that they are surrounded by figurative language. You can even seek out advertisements for the hottest new toy or craft that is popular with your students, to see if you can find figurative language. To expand students' notions of when and where they may confront figurative language, have them explore a range of multimodal texts in the Solar System model (see Figure 7.7) in which they can identify similes, metaphors, and/or alliteration. Some students who might struggle to access text with a metaphor can understand a visual metaphor. Others who struggle with identifying alliteration in print might more easily hear it when spoken or sung aloud. Moreover, in exploring a range of texts that exist outside of school, students will understand that figurative language is a tool that authors use to reach their audience regardless of their chosen genre or modality.

Visual Metaphor

Online, find an image of a person with a lightbulb overhead. Ask students what the lightbulb means. How do they know that a lightbulb signals an idea? Explain that this is a visual metaphor.

Metaphor in Theater

Read this quote from Shakespeare's play *As You Like It*, from the Poetry Foundation website:

> All the world's a stage,
> And all the men and women merely players.
> They have their exits and their entrances.

Ask your students what they think Shakespeare was trying to say with this excerpt. How is the world a stage? Who are players? What do exits and entrances mean in theater? What might Shakespeare be trying to say about life? **www.poetryfoundation.org/poems/56966/speech -all-the-worlds-a-stage**

Similes in Songs

Play your students "Firework," by Katy Perry. Project the lyrics from Genius.Com (**genius.com/Katy-perry-firework-lyrics**).

As students listen to the song and read the lyrics, ask them to think about what they are hearing.

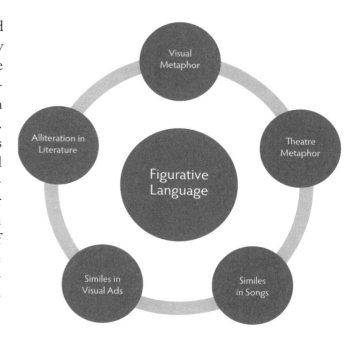

FIGURE 7.7 *This Solar System model explores figurative language in a range of real-world texts of different genres and modalities.*

Once you have listened to the song all the way through, have your students listen again and raise their hands when they hear/read a simile or a metaphor.

Why did Perry choose to use so many similes and metaphors in her song? How do they help the reader understand her message? What do they think her message is?

Similes in Visual Ads

Have students look at this image of a vintage Chevy Truck ad, with the slogan "Like a Rock" (Cook 2015) (**www.autoinfluence.com/four-best chevy-marketing-campaigns/**). Why would Chevy choose this simile? What does it say about the truck?

Alliteration in Literature

Ask your students to list as many Harry Potter characters as possible. As they share, ask them to consider how many names are alliterative. Some of the following names may appear on their list:

- Dudley Dursley
- Severus Snape
- Minerva McGonagall
- Luna Lovegood
- Filius Flitwick
- Peter Pettigrew
- Parvati and Padma Patil

Ask students to consider why J. K. Rowling may have chosen to create these names with alliteration.

Figurative Language Detectives: Creating a New Text Set

After you have had a chance to explore figurative language in the real world, have students create their own figurative language text set. Ask them to be "figurative language detectives" and collect figurative language that they see and hear in their everyday lives: sentences in their independent reading books; signs they see on the subway or out the window of buses and cars or in the aisles of the grocery store; advertisements they hear on the radio, see on television, or notice on webpages. Over a period of a week or two, have students document when they observe figurative language using a graphic organizer (see Figure 7.8). You can use the graphic organizer as a print document or a shared digital document, or even turn it into a bulletin board–sized graphic organizer chart that students write down their observations on the morning when they come into school and/or during the school day when they observe figurative language in books or other texts.

FIGURE 7.8 *Students can use this graphic organizer to track the figurative language they are finding in daily life.*

What I Read	Where I Found It	Type of Figurative Language	Why I Think the Author Used It
Example: "Our mattresses are as soft as a feather."	A window sign for a store that sells mattresses.	Simile	I think the store owners want people walking or driving by to think that the store sells really soft mattresses that are really comfortable for sleeping.

Create New Texts: Advertising Executives, Writers, and Designers

To further cement students' understanding of figurative language as a purposeful part of everyday life, have students create original advertisements that use figurative language to persuade people to do something. As a result, students will transition from *readers* of figurative language to *producers* of figurative language. Brainstorm a list of items that your students are interested in making advertisements about, or have students invent new imaginary products for which they can create advertisements. Challenge students working either alone, in pairs, or small groups, to include at least one example of figurative language in their advertisement.

Solar System Model: Figurative Language Author Study

In contrast to the pop-culture focus of the previous Solar System text sets, this next text set immerses students in the writing of Joyce Sidman (see Figure 7.9). Allow your students to explore these texts in whatever way you think works best. You can do whole-class read-alouds of one or two followed by small-group explorations of the others, or you could have students rotate through stations with each book over the course of a couple of days

Students will notice as they read one or more of these texts that Sidman utilizes similes, metaphors, and alliteration throughout her fiction and nonfiction. Most books in this Solar System model are poetry collections that have a poem on one side of the two-page spread and a nonfiction paragraph on the other. Sometimes the figurative language is just in the poem, sometimes in both the poem and the paragraph. Some use limited figurative language. For example, in *Ubiquitous* (Figure 7.10), Sidman (2010b) mostly utilizes alliteration in her poems. In *Before Morning*, a fictional book, Sidman (2016) focuses on metaphor as a young child wishes for snow: "Let the air turn to feathers, the earth turn to sugar" (n.p.). In contrast, in *Song of the Water Boatman*, Sidman (2005) uses similes, metaphors, and alliteration in her poems and her paragraphs (see Figure 7.11).

However you decide to explore the fiction and poetry and nonfiction included in this text set, keep track of what your students notice about Sidman's language and what they notice about the illustration techniques used by the different illustrators. What is similar and what is different about those techniques? How do they complement the mood of the written words? How does Sidman use similes, metaphors, and alliteration to create mood and/or

FIGURE 7.9 *This Solar System model explores author Joyce Sidman's use of figurative language.*

FIGURE 7.10

FIGURE 7.11

convey information? Use this graphic organizer in Figure 7.12 to provide your students with support in their note taking.

FIGURE 7.12 *Students can use this graphic organizer to document their observations of Sidman's use of figurative language.*

Figurative Language in: _____ (Book Title)		
What Kind of Figurative Language Do You Notice?	Copy the Simile, Metaphor, or Alliteration.	Describe What the Figurative Language Makes You Think About.

Once students have had the opportunity to explore Sidman's work over the course of a few days, have them come together to share some of their observations. You could create class anchor charts book by book. Or you could create an anchor chart for each of the three types of figurative language you've been exploring: similes, metaphors, and alliteration. Once students report out their observations on how Sidman has used figurative language, ask students to survey the anchor charts one more time. What are the different purposes for Sidman's figurative language? What kind of "jobs" did they have to do (to use a term used in *Seashells* [Stewart 2019], explored earlier in this chapter). Make a new author chart that lists these purposes, which can become a guide for students' own writing. These purposes will be explored in depth in the next section.

FIGURE 7.13

FIGURE 7.14 *This Tree Ring model explores the creation of Joyce Sidman's* (2014) Winter Bees and Other Poems of the Cold, *illustrated by Rick Allen.*

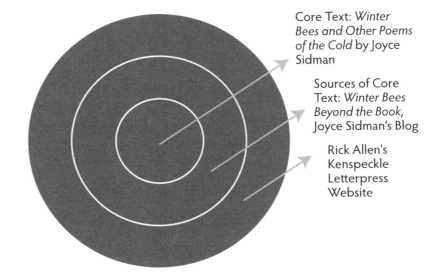

Core Text: *Winter Bees and Other Poems of the Cold* by Joyce Sidman

Sources of Core Text: *Winter Bees Beyond the Book,* Joyce Sidman's Blog

Rick Allen's Kenspeckle Letterpress Website

Extension: Exploring a Mentor Text and Mentor Processes

Tree Ring Model: Composing
Winter Bees and Other Poems of the Cold

Joyce Sidman's (2014) *Winter Bees and Other Poems of the Cold* (see Figure 7.13) is the core text for this Tree Ring text set (see Figure 7.14). You might choose to read the first two spreads, each containing a poem and a paragraph, by using a document camera. You could read these aloud and discuss what students notice in this collection compared with the other books by Sidman they have already explored. What is similar? What is different? Students could then explore the rest of the text in small groups. Or, you might feel that students are ready to dive into the work and read it independently in small groups from the start. Ask them to consider how this book aligns with what students have already noticed about her other work by placing sticky notes in places where they make connections. Come together as a class to discuss their observations.

Next, you will have your students explore some of the processes that Sidman followed to compose her poems and some of the processes that Rick Allen used to illustrate the book. This provides students with an in-depth exploration of how the book was created, which serves as a model for the methods they can use to create their own new texts. You could do all of this work as a whole class, projecting the PBS video, Sidman's blog, and

Allen's business website on the board. Or, you could do this work in stations, having students cycle through each source over the course of a few days in small groups.

MIDDLE RING: JOYCE SIDMAN'S MENTOR PROCESSES

When students watch the twenty-six-minute video from Twin Cities PBS, *Winter Bees Beyond the Book*, ask them what they learn about Sidman's love of nature. What do they learn about her process of writing? What do they learn about Rick Allen's methods of illustrating? What questions do they have about Sidman's writing process or Allen's illustrating process? As you explore Sidman's work, go for walks with your students around the school building. Regardless of whether you are in an urban, a suburban, or a rural environment, have students keep track of the natural world nearby. Have them take notes, take pictures, and/or draw their own. What do they notice about animal footprints, birds, insects, trees, and water? Do the same walk a couple of times to see what changes and what stays the same. Next, bring along someone really knowledgeable about the local environment, and have that local expert show you and your students what you might not have noticed, just as Sidman does in the video.

When students explore Sidman's blog, have them document what they learn about the ways in which Sidman notices the natural world around her through her daily long walks. How does her everyday routine help support her work as a writer? As a parallel, allow your students to select a topic from the natural world that they are curious about. Support your students as they research. You can have students compose a series of two-page spreads, featuring poems and paragraphs that each feature figurative language, as well as illustrations that convey important information. If you don't have enough time for students to create individual books that demonstrate their command of figurative language, have each student create a two-page spread for a class book. Work with your school or public librarian to find resources the students can use for research.

OUTER RING: RICK ALLEN'S MENTOR PROCESSES

Finally, when students explore Allen's business website, ask them what questions about Allen's illustrating process got answered, and what new questions they have. If you would like to experiment with block printing or scratchboard illustration, modeled on Rick Allen's illustrations as discussed in the various texts, collaborate with your art teacher or a local artist or arts organization. As Brooke did with her students in Chapter 6, you might want to provide time for students to begin illustrations before they are done with their writing. For some students, this will be their way into the writing.

- *Winter Bees Beyond the Book* Twin Cities PBS: **www.tpt.org/winter-bees-beyond-the-book/**
- Joyce Sidman's Blogs: **www.joycesidman.com/animals/**
- Rick Allen's Kenspeckle Letterpress Website: **kenspeckleletterpress.com/**

Conclusion

The text sets in this unit, which can be used as single text sets or in various combinations with one another, focus students like laser beams (pardon the simile!) on the concept of figurative language, specifically in the form of simile, metaphor, and alliteration. In setting up these text sets, we juxtaposed print books of different genres with one another and multimodal texts of different genres with one another. We asked students to become curators of figurative language. All of this was to demonstrate that figurative language is purposeful in its use, regardless of the genre in which the author is composing. By focusing on critical thinking, conceptual understanding of figurative language, and the mentor processes of Joyce Sidman and Rick Allen, we support students in their growing agency as readers and writers, and we offer them an opportunity to observe the natural world within their community, answer their own questions, and compose their own works.

Comprehensive Text Set

In Figure 7.15, you can find the complete list of texts discussed in this chapter.

FIGURE 7.15 *A comprehensive listing of texts from the unit.*

SCAFFOLD: INTRODUCING FIGURATIVE LANGUAGE	
Duet Model: Figurative Language in Fiction and Nonfiction	*Big Blue Whale* by Nicola Davies (1997) *Finn Throws a Fit!* by David Elliott (2009)
Duet Model: Figurative Language in Fiction and Nonfiction About the Natural World	*Over in the Wetlands: A Hurricane-on-the-Bayou Story* by Caroline Starr Rose (2015) *Seashells: More than a Home* by Melissa Stewart (2019)
IMMERSION: GOING DEEPER WITH FIGURATIVE LANGUAGE	
Solar System Model: Figurative Language in Multiple Genres and Modalities	William Shakespeare's *As You Like It* (**www.poetryfoundation.org/poems/56966/speech-all-the-worlds-a-stage**) "Firework," by Katy Perry. Project the lyrics from Genius.Com (**genius.com/Katy-perry-firework-lyrics**) "Like a Rock," Chevy Truck Ad (**www.autoinfluence.com/four-best-chevy-marketing-campaigns/**).
Solar System Model: Figurative Language Author Study	*Before Morning* by Joyce Sidman, illustrated by Beth Krommes (2016) *Dark Emperor and Other Poems of the Night* by Joyce Sidman, illustrated by Rick Allen (2010) *Round* by Joyce Sidman, illustrated by Taeeun Yoo (2017) *Song of the Water Boatman and Other Pond Poems* by Joyce Sidman, illustrated by Beckie Prange (2005) *Swirl by Swirl: Spirals in Nature* by Joyce Sidman, illustrated by Beth Krommes (2011) *Ubiquitous: Celebrating Nature's Survivors* by Joyce Sidman, illustrated by Beckie Prange (2010)
EXTENSION: EXPLORING A MENTOR TEXT AND MENTOR PROCESSES	
Tree Ring Model: Composing *Winter Bees and Other Poems of the Cold*	*Winter Bees and Other Poems of the Cold* by Joyce Sidman (2014), illustrated by Rick Allen "Winter Bees Beyond the Book" by Twin Cities PBS (**www.tpt.org/winter-bees-beyond-the-book/**) Joyce Sidman's blogs (**www.joycesidman.com/animals/**) Rick Allen's Kenspeckle Letterpress website (**kenspeckleletterpress.com/**)

CHAPTER 8

Social Studies Invitations
How Does Activism Lead Us to a "More Perfect Union" in Our Democracy?

Introduction

For thousands of years, hundreds of Native American nations lived in North America, in what is now the United States, under various governance structures. Many of those nations continue to this day. In the seventeenth century, European settlers came to North America to appropriate land and colonize; the result was genocide for many Native American nations. North American colonies followed the laws of their home nations: Spain, the Netherlands, France, and England. By the eighteenth century, the East Coast colonies were mostly English, and in the late eighteenth century, a new nation was created, through a written act of political rebellion, the Declaration of Independence, as well as a military victory. Since the inception of the United States, individuals, free and enslaved, from dominant and marginalized communities, have worked to improve conditions for themselves and others, to move the United States more closely toward the goal of a "more perfect union" called for by the Preamble of the Constitution (National Archives n.d.) (**www.archives.gov/founding-docs /constitution-transcript**)

In this text set exploration, students have the opportunity to explore fundamental questions about the rights of the individual in our democracy, and the ways in which social justice activists have always been working for change throughout the history of the United States.

Essential Questions

- How do we work toward a "more perfect union" in our democracy?
- How have changemakers of the past created change through protest and action?
- How can we become activists for social justice?

Within this text set, we work with two specific strands from the National Curriculum Standards for Social Studies (National Council for the Social Studies 2010): Time, Continuity, and Change, and Civic Ideals and Practices (see Figure 8.1).

FIGURE 8.1 *This chart documents the standards this unit was designed to meet.*

THE NATIONAL COUNCIL FOR THE SOCIAL STUDIES (2010) NATIONAL CURRICULUM STANDARDS FOR SOCIAL STUDIES	
Time, Continuity, and Change	*Knowledge—Learners will understand:* • That we can learn our personal past and the past of communities, nations, and the world by means of stories, biographies, interviews, and original sources such as documents, letters, photographs, and artifacts. • Key people, events, and places associated with the history of the community, nation, and world. • That historical events occurred in times that differed from our own, but often have lasting consequences for the present and future. *Processes—Learners will be able to:* • Use a variety of sources to learn about the past. • Identify examples of both continuity and change, as depicted in stories, photographs, and documents. • Use sources to learn about the past in order to inform decisions about actions on issues of importance today.
Civic Ideals and Practices	*Knowledge—Learners will understand:* • Concepts and ideas, such as individual dignity, fairness, freedom, the common good, rule of law, civic life, rights, and responsibilities. • The importance of gathering information as the basis for informed civic action. *Processes—Learners will be able to:* • Ask and find answers to questions about how to plan for action with others to improve life in school, community, and beyond. • Analyze how specific policies or citizen behaviors reflect ideals and practices consistent or inconsistent with democratic ideals. • Examine the influence of citizens and officials on policy decisions.

So here's our invitation: try out some or all of the text sets that follow. You can use them all, in combination with one another, or you can choose to use just one of the text sets to explore. It's up to you and how much time you have for this exploration of civic ideals and practices and individual and group rights. We created a logical progression of experiences, from an overview of activism over time, to a more specific examination of the efforts of individuals working for change in different times, to an exploration of contemporary issues about which students can become more knowledgeable and create a platform for change. Initially, we focus on activism here in the United States but then expand our focus to a global level. You might explore this exclusively in social studies, or you might seize this opportunity to combine some social studies and language arts learning. It's up to you.

Scaffold: Introducing Activists from History and Contemporary Life

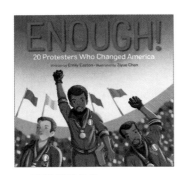

FIGURE 8.2

To begin the exploration of how activists have shaped our nation, read aloud *Enough! 20 Protesters Who Changed America* (see Figure 8.2) written by Emily Easton (2018) and illustrated by Ziyue Chen. The book presents twenty activists from American history, in chronological order. The book begins with the political rebellion of colonists against the crown, featuring a two-page spread of the Boston Tea Party and the words: "Samuel threw a tea party." On the next spread, Harriet Tubman leads self-emancipated people through the woods on the Underground Railroad; next, Susan B. Anthony casts an illegal vote. But the majority of the book's twenty protesters carve out change within the last fifty years, affirming for young readers that protest is a part of contemporary American life. Athletes from Muhammad Ali to Colin Kaepernick are featured, as are artists such as John Lennon, Yoko Ono, and Gilbert Baker, who created the first rainbow flag, now a symbol of LGBTQIA pride, and women from Hollywood who founded the TIME'S UP movement to fight sexual harassment in the workplace. Young people from Jazz Jennings, the youngest transgender activist in the public realm, to the Parkland students are also celebrated.

After reading this simple and accessible book aloud, ask your students why they think the author wrote this book. Why is it important to commemorate those who protest? Ask students what they think they know about the individuals featured in this book, and what questions they have. You might want to ask students if they can think of other people who could or should be in this book. Next, ask students, in small groups, to review the back matter, which provides a paragraph on each individual featured, and the obstacles and opportunities each experienced as a result of their activism. Depending on the age of your students, you may also choose to share the author's personal connection to the Parkland shooting, as referenced in her author's note at the start of the book. Easton's cousin Ryan Deitsch was one of the Parkland students who organized the March for Our Lives, and she writes, "I was moved to make a list of other protestors who stood up and said 'Enough!' and was reminded that America itself was formed as a protest against England. Protest is part of America's DNA, and I wanted to share this realization in a book for young people. I especially wanted to show the many ways protestors have stood, marched, sat, or knelt for change" (n.p.).

Use this book as an opportunity for your students to begin to think about the curriculum strand of Continuity and Change. Create an anchor chart with one side labeled "Continuity: What Do Protesters Have in Common?" and the other side labeled "Change: What Is Different About Protester's Experiences?"

You can also use this book as an opportunity for your students to begin to think about the curriculum strand of Civic Ideals and Practices. Work with students to create kid-friendly definitions of the words *protest* and *act* on an anchor chart. You might want to start by sharing their Latin origins. The Latin origin of *act* is "to do," and the Latin origins of *protest* is to "publicly declare." Use those basic definitions as a foundation for also defining the words *protester* and *activist*. Next, ask students what big questions they have about people who protest. Document these questions on another anchor chart, to guide students' thinking throughout the unit and so that you can add new questions as they emerge.

Immersion: Exploring the Stories of Individual Activists

Sunburst Models of Individual Activists

Throughout this book, we have not written much about using the Sunburst instructional model; although the Sunburst is the most commonly used model in classrooms, it is typically not labeled as such by educators. In the Sunburst model, there is one book that is at the core of the exploration. All the other multimodal texts serve to support readers' ability to access, understand, and critique the core text.

You can choose to have students explore any combination of activists. You might assign students to small groups, and each group is responsible for sharing information with the class about one activist. Or you might choose to have the students make their way through more than one text set, over a period of several days, depending on how much time you have. The activist Sunburst models are presented in the chronological order of the major events depicted in the core texts. Each Sunburst model contains links to digital texts. Some of these texts we discovered through our own research, and some were part of the back matter within the books. This set of texts is not comprehensive. For example, there are not enough books about contemporary or historic Native Americans, let alone books written about Native Americans by Native American authors. There are so many stories of activism that we have yet to hear in picture book format. Hopefully, by time you are reading this book, there will be more.

Sunburst Model: Hiawatha, Member of the Mohawk Nation, Before the Fourteenth Century

The historical fiction picture book *Hiawatha and the Peacemaker* (Robertson 2015) at the core of the Sunburst model (see Figure 8.8) tells the story of Hiawatha, a Mohawk warrior and talented speaker living sometime before the fourteenth century. Hiawatha traveled with the Peacemaker, sent by the Creator, to convince the Cayugas, the Senecas, the Oneidas, the Mohawks, and the Onondagas to establish the Haudenosaunee, or People of the Long House, a union of five different nations. In the Historical Note in the back matter, author Robbie Roberston, himself a descendent of the Mohawk and Cayuga Nations, states that "in 1722 the Tuscarora nation joined this united league, and it became the Six Nations Iroquois Confederacy" (n.p.). The Iroquois Confederacy, known more accurately as the Haudenosaunee Confederacy, was inspirational for the separation of powers and the government structures outlined in the Constitution of the United States. Through this fictional representation of Hiawatha, students can explore the activist role that Hiawatha played in an effort to establish long-lasting peace and create a new governance structure that benefited the citizens of the Iroquois nations and was influential to our current governance structures.

FIGURE 8.3 *The texts in this Sunburst model explore the historical Hiawatha*

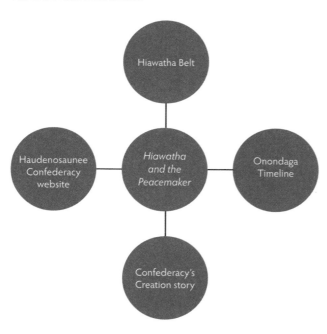

- Timeline of Onondaga Nation, Connection to American Revolution **www.onondaganation.org/history/timeline/**

- Description of the "Hiawatha Belt," returned to the Onondaga Nation in 2012 **www.onondaganation.org/culture/wampum /hiawatha-belt/**

- Haudenosaunee Confederacy Website **www.haudenosauneeconfederacy.com/**

- Haudenosaunee Confederacy's Creation story **www.haudenosauneeconfederacy.com/confederacys-creation/**

Sunburst Model: Elizabeth Freeman, Self-Emancipated Woman, 1780–1783

The historical fiction picture book *Mumbet's Declaration of Independence* by Gretchen Woelfle (2014), at the core of this second Sunburst model (see Figure 8.4), tells the story of Mumbet, later known by the name she gave herself: Elizabeth Freeman. Elizabeth was born into slavery in the mid-eighteenth century in central Massachusetts. The Massachusetts state constitution in 1780 inspired her to sue the state in 1781 for her freedom. Her winning court case paved the way for slavery to be outlawed by the Massachusetts Supreme Court in 1783.

- Catharine Sedgwick's 1853 draft of Freeman's life, from the Massachusetts Historical Society: **www.masshist.org/database/viewer .php?old=1&ft=End+of+Slavery& from=%2Fendofslavery%2Findex .php%3Fid%3D54&item_id=587**

- 1811 Portrait of Elizabeth Freeman from the Massachusetts Historical Society: **www.masshist.org/database/viewer .php?old=1&ft=End+of+Slavery& from=%2Fendofslavery%2Finde .php%3Fid%3D54&item_id=25**

FIGURE 8.4 *The texts in this Sunburst model explore Elizabeth Freeman's efforts to self-emancipate by changing the laws regarding slavery in Massachusetts.*

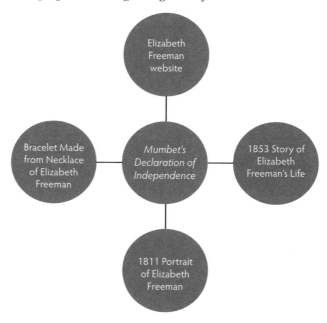

- Bracelet made from a necklace owned by Elizabeth Freeman, also from the Massachusetts Historical Society: **www.masshist.org/database/548**

- Website devoted to Elizabeth Freeman, which includes links to various sites related to her life as well as the court transcripts: **elizabethfreeman.mumbet.com/**

- Elizabeth Freeman exhibit at the National Museum of African American History and Culture: **nmaahc.tumblr.com/post /163991306641/petitioning-for-freedom-elizabeth-freeman**

FIGURE 8.5

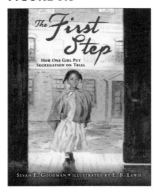

Sunburst Model: Sarah Roberts, African American Student, 1847–1855

The picture book biography *The First Step: How One Girl Put Segregation on Trial* (see Figure 8.5) by Susan Goodman (2016), in the third Sunburst model (see Figure 8.6), features Sarah Roberts, who was just four years old in 1847 when she was told that she was not allowed to attend Boston's Otis School because it was for white children only. Sarah's parents, along with the country's second African American lawyer, Robert Morris, mounted a court case. Although they were not successful initially, their efforts were ultimately rewarded in 1855 when Boston integrated its schools; American schools remain quite segregated even today.

FIGURE 8.6
The texts in this Sunburst model explore Sarah Roberts's efforts to desegregate Boston's public schools in the mid-nineteenth century.

- On this webpage, created in partnership with the Massachusetts Historical Society, readers can see a photograph of Robert Morris and learn more about the case: **www.longroadtojustice.org/topics /education/sarah-roberts.php**

- A WBUR Interview with Susan Goodman, author of *The First Step*, about writing the book: **www.wbur.org/radioboston/2017/02/24 /the-first-step**.

Sunburst Model: Sylvia Mendez, Mexican American Student, 1945–1947

The picture book biography *Separate Is Never Equal: Sylvia Mendez and Her Family's Fight for Desegregation* (Tonatiuh 2014), in the fourth Sunburst model (see Figure 8.7), features Sylvia Mendez, who, like Sarah Roberts a century before her, also faced school segregation. In this case, Sylvia and her siblings and cousins were told that they could not attend their neighborhood school. Instead, they had to attend the dilapidated, underfunded

"Mexican" school, even though Sylvia's family were American citizens. In 1945, the family filed a lawsuit, and in 1947, California banned segregation in schools.

- Your students can listen to Sylvia and Sandra Mendez Duran talk about their memories of the trial on NPR Story-Corps: **storycorps.org/stories/sylvia -mendez-and-sandra-mendez-duran/**

- News story on Sylvia Mendez getting the Presidential Medal of Freedom: **www.ocregister.com/2011/02/15/oc-civil -rights-icon-mendez-awarded-medal-of -freedom/**

- Sylvia Mendez talking about winning the Presidential Medal of Freedom in 2011: **www.youtube.com /watch?v=eMoAXggpj_0**

Sunburst Model: Anna May Wong, Chinese American Actress, 1940s

The picture book biography *Shining Star: The Anna Wong Story* by Paula Yoo (2009) (see Figure 8.9), in the fifth Sunburst model (see Figure 8.8), features Anna May Wong, born in Los Angeles in 1905. Growing up, she worked in her parents' laundry but dreamed of a career in film. For years, Anna played stereotyped roles, demeaning to Chinese Americans, in Hollywood films. But then, a 1936 trip to China allowed Anna to see her culture and heritage in a new light, and from then on, she was an advocate for more authentic representation of Chinese Americans in the movie and television.

- Students can watch an eight-minute silent video of Anna Wong visiting China in 1936 from the UCLA Film Archive: **www.youtube.com /watch?v=9mDJDt2vD7w**

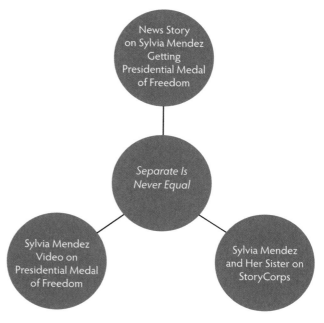

FIGURE 8.7 *The texts in this Sunburst model explore Sylvia Mendez's efforts to desegregate in schools in her California community in the mid–twentieth century.*

FIGURE 8.8 *The texts in this Sunburst model explore Chinese American actress Anna May Wong's advocacy for more authentic representations of Chinese culture in television and movies.*

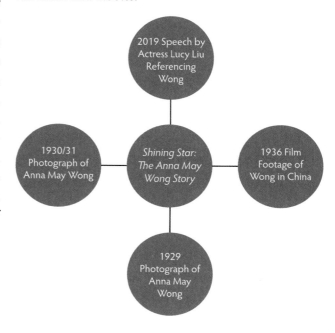

- Students can watch this *Variety* film clip from May 2019, in which actress Lucy Liu celebrates becoming the second Asian American to get a star on the Hollywood Walk of Fame, the first being Anna Wong: **variety.com/2019/film/news/lucy-liu-hollywood-walk-of -fame-second-asian-american-actress-1203202691/**

- Students can view this 1929 photograph of Anna May Wong from London's National Portrait Gallery: **www.npg.org.uk/collections /search/portrait/mw66914/Anna-May-Wong**

- Students can view this 1930/31 photograph of Anna May Wong from the Art Institute of Chicago: **www.artic.edu/artworks/137078 /anna-may-wong**

Sunburst Model: Ella Baker, Joseph McNeil, Franklin McCain, David Richmond, and Ezell Blair, Civil Rights Activists, 1960

The picture book *Sit-In: How Four Friends Stood Up by Sitting Down* by Andrea Davis Pinkney (2010), in the sixth Sunburst model (see Figure 8.9), features four young African American students at North Carolina Agricultural and Technical State University, mentored by NAACP activist Ella Baker, who became a catalyst for desegregation when they sat down at the whites-only lunch counter at their local Woolworth's store. Soon, other students across the South also began to sit at lunch counters in nonviolent protest. By spring of 1960, Ella Baker and college students from across the country created the Student Nonviolent Coordinating Campaign Committee, a major arm of the Civil Rights Movement.

FIGURE 8.9 *The texts in this Sunburst model explore the lunch counter sit-ins of the Civil Rights Movement.*

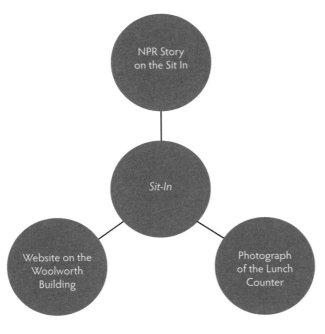

- Have students listen to this short NPR story "The Woolworth Sit-In That Launched a Movement:" **www.npr.org /templates/story/story .php?storyId=18615556**

- Students can see the lunch counter from the protest at the National Museum of American History: **americanhistory.si.edu/exhibitions /greensboro-lunch-counter**

- Students can explore the website of the International Civil Rights Center and Museum, now house in the Woolworth Building in which the sit-ins took place: **www.sitinmovement.org/**.

Sunburst Model: Ruth Bader Ginsburg, Women's Rights Activist and Supreme Court Justice, 1970s–2020

The picture book biography *I Dissent: Ruth Bader Ginsburg Makes Her Mark* by Debbie Levy (2016), in the seventh Sunburst model (see Figure 8.10), features Ruth Bader Ginsburg, a lawyer and the second female Supreme Court justice. Ginsburg, born in 1933, fought gender discrimination in school and the workplace as a student, a professional, and a lawyer advocating for equal rights for women. Appointed to the Supreme Court in 1993, Justice Ginsburg continued to serve the citizens of the United States until her death in 2020.

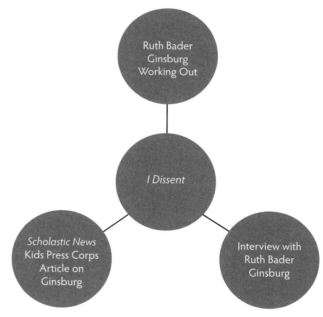

FIGURE 8.10 *The texts in this Sunburst model explore Ruth Bader Ginsburg's career advocating for the removal of legal barriers that prevented women from participating fully in American schools and places of employment.*

- Watch author Debbie Levy interview Ruth Bader Ginsburg at the at the Young Reader's Center of the Library of Congress: **www.youtube.com /watch?v=OrxCs4gRJNI**

- Students can watch this *ABC News* video clip of Ruth Bader Ginsburg working out with comedian Stephen Colbert in 2018: **www.youtube.com /watch?v=aSRTx3jg4RA**

- Students can read this Scholastic News Kids Press Corps 2018 article on Ruth Bader Ginsburg: **kpcnotebook .scholastic.com/post/making-rbg**

Sunburst Model: Dolores Huerta, 1962–Present and César Chávez, 1962–1993, Labor Rights Activists

The picture book biography *Side by Side: The Story of Dolores Huerta and César Chávez / Lado e Lado: El Historia de Dolores Huerta y César Chávez* by Monica Brown (2009) in the eighth Sunburst model (see Figure 8.11) features César Chávez , born in 1927 in Arizona, and Dolores Huerta, born in New Mexico in 1930. The two activists cofounded the National Farm Workers

Association in 1962 to organize migrant workers in America's west, advocating for fair pay, safe working conditions, and access to health care and benefits. For decades, the pair continued to fight for the rights of the working poor. Although Chávez died in 1993, Dolores continues to work for social justice.

FIGURE 8.11 *The texts in this Sunburst model explore the joint efforts of Dolores Huerta and César Chávez to support Mexican and Mexican American laborers organize and unionize for safer working conditions and better pay in the mid-twentieth century.*

- Students can watch this short video, featuring Dolores Huerta talking about getting the Presidential Medal of Freedom in 2011: **www.youtube.com /watch?v=pDtKc4BDQFY**

- Students can watch this short video, featuring the work of the Dolores Huerta Foundation in communities today: **doloreshuerta.org/dhf-promo-video/**

- Students can watch Dolores Huerta's 2019 TED Talk: **www.ted.com/talks /dolores_huerta_how_to_overcome _apathy_and_find_your_power**

- Students can read more about César Chávez 's life on the webpage of the César Chávez Foundation: **chavezfoundation.org/about-cesar -chavez/#1517518227969-596aaa83-bbbe**

- Students can read about the current and historical work of the César Chávez Foundation: **chavezfoundation.org/history/**

- Students can explore the online resources of the César Chávez National Monument, including a virtual tour, on the National Park Service website: **www.nps.gov/cech/index.htm**

Sunburst Model: Gloria Steinem, Women's Rights Activist, 1960s–Present

The picture book biography *Gloria Takes a Stand: How Gloria Steinem Listened, Wrote, and Changed the World* by Jessica Rinker (2019) in the final Sunburst model (see Figure 8.12) features Gloria Steinem, a writer and an activist who has worked for women's rights and gender equality. As a leader of the women's liberation movement, Steinem, with Dorothy Pitman Hughes, cofounded *Ms.* magazine in 1971, the first magazine in the United States "owned and written by women" (n.p.) (Rinker 2019). Steinem continues to advocate for gender equality today.

- Students can watch this video of children discussing equal pay: **youtu.be /snUE2jm_nFA**

- Students can read this short 2018 *Time Magazine* article about equal pay standards in Iceland, and the gender gap that exists in Europe and the United States: **time.com/5087354/iceland-makes -equal-pay-the-law/**

- Have students explore the Girls Who Code website (**girlswhocode.com/**) and consider why there is a gender gap in the tech industry.

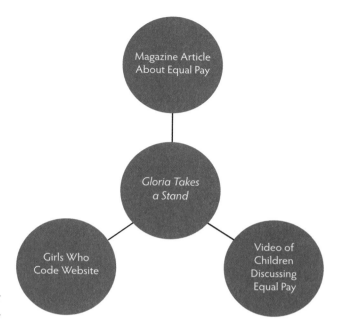

FIGURE 8.12 *The texts in this Sunburst model explore Gloria Steinem's advocacy on behalf of women's equality.*

To help your students document their thinking about each Sunburst text set and allow for conversations across the different text sets, we have created a graphic organizer (see Figure 8.13). Have students share their findings to identify what the various activists have in common (continuity) and the ways in which they and their circumstances differ from one another (change).

FIGURE 8.13 *Students can use this graphic organizer to explore activism within each Sunburst model. Size the boxes appropriately so that students have space to write.*

BOOK TITLE: _____	
Specific Challenges Faced	**What the Activist(s) Did in Response**
Long-Lasting Change Describe the long-lasting change that happened as a result of the activist(s)' actions.	

Extension: Exploring Malala Yousafzai, Contemporary Activist for Girls' Global Education

Solar System Model: Primary and Secondary Sources About Malala's Work

To transition from activists who worked for change before your students were born to contemporary activists, explore a Solar System text set (see Figures 8.14 and 8.15) on Malala Yousafzai, a global activist on behalf of education for children, particularly girls. Some texts are written about Malala, while others are written by Malala. Born in Swat Valley of Pakistan in 1997, Malala grew up in a household in which both her mother and father supported her education. But under Taliban rule, Malala and other girls were denied an education. In 2009, Malala began to blog anonymously about life under the Taliban. In 2011, she stopped writing anonymously, and in October of 2012, Malala was shot by members of the Taliban on

FIGURE 8.14

FIGURE 8.15

This text set allows students to learn about Malala's life and advocacy work from a range of different text types.

her way home from school. Since then, Malala and her family have lived as refugees in England. In 2014, Malala was awarded the Nobel Peace Prize. She continues to study in England and run the Malala Fund, to support girls' education globally.

As with the other text sets, you can have all students read all or some of the texts or focus on small groups reading one text and sharing out to the rest of the class using the jigsaw method. Keep a class anchor chart that compares and contrasts the challenges that Malala experiences and the decisions that she makes, similar to the big ideas of the graphic organizer in the previous section. Have students consider what Malala has accomplished already through her activism and what work she continues to focus on.

- Malala's Life Story on the Malala Fund Website: **www.malala.org /malalas-story**

- Interview with Malala Yousafzai about her 2019 book *We Are Displaced* on *ABC News*: **www.youtube.com/watch?v=2afKvjMc5lw**

- Malala's Nobel Peace Prize Speech, 2014 on video and transcript: **www.youtube.com/watch?v=MOqlotJrFVM**

Create New Texts: Student-Created Texts— Becoming Activists

Ask your student to review the different reasons that people became activists and the causes for which they took action. Are these causes ones that the students are interested in learning about in our contemporary world? What new causes are students interested in learning more about, and why? What connections can they make between the challenges of the past and the challenges of the present? For example, access to public education is a topic that runs through several of the Sunburst text sets. Students may want to identify a problem or concern in your educational community that they would like to change.

Make an anchor chart of problems that your students see in your community, nationally, and/or globally. Decide on your own, or with your students, whether they will work collectively on the same topic or pursue research in small groups, pairs, or individually. Topics may include a local concern, such as a polluted playground or a library branch closure. Nationally, many communities around the country are grappling with ground water contamination. Globally, the challenges of climate change and ocean plastics are becoming increasingly evident. These are all topics your students may be interested in researching to create change. Or they may be

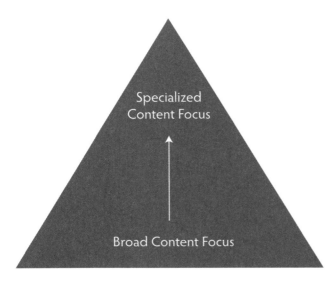

FIGURE 8.16 *Using the Mountain model, students researching a cause of their choice move from more general information to more specific.*

inspired to consider issues of equity they learned about while exploring the text sets in this unit or that they have experienced themselves or witnessed within their community.

Once you have established the problem or problems that your students want to research, work with your school or public librarian to identify manageable sources of information on the problem(s) that students will explore (see Figure 8.16).

Taking Notes

You should feel free to have your students take notes in whatever format works best for them. But if it is helpful, we have created a graphic organizer (see Figure 8.17) that your students could use to take notes.

You'll notice that this graphic organizer asks students to extract information and make sense of that information as part of the note-taking process. Some of your students might be able to read, listen, or view texts; discuss in small groups; and take notes independently. Some of your students may need additional supports or graphic organizers that focus on the

FIGURE 8.17 *Share this graphic organizer with your students so that they can take notes that focus specifically on activism and problem solving.*

INFORMATION SOURCE: _____
PROBLEM: _____

What are the causes of the problem?	What are possible solutions to the problem? What are some people already doing?	Why are the solutions hard to make happen?

main idea and details as a scaffold toward the kind of synthesis that this graphic organizer requires. Differentiate as needed to support students as they access and interpret new information through a range of texts.

Taking a Stand: Multigenre, Multimodal Texts

As your students learn more about the problem they are researching, you will want to turn the focus of your work toward possible solutions. Go back to the texts read in the various text sets for "mentor methods" of activism. Some people challenged the system with lawyers. Some wrote letters, blogs, and speeches. What is within reach of your students? What can they write or create to help solve the problem? Students might want to make infographics, like Brooke's students did, to inform their community of the problem and the possible solutions. Students might want to write and record a podcast that could be shared on the school website as a public service announcement. Students might want to host an event that informs parents and community members and allows people to take action. They could write and perform a play, like the fifth graders in Haley and Taylor's classes did, using the power of the written word like Malala to enact change. They could write to and speak to your local school committee about education funding or to the town or city government about concerns about playground safety or library access, like Charlotte's students did when they successfully petitioned their local library to stop charging fines for overdue library books in the summer. Encourage your students to create multimodal forms of activism whenever possible.

Conclusion

The text sets in this unit, which can be used as single text sets or in various combinations with one another, focus students on Civic Ideals and Practices through the concept of activism. By looking at activism over a period of hundreds of years, students can see yet another strand of social studies instruction: Time, Continuity, and Change. In organizing these text sets, we went from a broad introduction to activism and protest over the history of the United States to a more in-depth look at specific activists. Students then considered the life work of a contemporary student activist, Malala Yousafzai. By focusing on critical thinking, conceptual understanding of activism, and the methods of activism modeled by various historical and contemporary figures, we support students in their growing agency as readers, researchers, writers, and citizens, offering them the opportunity to work for change on issues of personal significance or as allies to others.

Comprehensive Text Sets

In Figure 8.18, you can find the complete list of texts discussed in this chapter.

FIGURE 8.18 *A comprehensive listing of texts from the unit.*

SCAFFOLD: INTRODUCING ACTIVISTS FROM HISTORY AND CONTEMPORARY LIFE
Enough! 20 Protesters Who Changed America written by Emily Easton (2018) and illustrated by Ziyue Chen

IMMERSION: EXPLORING THE STORIES OF INDIVIDUAL ACTIVISTS	
Sunburst Model: Hiawatha	*Hiawatha and the Peacemaker* by Robbie Robertson (2015), illustrated by David Shannon
	Timeline of Onondaga Nation, connection to American Revolution: **www.onondaganation.org/history/timeline/**
	Description of the "Hiawatha Belt," returned to the Onondaga Nation in 2012: **www.onondaganation.org/culture/wampum/hiawatha-belt/**
	Haudenosaunee Confederacy website: **www.haudenosauneeconfederacy.com/**
	Haudenosaunee Confederacy's creation story: **www.haudenosauneeconfederacy.com/confederacys-creation/**
Sunburst Model: Elizabeth Freeman	*Mumbet's Declaration of Independence* by Gretchen Woelfle, illustrated by Alix Delinois 2014
	Catharine Sedgwick's 1853 draft of Freeman's life, from the Massachusetts Historical Society: **www.masshist.org/database/viewer.php?old=1&ft=End+of+Slavery&from=%2Fendofslavery%2Findex.php%3Fid%3D54&item_id=587**
	1811 Portrait of Elizabeth Freeman from the Massachusetts Historical Society: **www.masshist.org/database/viewer.php?old=1&ft=End+of+Slavery&from=%2Fendofslavery%2Findex.php%3Fid%3D54&item_id=25**
	Bracelet made from a necklace owned by Elizabeth Freeman, also from the Massachusetts Historical Society: **www.masshist.org/database/548**
	Website devoted to Elizabeth Freeman and includes links to various sites related to her life as well as the court transcripts: **elizabethfreeman.mumbet.com/**
	Elizabeth Freeman exhibit at the National Museum of African American History and Culture: **nmaahc.tumblr.com/post/163991306641/petitioning-for-freedom-elizabeth-freeman**

Sunburst Model: Sarah Roberts	*The First Step: How One Girl Put Segregation on Trial* by Susan Goodman (2016), illustrated by E. B. Lewis On this webpage, created in partnership with the Massachusetts Historical Society, readers can see a photograph of Robert Morris and learn more about the case: **www.longroadtojustice.org/topics/education/sarah-roberts.php** A WBUR interview with Susan Goodman, author of *The First Step,* about writing the book: **www.wbur.org/radioboston/2017/02/24/the-first-step**
Sunburst Model: Sylvia Mendez	*Separate Is Never Equal: Sylvia Mendez & Her Family's Fight for Desegregation* by Duncan Tonatiuh (2014) Your students can listen to Sylvia and Sandra Mendez Duran talk about their memories of the trial on NPR *StoryCorps:* **storycorps.org/stories /sylvia-mendez-and-sandra-mendez-duran/**. News story on Sylvia Mendez getting the Presidential Medal of Freedom: **www.ocregister.com/2011/02/15/oc-civil-rights-icon-mendez-awarded -medal-of-freedom/** Sylvia Mendez talking about winning the Presidential Medal of Freedom in 2011: **www.youtube.com/watch?v=eMoAXggpj_0**
Sunburst Model: Anna May Wong	*Shining Star: The Anna Wong Story* by Paula Yoo (2009) Students can watch an eight-minute silent video of Anna Wong visiting China in 1936 from the UCLA Film Archive: **www.youtube.com/watch?v=9mDJDt2vD7w** Students can watch this *Variety* film clip from May 2019, in which actress Lucy Liu celebrates becoming the second Asian American to get a star on the Hollywood Walk of Fame, the first being Anna Wong: **variety.com/2019/film/news/lucy-liu-hollywood-walk-of-fame-second -asian-american-actress-1203202691/** Students can view this 1929 photograph of Anna May Wong from London's National Portrait Gallery: **www.npg.org.uk/collections/search/portrait /mw66914/Anna-May-Wong**. Students can view this 1930/31 photograph of Anna May Wong from the Art Institute of Chicago: **www.artic.edu/artworks/137078/anna-may-wong**
Sunburst Model: Ella Baker, Joseph McNeil, Franklin McCain, David Richmond, and Ezell Blair, Civil Rights Activists	*Sit-In: How Four Friends Stood Up by Sitting Down* by Andrea Davis Pinkney (2010), illustrated by Brian Pinkney Have students listen to this short NPR story "The Woolworth Sit-In That Launched a Movement": **www.npr.org/templates/story/story.php?storyId=18615556**. Students can see the lunch counter from the protest at the National Museum of American History: **americanhistory.si.edu/exhibitions/greensboro-lunch-counter** Students can explore the website of the International Civil Rights Center and Museum, now housed in the Woolworth Building in which the sit-ins took place: **www.sitinmovement.org/**

Sunburst Model: Ruth Bader Ginsburg	*I Dissent: Ruth Bader Ginsburg Makes Her Mark* by Debbie Levy (2016), illustrated by Elizabeth Baddeley
	Watch author Debbie Levy interview Ruth Bader Ginsburg at the at the Young Reader's Center of the Library of Congress: **www.youtube.com/watch?v=OrxCs4gRJNI**
	Students can watch this *ABC News* video clip of Ruth Bader Ginsburg working out with comedian Stephen Colbert in 2018: **www.youtube.com/watch?v=aSRTx3jg4RA**
	Students can read this Scholastic News Kids Press Corps 2018 article on Ruth Bader Ginsburg: **kpcnotebook.scholastic.com/post/making-rbg**.
Sunburst Model: Dolores Huerta and César Chávez	*Side by Side: The Story of Dolores Huerta and César Chávez / Lado e Lado: El Historia de Dolores Huerta y César Chávez* by Monica Brown (2009), illustrated by Joe Cepeda
	Students can watch this short video, featuring Dolores Huerta talking about getting the Presidential Medal of Freedom in 2011: **www.youtube.com/watch?v=pDtKc4BDQFY**
	Students can watch this short video, featuring the work of the Dolores Huerta Foundation in communities today: **doloreshuerta.org/dhf-promo-video/**
	Students can watch Dolores Huerta's 2019 TED Talk: **www.ted.com/talks /dolores_huerta_how_to_overcome_apathy_and_find_your_power**
	Students can read more about César Chávez 's life on the webpage of the César Chávez Foundation: **chavezfoundation.org /about-cesar-chavez/#1517518227969-596aaa83-bbbe**
	Students can read about the current and historical work of the César Chávez Foundation: **chavezfoundation.org/history/**
	Students can explore the online resources of the César Chávez National Monument, including a virtual tour, on the National Park Service website: **www.nps.gov/cech/index.htm**
Sunburst Model: Gloria Steinem	*Gloria Takes a Stand: How Gloria Steinem Listened, Wrote, and Changed the World* by Jessica Rinker (2019), illustrated by Daria Peoples-Riley
	Students can watch this video of children discussing equal pay: **youtu.be/snUE2jm_nFA**
	Students can read this short 2018 *Time Magazine* article about equal pay standards in Iceland, and the gender gap that exists in Europe and the United States: **time.com/5087354/iceland-makes-equal-pay-the-law/**
	Have students explore the Girls Who Code website and consider why there is a gender gap in the tech industry: **girlswhocode.com/**

EXTENSION: EXPLORING MALALA YOUSAFZAI, CONTEMPORARY ACTIVIST FOR GIRLS' GLOBAL EDUCATION

Solar System Model: Malala Yousafzai	*Malala Yousafzai: Warrior with Words* by Karen Leggett Abouraya, illustrated by Susan Roth (2014/2019)
	Malala's Magic Pencil by Malala Yousafzai, illustrated by Kerascoët (2017)
	Malala: Activist for Girls' Education by Raphaële Frier, illustrated by Aurélia Fronty (2017)
	Malala, a Brave Girl from Pakistan/Iqbal: A Brave Boy from Pakistan by Jeanette Winter (2014)
	Malala's life story on the Malala Fund Website: **www.malala.org/malalas-story**
	Malala's Nobel Peace Prize Speech, 2014 on video and transcript: **www.youtube.com/watch?v=MOqIotJrFVM**
	Interview with Malala Yousafzai about her 2019 book *We Are Displaced* on *ABC News:* **www.youtube.com/watch?v=2afKvjMc5lw**

CHAPTER 9

Science Invitations: Ocean Interdependencies
How Does the Health of the Ocean Relate to the Health of the Planet?

Introduction

Although it may seem like a cliché to say that the ocean is vast and full of wonders—it's true! And it's also true that the oceans may hold secrets to planetary health and human well-being. The text sets that follow are designed to support students in understanding the delicate balance of ocean ecosystems. These texts will also pique students' interest in the fascinating animals that make the ocean their home. There is a stance of activism embedded in these text sets, expressed through the lens of conservation and current efforts to preserve animals, plants, and habitats.

As we noted in Chapters 2 and 5, effective science instruction combines texts and experiential learning. In this chapter, we are focusing on texts that model the disciplinary literacies of science and that offer content knowledge of ocean habitats. You will want to complement these text set experiences with opportunities for students to observe ocean animals (at an aquarium or through videos), to talk with oceanographers and marine biologists (in-person or Skype interviews), and to conduct investigations that explore the health of water environments. The suggested text sets below were designed with the Next Generation Science Standards for Grades 3–5 in mind (see Figure 9.1).

FIGURE 9.1 *The Next Generation Science Standards for Matter and Energy in Organisms and Ecosystems.*

NEXT GENERATION SCIENCE STANDARDS GRADES 3–5: MATTER AND ENERGY IN ORGANISMS AND ECOSYSTEMS	
5-PS3-1.	Use models to describe that energy in animals' food (used for body repair, growth, and motion and to maintain body warmth) was once energy from the sun.
5-LS1-1.	Support an argument that plants get the materials they need for growth chiefly from air and water.
5-LS2-1.	Develop a model to describe the movement of matter among plants, animals, decomposers, and the environment.
LS2.A: Interdependent Relationships in Ecosystems	The food of almost any kind of animal can be traced back to plants. Organisms are related in food webs in which some animals eat plants for food and other animals eat the animals that eat plants. Some organisms, such as fungi and bacteria, break down dead organisms (both plants or plants parts and animals) and therefore operate as "decomposers." Decomposition eventually restores (recycles) some materials back to the soil. Organisms can survive only in environments in which their particular needs are met. A healthy ecosystem is one in which multiple species of different types are each able to meet their needs in a relatively stable web of life. Newly introduced species can damage the balance of an ecosystem. (5-LS2-1)
LS2.B: Cycles of Matter and Energy Transfer in Ecosystems	Matter cycles between the air and soil and among plants, animals, and microbes as these organisms live and die. Organisms obtain gases and water from the environment, and release waste matter (gas, liquid, or solid) back into the environment. (5-LS2-1)
3-LS2-1 Ecosystems: Interactions, Energy, and Dynamics	Construct an argument that some animals form groups that help members survive.
3-LS4-4 Biological Evolution: Unity and Diversity	Make a claim about the merit of a solution to a problem caused when the environment changes and the types of plants and animals that live there may change.
5-ESS3-1 Earth and Human Activity	Obtain and combine information about ways individual communities use science ideas to protect the Earth's resources and environment.

So here's our invitation: try out some, or all, of the text sets that follow. You can use them all, in combination with one another, or you can choose to use just one of the text sets to explore. It's up to you and how much time you have to devote to ocean ecosystems. We created a logical progression of experiences, from an overview of the interdependency of species in the ocean, to a more focused look at specific ocean animals currently facing environmental threats, to a look at the life stories of oceanographers and environmental activists who are committed to preserving ocean habitats. Finally, we invite students to go deeper, selecting an ocean animal to learn more about through research. We also know that you may see other ways to use these text sets in a different order. You might explore this exclusively in science, or you might seize this opportunity to combine some science and language arts learning. It's up to you.

Scaffold: Ocean Habitats

Duet Model: The Importance of Our Oceans— A Pairing of TED Talks

Introduce the importance of healthy oceans with a Duet model of two TED Talks (see Figure 9.2). In the first TED Talk, oceanographer Sylvia Earle eloquently describes the delicate interdependent relations among ocean animals and plants and humans. In the second TED Talk, oceanographer Asha de Vos suggests concrete action that could be taken to improve the health of ocean ecosystems and by extension, the health of our planet. Provide students with a two-column graphic organizer that includes places to make notes on why the health of the ocean matters and what we might do to keep our oceans healthy (see Figure 9.3).

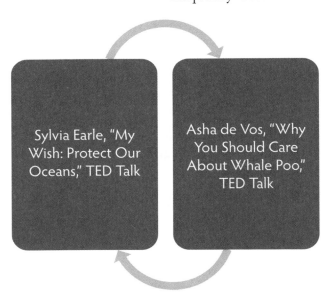

FIGURE 9.2 *In this Duet model, students compare and contrast two TED Talks about ocean habitats.*

- Sylvia Earle's TED Talk: **www.ted.com /talks/sylvia_earle_s_ted_prize_wish_to _protect_our_oceans#t-333114**

- Asha de Vos's TED Talk: **www.ted.com /talks/asha_de_vos_why_you_should _care_about_whale_poo#t-363080**

- **marinesanctuary.org/blog/whale-poop -and-climate-change/**

Immersion: Life in the Ocean

Following a framing of the challenges that are currently impacting ocean ecosystems, offer your students the opportunity to learn more about ocean habitats through a Duet model of two nonfiction picture books (see Figure 9.4). Begin with Steve Jenkins's *Down Down Down: A Journey to the*

FIGURE 9.3 *Students can use this graphic organizer to record their understandings from the two TED Talks in the Duet model about ocean habitats.*

"Health for the ocean means health for us."—Sylvia Earle (TED Talk)	
Why Does the Health of the Ocean Matter?	What We Might Do to Keep Our Oceans Healthy?

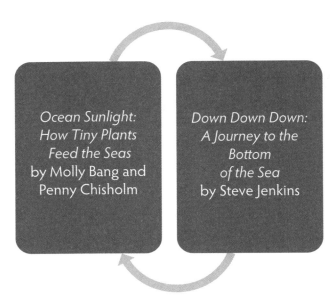

FIGURE 9.4 *The two nonfiction books in this Duet model explore ocean regions and cycles of interdependency within these habitats.*

Bottom of the Sea (Jenkins 2009) to provide an overview of the ocean zones from the surface to the depths of the Mariana Trench. Follow this orientation to the ocean depths with Molly Bang and Penny Chisholm's (2012) *Ocean Sunlight: How Tiny Plants Feed the Seas*. This text includes a fictional narrator (the sun) and offers a concise and clear explanation of the role of photosynthesis in sustaining food chains and ecosystems in the ocean environment. Bang and Chisholm make a visceral connection between ocean plants and human health: "Take a deep breath. HALF the oxygen you breathe every day comes from green plants on land. The OTHER HALF is bubbling out of all the tiny phytoplankton floating in your seas" (n.p.). Ideally, you will obtain multiple copies of this title so that you can follow a teacher read-aloud with small-group exploration of the title.

As you read *Ocean Sunlight: How Tiny Plants Feed the Seas* (Bang and Chisolm 2012), pause to allow students to turn and talk to a classmate, providing an opportunity for students to explore the ideas that they are taking away from the text. Encourage students to make connections with the texts they have experienced in the unit thus far, the two TED Talks, and *Down Down Down: A Journey to the Bottom of the Sea* (Jenkins 2009). At the conclusion of the reading, create an anchor chart and ask students to share the science ideas that they are taking away, posing the question: "How do tiny plants feed the seas?" Bang and Chisholm's text includes three double-page spreads of back matter, which elaborate the processes and relationships described in the main text. Divide students up into smaller groups and ask them to read this back matter together. Provide each group with a large piece of chart paper and ask them to:

1. Create a visual representation of the ocean zones as they are described in *Down Down Down: A Journey to the Bottom of the Sea* (Jenkins 2009);

2. Create a visual representation of the interdependency cycle that is described in *Ocean Sunlight: How Tiny Plants Feed the Seas* (Bang and Chisolm 2012);

3. Record any questions that arise while they are working on sticky notes, and attach these sticky notes to the visual representations.

As students complete their visual representations, post them around the room and invite students to tour this gallery of images. Students should travel with their working group and discuss what they see represented in the work of other groups. You could conclude this activity by having each group report out on the work of another group, noting strengths in the representation and any questions they may have about what they have viewed.

Solar System Model: Endangered Ocean Animals

The next text set, a Solar System model of texts about endangered ocean animals (see Figure 9.5) affords an opportunity to appreciate how animals are uniquely adapted to an ocean environment and to understand the consequences of a disruption to that environment.

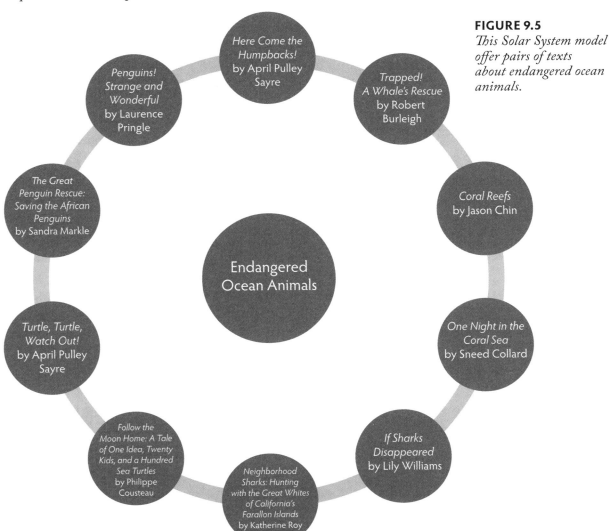

FIGURE 9.5
This Solar System model offer pairs of texts about endangered ocean animals.

Launch this text set exploration with a read-aloud of Lily Williams's (2017) *If Sharks Disappeared*. This illustrated nonfiction picture book presents sharks as apex predators, "the top of the food chain in their ecosystem, the ocean" (n.p.). Noting that more than a quarter and as much as a third of shark species are endangered, Williams poses a scenario in which the species disappears, setting off a chain reaction of imbalance and subsequent species die out known as trophic cascade. In back matter, Williams's further describes existing threats to shark species and provides a list of action steps to help save sharks. These include consumer actions (don't buy products containing shark, but do buy sustainably caught fish) and advocacy actions (tell your representatives you want increased protection for marine life).

FIGURE 9.6

Following the read-aloud, work together to complete an enlarged version of the graphic organizer Endangered Ocean Animals (see Figure 9.7). This organizer asks students to note the species' adaptations and role in the ocean ecosystem, threats to the species survival, and further questions they have about the species. After completing this graphic organizer as a group for *If Sharks Disappeared* (Williams 2017), divide students into small groups to read the additional titles in this Solar System model, completing the graphic organizer for their title. These titles focus on whales, coral reefs, penguins, and sharks and there are a pair of titles for each animal (see Figure 9.6).

When each group has completed the organizer, groups that have focused on the same animals should meet together. Provide each group with a large piece of chart paper. After sharing what they have learned about the species from each book, the group should then work collaboratively to create a visual representation of their learning, making sure to include the species' place in the food chain and threats to the species' survival. Reconvene as a whole group and ask the students to share the visuals that they have created. Look for common threats across the species and consider the relationships and interdependencies discussed in the books. Create an anchor chart to record your findings. If time allows, students could collaborate to create a large mural scene that includes all the species that represents the food chain and elements of interdependency.

Solar System Model: Ocean Explorers and Activists

The next text set, a Solar System model of texts, focuses on individuals who have devoted their life's work to the exploration of the ocean and to advocacy for the health of the ocean (see Figure 9.8). Each of these individuals had a strong childhood interest in the study of nature and each developed deep respect for ocean ecosystems. Sylvia Earle and Jacques

FIGURE 9.7 *Students can use this graphic organizer to record their learning about endangered ocean animals and their characteristics.*

Book Title and Author:	Featured Animal:
Animal Characteristics and Behavior (Adaptations):	**Relationships with Other Ocean Species (Role in the Ecosystem):**
Threats to the Species:	**Questions We Have About This Animal:**

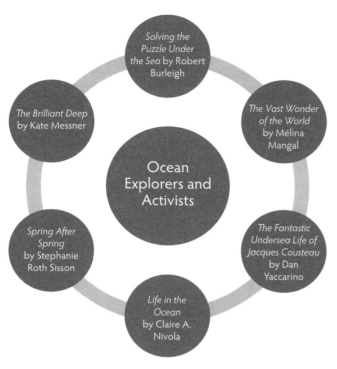

FIGURE 9.8 *This Solar System text set is comprised of picture book biographies of ocean explorers and activists.*

Cousteau explored the ocean depths and spoke out to raise awareness of the critical importance of healthy ocean environments. Ernest Everett Just, an African American biologist, was a pioneer in the study of microorganisms and cell biology. Rachel Carson, also a biologist, was an eloquent writer, who sounded alarm bells about the harmful effects of chemicals and the dangers of disrupting the balance of nature. Ken Nedimyer grew up exploring the oceans of Florida and founded an organization dedicated to the restoration of coral reefs. We have also included in this collection of life stories a fictionalized biography of Marie Tharp; her exploration of the ocean involved studies to map the ocean floor. Although activism is less visible in this text, students will learn about her unique contribution to our understanding of the ocean and her role as a scientific thinker.

Divide students into small groups to read these life stories. Students can complete graphic organizers to record their learning (see Figure 9.9), recording the subject's childhood interests and character traits, how they came to study the ocean, and their challenges and accomplishments. Remind students to consider the role of illustrations in these picture book biographies as they read and to be certain to read the back matter of the texts. If time allows, have students create character maps for these individuals (see Chapter 3 for a discussion of character mapping).

If you are able, extend this text set exploration by inviting an ocean scientist to speak with your students, either in person or through video conferencing technology. Prep for the interview by developing a list of questions for this scientist and invite your students to share what they have been learning about interdependence in ocean ecosystems.

Create New Texts

Extension: A Deeper Exploration—Becoming an Expert on an Ocean Animal

In Chapter 2, we described Candace Fleming (2016) and Eric Rohmann's award winning title, *Giant Squid* (see Figure 9.10), as a model for how the disciplinary literacies of science can be conveyed in picture book form. In

FIGURE 9.9 *Students can use this graphic organizer to record information about ocean explorers, including notes about their childhood, challenges, and accomplishments.*

Title:
Subject of the biography:
What childhood interests are described?
What character traits stand out in this book? How are they revealed in the text and in the illustrations?
How did the subject learn how to study the ocean?
What challenges did the subject face?
What accomplishments are featured in the book?
How did this individual further our knowledge of the ocean and serve as an activist for the health of the ocean?
What kinds of information did the author include in the back matter?

FIGURE 9.10

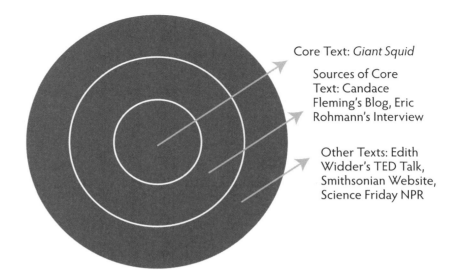

Core Text: *Giant Squid*

Sources of Core Text: Candace Fleming's Blog, Eric Rohmann's Interview

Other Texts: Edith Widder's TED Talk, Smithsonian Website, Science Friday NPR

FIGURE 9.11 *In this Tree Ring model, students learn more about* Giant Squid *and the choices and process of author Candace Fleming and illustrator Eric Rohmann.*

Chapter 6 we discussed the book as a nonfiction mentor text for student writing and illustrating. *Giant Squid* can also serve as a mentor text as students research and write about an ocean animal of their choosing. Launch this process by reading *Giant Squid* aloud. Be sure to discuss both the text and the illustrations—how they work in tandem to offer readers visual images of and information about this mysterious creature. Revisit Chapter 6 for a snapshot of a discussion of *Giant Squid* in a third-grade classroom.

The Tree Ring model for text sets is used when you want students to come to understand the processes that authors and illustrators have engaged in to create their work. In this model, the core text is the scaffold, texts used to research and create the text provide the immersion, and additional texts on the topic serve as extensions. A focus here is on author and illustrator processes; examining the sources and choices made by the author or illustrator supports students as they make their own compositional choices. After reading and discussing *Giant Squid*, you and your students can read Candace Fleming's blog description of how this book came to be and watch a video interview in which Eric Rohmann talks about creating the pictures (see Figure 9.11). Finally, investigate some of the source material that is included in the back matter of *Giant Squid*. Discuss what you have learned about the content choices made by Fleming and Rohmann (what to include and what to leave out) and the aesthetic choices (how to create imagery through words and illustration).

Sources of/About Core Text:

- Candace Fleming's blog: *New Book: Giant Squid*
  www.candacefleming.com/blog/2015/04/28/new-book-giant-squid/

- LadyBird & Friends: Betsy Bird interviews Eric Rohmann
  www.youtube.com/watch?v=bYBtr4L8CnA

Other texts on giant squids:

- Edith Widder: TED Talk: How We Found the Giant Squid
  **www.ted.com/talks/edith_widder_how_we_found_the_giant
  _squid#t-438807**

- Smithsonian: Giant Squid
  ocean.si.edu/ocean-life/invertebrates/giant-squid

- Science Friday: The Giant Squid's Biggest Mystery
  www.sciencefriday.com/videos/giant-squid-vid/

Following this exploration of *Giant Squid* ask students to identify an ocean animal about which they would like to create a picture book. Provide students with a broad range of print and digital texts and encourage students to build on their understandings of the interdependence of ocean creatures and healthy ecosystems as they draft a nonfiction text. In Chapter 6, you can read about the steps taken by third-grade teacher Brooke to guide her students from note taking, to drafting, to creating illustrations, to publishing.

Conclusion

Whether your students experience a couple of these text set models or the unit as whole, your students will gain a sense of the balance that exists within a healthy ocean environment and an appreciation for the impact of disruptions caused by pollution, overfishing, and climate change. Additionally, these texts offer windows into the work of scientists who study the ocean, showcasing the ongoing research into the vast and varied wonders of our oceans and developing students' understandings of the disciplinary literacies of inquiry and evidence in science.

Comprehensive Text Sets

In Figure 9.12, you can find the complete list of texts discussed in this chapter.

FIGURE 9.12 *A complete listing of the texts suggested for this series of invitations focusing on science and ocean ecosystems*

SCAFFOLD TEXTS: OCEAN HABITATS	
Duet Model: The Importance of Our Oceans: A Pairing of TED Talks	Sylvia Earle TED Talk: My Wish: Protect Our Oceans www.ted.com/talks/sylvia_earle_s_ted_prize_wish_to_protect_our_oceans#t-333114
	Asha de Vos TED Talk: Why You Should Care About Whale Poo www.ted.com/talks/asha_de_vos_why_you_should_care_about_whale_poo#t-363080
	marinesanctuary.org/blog/whale-poop-and-climate-change/

IMMERSION TEXTS: LIFE IN THE OCEAN	
Duet Model: Ocean Ecosystems and Relationships	*Ocean Sunlight: How Tiny Plants Feed the Seas.* Written by Molly Bang and Penny Chisholm and illustrated by Molly Bang (2012).
	Down Down Down: A Journey to the Bottom of the Sea. Written and illustrated by Steve Jenkins (2009).
Solar System Model: Endangered Ocean Animals	*Here Come the Humpbacks!* Written by April Pulley Sayre and illustrated by Jaime Hogan (2013).
	Trapped! A Whale's Rescue. Written by Robert Burleigh and illustrated by Wendell Minor (2015).
	Coral Reefs. Written and illustrated by Jason Chin (2011).
	The Great Penguin Rescue: Saving the African Penguins. Written by Sandra Markle (2018).
	If Sharks Disappeared. Written and illustrated by Lily Williams (2017).
	Neighborhood Sharks: Hunting with the Great Whites of California's Farallon Islands. Written and illustrated by Katherine Roy (2014).
	Turtle, Turtle, Watch Out! Written by April Pulley Sayre and illustrated by Annie Patterson (2010).
	Follow the Moon Home: A Tale of One Idea, Twenty Kids, and a Hundred Sea Turtles. Written by Philippe Cousteau and illustrated by Meilo So (2016).
	Penguins! Strange and Wonderful. Written by Laurence Pringle and illustrated by Meryl Henderson (2013).
	One Night in the Coral Sea. Written by Sneed Collard III and illustrated by Robin Brickman (2005).

Solar System Text Set: Picture Book Biographies of Ocean Explorers	*Life in the Ocean: The Story of Oceanographer Sylvia Earle.* Written and illustrated by Claire A. Nivola (2012).
	The Vast Wonder of the World: Biologist Ernest Everett Just. Written by Mélina Mangal and illustrated by Luisa Uribe (2018).
	The Fantastic Undersea Life of Jacques Cousteau. Written and illustrated by Dan Yaccarino (2009).
	Solving the Puzzle Under the Sea: Marie Tharp Maps the Ocean Floor. Written by Robert Burleigh and illustrated by Raul Colon (2016).
	Spring After Spring: How Rachel Carson Inspired the Environmental Movement. Written and illustrated by Stephanie Roth Sisson (2018).
	The Brilliant Deep: Rebuilding the World's Coral Reefs: The Story of Ken Nedimyer and the Coral Restoration Foundation. Written by Kate Messner and illustrated by Matthew Forsythe (2018).

EXTENSION TEXTS: A DEEPER EXPLORATION: BECOMING AN EXPERT ON AN OCEAN ANIMAL

Tree Ring Model: *Giant Squid*	*Giant Squid.* Written by Candace Fleming and illustrated by Eric Rohmann (2016).
	Candace Fleming's blog: *New Book: Giant Squid* **www.candacefleming.com/blog/2015/04/28/new-book-giant-squid/**
	LadyBird & Friends: Betsy Bird interviews Eric Rohmann **www.youtube.com/watch?v=bYBtr4L8CnA**
	Resources listed in the back matter of *Giant Squid*
	Edith Widder: TED Talk: How We Found the Giant Squid **www.ted.com/talks/edith_widder_how_we_found_the_giant _squid#t-438807**
	Smithsonian: Giant Squid **ocean.si.edu/ocean-life/invertebrates/giant-squid**
	Science Friday: "The Giant Squid's Biggest Mystery" **www.sciencefriday.com/videos/giant-squid-vid/**
Mountain Model: Research Texts	A variety of multimodal, multigenre texts to support students' individual or group research on ocean species

Mathematics Invitations: Geometry and Design
How Is an Architect an Artist?

Introduction

Have you ever marveled at the soaring profile of a skyscraper? Enjoyed a cozy window seat? Walked under an archway in a flower-filled public garden? Admired the towers that anchor a river-spanning bridge? As you observed these structures, did you think about math? The architects who designed these structures and the builders who built them used math in every step of the process. The text set exploration in this chapter invites you and your students to learn about geometry and design in architecture. Three concepts are explored:

1. Aesthetics—how architects design buildings and outdoor spaces that are pleasing visually;

2. Functionality—how architects design buildings and outdoor spaces for different purposes; and

3. Elements of design—line, color, shape, light, perspective, and materials.

Architects are artists who focus on creating spaces in which we live, play, and work. Using the elements of design, along with their knowledge of geometry and measurement, architects design spaces that inspire ideas, emotions, and contemplation.

We've outlined a series of text set experiences that encourage students to explore geometry concepts at work in architecture by focusing on architects, the structures they design, and the processes they follow. Students move from an examination of shape and pattern in buildings, to a look at the lives of architects and how their artistic sensibilities drive their work, to a more specific look at how structures go from design to reality using calculations of length, area, and volume. Finally, we offer a text set that features kid designers and, as an extension, engages students in designing a building or a structure that meets a community need. These text set experiences are meant to parallel your mathematics instruction in geometry. The texts that we have selected support disciplinary literacy in mathematics by demonstrating how the standards (see Figure 10.1) are applied in the design and construction of buildings and outdoor spaces. We invite you to try out this sequence as a whole or to choose the text sets that best serve your purposes. The text sets are meant to be used flexibly in combination with your math lessons on geometry and measurement as you work with the standards in Figure 10.1.

FIGURE 10.1 *The National Council of Teachers of Mathematics' Standards for Geometry.*

NATIONAL COUNCIL OF TEACHERS OF MATHEMATICS STANDARDS (2002): GEOMETRY	
In grades 3–5 each and every student should–	• Use visualization, spatial reasoning, and geometric modeling to solve problems; • build and draw geometric objects; • create and describe mental images of objects, patterns, and paths; • identify and build a three-dimensional object from two-dimensional representations of that object; • identify and draw a two-dimensional representation of a three-dimensional object; • use geometric models to solve problems in other areas of mathematics, such as number and measurement; • recognize geometric ideas and relationships and apply them to other disciplines and to problems that arise in the classroom or in everyday life.

Photographer and lecturer Philip Isaacson describes a kind of magic in architecture, noting that new forms continuously emerge: "Like the grand buildings of history or the simple buildings that are close to the hearts of their builders, the new forms will share in the magic that comes from harmony. They will be works of art because their ingredients—their materials, colors, and shapes—will unite with their settings to lift us above the ordinary"

(Isaacson 1988, 109). This view of buildings and structures as works of art and of architects as artists who use geometry to create something magical is infused throughout the texts that we have selected for this unit.

Scaffold: Introducing Architecture as Worldview

To open a unit of study on geometry, architecture, and design, arrange an opportunity for a walking tour of the center of your community. Equip students with iPads or digital cameras and invite them to take photographs of the buildings that interest them. Ask students to zoom out, capturing buildings in their entirety, and to zoom in, documenting aspects of buildings and structures that they find to be particularly interesting. When you return to the classroom, create an opportunity for students to share two favorite photos each, describing what appealed to them about this particular building and what they know and wonder about the function of the building. (Note: If it is not possible to visit your community center, you could carry out this same activity within and outside of your school building.) Next, invite your students to work in small groups to examine the photographs they have taken. Provide each group with a large piece of chart paper and ask them to make note of the shapes that they see in the buildings and any patterns they see in the design.

FIGURE 10.2 *In this Duet model, students examine unusual buildings and begin to think about how art and architecture are related.*

Duet Model: Shaping Our World

After an opportunity to observe shape and pattern at work in the design of buildings in your community, use a Duet model of two nonfiction picture books that explore the way architects view their world and express their worldviews through design (see Figure 10.2).

Begin with *The World Is Not a Rectangle: A Portrait of Architect Zaha Hadid*, written and illustrated by Jeanette Winter (2017). Growing up in Baghdad, Iraq, young Zaha observed the forms of the natural elements around her—the flow of rivers through the reeds and the shapes created by wind in the sand dunes. She was a child who loved to design and create, playing with color and shape and resisting corners and regularity. Winter describes Hadid's love for

FIGURE 10.3 *Create an anchor chart to record students' observations about buildings designed by Hadid.*

Buildings Designed by Hadid			
Building Name and Location	**Shapes We See**	**Patterns We See**	**Materials Used**

math, her studies in London, and the persistence she demonstrates when her unusual plans for buildings are initially rejected. The back matter of this inspiring book includes Winter's drawings of the buildings and structures Hadid designed during her career as an architect. Following this read-aloud, project images of buildings designed by Hadid and her colleagues accessible on the firm's website **www.zaha-hadid.com**. Create an anchor chart to record the name of the building, the shapes and patterns students observe, and what materials students think were used to build the building (see Figure 10.3).

Pair *The World Is Not a Rectangle* with a reading of Christy Hale's (2012) picture book poetry collection *Dreaming Up: A Celebration of Building*. Hale pairs concrete poems about child builders with photographs of adult-designed buildings that incorporate the techniques and shapes used by the child designers. This versatile picture book is appropriate for a wide audience. Although primary-grade readers will immediately identify with the children and their building techniques that form the basis for the concrete forms, intermediate-grade readers will have fond memories of past building projects (and hopefully current ones, as well) and will be fascinated by the buildings that Hale has chosen that reflect the child building projects. The back matter includes additional information about each real-life building and the architect who designed it. This title expands students' conceptions about architecture, introducing a range of new designers. You could either use this book as a read-aloud or use multiple copies for a small-group read. Create a second anchor chart, similar to the one described previously for the buildings that are featured in *The World Is Not a Rectangle*, reinforcing students' recognition of shape and pattern in architecture (see Figure 10.3).

Immersion: Architects—Their Stories, Their Processes, and Their Creations

Following this introduction to the habits of mind of architects and to the diverse range of design types, immerse your students in the study of architecture with the following series of text sets. These texts sets focus on the life stories of architects, the design and building processes of famous structures, and the creative processes of architecture.

Solar System Model: Picture Book Biographies of Architects

There are a range of picture book biographies about notable architects. The Solar System model in Figure 10.4 includes architects with diverse backgrounds and a range of artistic styles. Each describes the architects' childhood interests, their career path, and how their sense of aesthetics shaped the artistic style for which they are noted.

As students read these life stories, guide them to consider what they learn about architecture as an art form and the functionality of architecture. Divide students into small groups to read these biographies. To prepare to compare and contrast these life stories, students can complete a graphic organizer (see Figure 10.5). You will note that the organizer asks students to capture their thoughts on what the book reveals about the architect's style (for example, use of shape, color, line, light and shadow, perspectives, materials) and about the architect's work process (how they create plans, how they share plans, how they go from plans to reality).

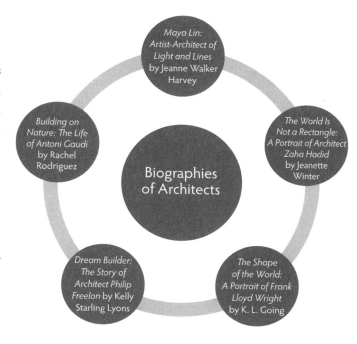

FIGURE 10.4 *This Solar System model consists of picture book biographies of architects.*

Each group should then share what they have learned about the subject of their biography. Next, create an anchor chart to consider similarities and differences in the lives and work of these architects/designers. As you compare and contrast, consider the following questions:

- In what ways did childhood experiences influence these subjects' decisions to become architects/designers?
- What challenges did these subjects face in pursuing their interest in architecture?
- How is architecture art?
- How do architects work?
- How do architects use geometry?

FIGURE 10.5 *Students can use this graphic organizer to record notes about the architect featured in the picture book biography they have read.*

Book Title:	Architect:
Childhood Interests:	Path to Becoming an Architect and Challenges Faced:
Stylistic Elements: What Makes the Architect's Work Distinct?	How the Architect Works:
Accomplishments:	Further Questions:

Duet Model: Artists Who Shape Landscapes

As an extension of this activity, you might also invite children to consider how artists who shape landscapes use geometry and measurement in their art. The Duet model of picture book biographies in Figure 10.6 describes the life and work of two artists who imagined and created unique outdoor spaces. These artists used geometry (shape, pattern, and measurement) as they created.

Following read-alouds of these two texts, create an anchor chart to record students' observations about the processes used by these artists. Consider these questions: How is an artist like an architect? How is an architect like an artist? How are architects and artists mathematicians? The Center for the Study of Art and Architecture offers a helpful online resource, Architeacher: Architecture and Aesthetics: Exploring Architecture as an Art Form (Architeacher, n.d.) (**www.architeacher.org/aesthetics/archi-main.html**) that can provide you and your students with additional context for how the elements of design are expressed in buildings and structures.

FIGURE 10.6 *This Duet model features artists who shaped landscapes.*

Solar System Model: Structures, Design Process, and Construction

To engage students with a closer look at the mathematics at work in design and building processes, arrange an opportunity for students to interview a local architect and a local builder (perhaps a pair who regularly work together). Prep for the interview by preparing a list of questions, making sure to include questions about how mathematics is applied in their work. Consider including question such as the following: How do you begin the work of designing a building? How do you move from plans to construction? What are some of the ways that you use math as you do your work? Following the visit, create an anchor chart listing of what students learned about how buildings go from design to habitable structures.

Each of the titles in the Solar System text set that follows (see Figure 10.7) features buildings and the processes of constructing these buildings. Additionally, each one is paired with a video presentation of the featured structure. You will note that these texts vary in complexity,

FIGURE 10.7

This Solar System model features the design and construction processes for different types of structures.

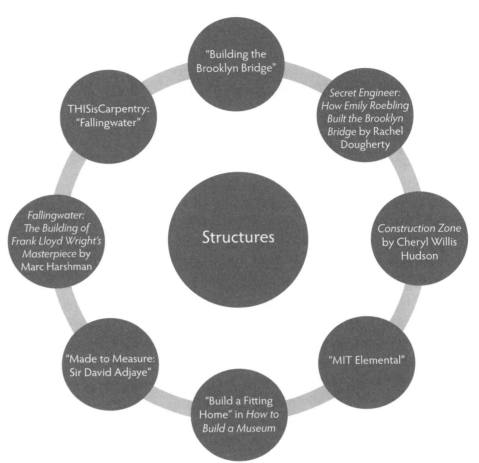

FIGURE 10.8

offering you an opportunity to match students with texts with which they can be most successful.

These texts provide an forum to unpack the mathematics at work in design and construction. A less complex text, Hudson and Sobol's (2017) photo essay *Construction Zone* (see Figure 10.8), prompts discussion of the unusual shapes and patterns in the design of MIT's Ray and Maria Stata Center and to note the calculation of materials required in a large construction project. For example, the poetic text reads: "Between the walls and under the floors, miles and miles of cable and cords, and wires, and pipes and vents are laid" (n.d.). *Fallingwater*, by Harshman and Smucker (2017), offers another opportunity to notice shape and pattern and includes images of plans that note placements and measurement. This text also highlights a conflict between the artist/architect's vision and the engineers' structural concerns. In *Secret Engineer: How Emily Roebling Built the Brooklyn Bridge*, author Rachel Dougherty (2019) describes the volume of the caissons that were plunged underwater to make air spaces for men digging holes for the bridge's towers. The illustrations for this fascinating text include sketches showing measurements and equations for calculating tension and strength.

This text set also includes a book chapter, chapter four of Bolden's (2016) *How to Build a Museum: Smithsonian's National Museum of African American History and Culture*, which describes the design and construction process of the Smithsonian's National Museum of African American History and Culture in Washington, DC. Appropriate for your more experienced readers, this chapter describes the origins of the building, the dreams and hopes that the building would express, as well as the constraints of budget and space. Photographs of the construction project are included as well as statistics related to the height, square footage, and amount of materials required. As your students are learning to calculate distance, area, and/or volume, the stories of these buildings help to demonstrate how these calculations are used in the process of creating the structures featured in these texts.

Video Pairings

- TeenKidsNews: "Building the Brooklyn Bridge"
  www.youtube.com/watch?v=HWw4tPUzk8c

- Elemental MIT: "Ray and Maria Stata Center"
  www.youtube.com/watch?v=nwK4dsUdgA8

- Made to Measure: "Sir David Adjaye, Creator of The National Museum of African History [National Museum of African American History and Culture]"
  www.youtube.com/watch?v=07PoOQw2U6Q

- THISisCarpentry: "Fallingwater"
  www.youtube.com/watch?v=EBH7vlPqX6M

Divide students into small groups to read these titles. Each group should be prepared to report out on what they have learned about mathematics in the design and building process. To prepare to share this information, groups can complete the following graphic organizer (see Figure 10.9).

FIGURE 10.9 *Students can use this graphic organizer to unpack the mathematics involved in the design and construction of the structure featured in the text they read.*

Book Title:
Building/Structure Featured:
What need/want did this building or structure address?
Who designed this building/structure?
How was math used in the design of this building (geometry: shape and measurement)?
How was math used in the construction of this building (geometry: shape and measurement)?
What did you learn about the design and construction process?
What new questions do you have?

Solar System Model: Fictional Books Featuring Kid Designers

The Solar System text set in Figure 10.10 features fictional titles about kid designers. In each of these titles, a child protagonist takes a building project from idea to reality. You may note in reviewing these titles that a broader representation of gender and diversity would be desirable. Hopefully by the time you are reading this, more titles featuring diverse kid builders will be available. Divide students up into small groups to read these titles. After reading, ask the students to work as a group to create a three-dimensional rendering of the constructions made by these kid builders. Have students collect recycled materials in advance and use them to build in class. As they construct, guide students to identify how they use mathematics (geometry and measurement) in the process.

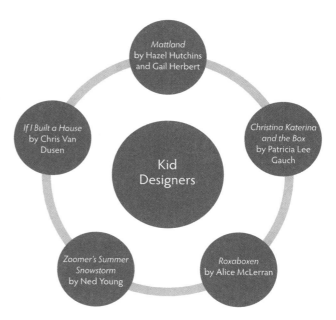

FIGURE 10.10 *This Solar System model consists of fictional picture books that feature kid designers and builders.*

Create New Texts

Extension: Designing for Your Community

As a culminating project, engage your students with an opportunity to create a design for a building or an outdoor space in your community. The extension activity works toward the following National Council of Teachers of Mathematics standards (see Figure 10.11).

FIGURE 10.11 *The National Council of Teachers of Mathematics Standards for Engineering Design.*

NATIONAL COUNCIL OF TEACHERS OF MATHEMATICS STANDARDS FOR ENGINEERING DESIGN	
3-5-ETS1-1 Engineering Design	Define a simple design problem reflecting a need or a want that includes specified criteria for success and constraints on materials, time, or cost.
3-5-ETS1-2 Engineering Design	Generate and compare multiple possible solutions to a problem based on how well each is likely to meet the criteria and constraints of the problem.

FIGURE 10.12 *Caption: A Duet Model of texts featuring community building projects.*

You could launch this project with a Duet model of picture books that include the full scope of the design process (see Figure 10.12). In *Green City*, Drummond (2016) describes how a community regrouped and rebuilt following the devastation of a tornado, keeping environmental concerns at the center of their design process. *Let's Build a Playground* (Rosen 2013) addresses a different community need—the design of a playground for children's recreation. This photo essay takes readers through the processes of dreaming, designing, and building.

After reading these titles, ask your students to consider building-related needs/wants within your community. Invite your town/city planner in to discuss the students' ideas. Decide whether you want to take an environmental angle and plan for green construction. If you do, see if you can arrange in-person or Skype visits from architects and construction firms that specialize in green building. After this prep work, have students work in groups to take their projects through the initial stages of design and planning. Depending on the age of your students and the extent to which you have worked on measurement, decide how much calculation students will do to create blueprints for their ideas and to estimate construction costs.

Conclusion

This sequence of text sets was designed to engage students in an investigation of how geometry is used in architecture. The disciplinary literacies of mathematics are developed as students practice visual literacy, calculation, and representation. As a whole, this text set–based unit goes beyond an examination of shape and pattern, and length, area, and volume, to offer a sense of architecture as an art form, describing architects as artists with dreams and visions of how to create beautiful and functional spaces in which people will live, work, and reflect.

Comprehensive Text Sets

In Figure 10.13, you can find the complete list of texts discussed in this chapter.

FIGURE 10.13 *A complete listing of the texts suggested for this series of invitations focusing on mathematics, architecture, art, and geometry.*

SCAFFOLD TEXTS: INTRODUCING ARCHITECTURE AS WORLDVIEW	
Duet Model: Shaping Our World	*The World Is Not a Rectangle: A Portrait of Architect Zaha Hadid.* Written and Illustrated by Jeanette Winter (2017).
	Dreaming Up: A Celebration of Building. Written and illustrated by Christy Hale (2012).

IMMERSION TEXTS: ARCHITECTS: THEIR STORIES, THEIR PROCESSES, AND THEIR CREATIONS	
Solar System: Biographies of Architects	*Building on Nature: The Life of Antoni Gaudi.* Written by Rachel Rodriguez and illustrated by Julie Paschkis (2008).
	Maya Lin: Architect of Light and Lines. Written by Jeanne Walker Harvey and illustrated by Dow Phumurik (2017).
	The World Is Not a Rectangle: A Portrait of Architect Zaha Hadid. Written and illustrated by Jeanette Winter (2017).
	The Shape of the World: A Portrait of Frank Lloyd Wright. Written by K. L. Going and illustrated by Lauren Stringer (2017).
	Dream Builder: The Story of Architect Philip Freelon by Kelly Starling Lyons and illustrated by Laura Freeman (2020).
Duet Model: Artists Who Shape Landscapes	*In Mary's Garden.* Written and illustrated by Tina and Carson Kügler (2015).
	The Secret Kingdom: Nek Chand, a Changing India, and a Hidden World of Art. Written by Barbara Rosenstock and illustrated by Claire A. Nivola (2018).
Solar System Model: Structures Text Set	*Secret Engineer: How Emily Roebling Built the Brooklyn Bridge.* Written and illustrated by Rachel Dougherty (2019).
	TeenKidsNews: Building the Brooklyn Bridge: **www.youtube.com/watch?v=HWw4tPUzk8c**
	Construction Zone. Written by Cheryl Willis Hudson with photographs by Richard Sobol (2017).
	MIT Elemental: Ray and Maria Stata Center: **www.youtube.com/watch?v=nwK4dsUdgA8**
	Chapter 4: "Build a Fitting Home" in *How to Build a Museum: Smithsonian's National Museum of African American History and Culture.* Written by Tanya Bolden (2016).
	Made to Measure: Sir David Adjaye, Creator of The National Museum of African History [National Museum of African American History and Culture]: **www.youtube.com/watch?v=07PoOQw2U6Q**
	Fallingwater: The Building of Frank Lloyd Wright's Masterpiece. Written by Marc Harshman and illustrated by LeUyen Pham (2017).
	THISisCarpentry: Fallingwater: **www.youtube.com/watch?v=EBH7vIPqX6M**

Solar System Model: Books Featuring Kid Designers	*Roxaboxen.* Written by Alice McLerran and illustrated by Barbara Cooney (1991).
	Zoomer's Summer Snowstorm. Written and illustrated by Ned Young (2011).
	Mattland. Written by Hazel Hutchins and Gail Herbert and illustrated by Dusan Petricic (2008).
	If I Built a House. Written and illustrated by Chris Van Dusen (2012).
	Christina Katerina and the Box. Written by Patricia Lee Gauch and illustrated by Doris Burns (1971/2012).

EXTENSION TEXTS: DESIGNING FOR YOUR COMMUNITY

Duet Model: From Design to Reality	*Green City: How One Community Survived a Tornado and Rebuilt for a Sustainable Future.* Written and illustrated by Allan Drummond (2016).
	Let's Build a Playground. Written by Michael J. Rosen with photographs by Ellen Kelson and Jennifer Cecil (2013).

ADDITIONAL TEXT RESOURCES

Books

- Bean, Jonathan. 2013. *Building Our House.* New York: Farrar, Straus and Giroux.
- Isaacson, Philip M. 1988. *Round Buildings, Square Buildings, & Buildings That Wiggle Like a Fish.* New York: Knopf.
- Laroche, Giles. 2011. *If You Lived Here: Houses of the World.* Boston: Houghton Mifflin.

Digital Texts

- Architeacher: Architecture and Aesthetics: Exploring Architecture as an Art Form www.architeacher.org/aesthetics/archi-main.html
- ArchDaily www.archdaily.com/search/projects

References

Abigail Adams Historical Society. n.d. Accessed July 25, 2019. **www.abigailadamsbirthplace.com/**.

Adichie, Chimamanda. 2009. "The Danger of a Single Story." TED video, 18:43. **www.ted.com/talks/chimamanda_adichie_the_danger_of_a_single_story**.

Alderson, Alula. 2018. "The Making of RBG." Scholastic Kids Press. Kid Reporters' Notebook. **kpcnotebook.scholastic.com/post/making-rbg**.

American Library Association. n.d. "Great Websites for Kids." Accessed July 25, 2019. **gws.ala.org/**.

American Library Association. n.d. "Youth Media Awards." Accessed July 25, 2019. **www.ala.org/awardsgrants/awards/browse/yma?showfilter=no**.

American Library Association. n.d. "Notable Children's Digital Media." Accessed July 25, 2019. **www.ala.org/alsc/awardsgrants/notalists/ncdm**.

American Museum of Natural History. n.d. "Dinosaurs Among Us." Accessed August 2, 2019. **www.amnh.org/exhibitions/dinosaurs-among-us**.

American Public Health Association. n.d. "Gun Violence." Accessed July 25, 2019. **www.apha.org/topics-and-issues/gun-violence**.

Amherst College. n.d. "Berneski Museum of Natural History." **www.amherst.edu/museums/naturalhistory**. Accessed August 2, 2019.

Animal Planet. n.d. "Wild Animals: Top 10 Adaptations Slideshow." Accessed August 2, 2019. **www.animalplanet.com/wild-animals/animal-adaptations/**.

Annotated Newspapers of Harbottle Dorr, Jr. n.d. *Boston-Gazette and Country Journal,* October 7, 1765. Accessed July 25, 2019. **www.masshist.org/dorr/volume/1/sequence/221**.

ArchDaily. n.d. "Search in Projects." Accessed August 2, 2019. **www.archdaily.com/search/projects**.

Architeacher. n.d. "Architecture and Aesthetics: Exploring Architecture as an Art Form." Accessed August 2, 2019. **www.architeawww.npr.org /templates/story/story.php?storyId=18615556cher.org/aesthetics /archi-main.html**

Audubon. n.d. "Guide to North American Birds." Accessed August 2, 2019. **www.audubon.org/bird-guide**.

Author's Voice. 2016. "LadyBird & Friends, S. 1 Ep. 3, Eric Rohmann." YouTube video, 30:45. **www.youtube.com/watch?v=bYBtr4L8CnA**.

Barber, Michaela. 2016. "Rockin Robin: The Life Cycle." YouTube video, 1:10. **www.youtube.com/watch?v=tfDSnT9nCdg**.

BrainPOP. n.d. "Charles Darwin." Accessed August 2, 2019. **www.brainpop.com/science/famousscientists/charlesdarwin/**.

———. n.d. "Natural Selection." Accessed August 2, 2019. **www.brainpop.com/science/cellularlifeandgenetics/naturalselection/**.

Buehl, Doug. 2017. *Developing Readers in the Academic Disciplines*. 2nd ed. Portland, ME: Stenhouse.

Calkins, Lucy. 2016. *Units of Study in Opinion, Information, and Narrative Writing*. Portsmouth, NH: Heinemann.

Cape Abilities. 2009. "Cape Abilities Farm at Plimoth Plantation." YouTube video, 2:15. **www.youtube.com/watch?v=ZbiVR8PFdp8**.

Cappiello, Mary Ann, and Erika Thulin Dawes. n.d. "Teaching with Trade Books." Accessed July 25, 2019. **www.teachingwithtradebooks.com**.

———. 2013. *Teaching with Text Sets*. Huntington Beach, CA: Shell Education.

———. 2015. *Teaching to Complexity: A Framework to Evaluate Literary and Content-Area Texts*. Huntington Beach, CA: Shell Education.

Cappiello, Mary Ann, and Melissa Stewart. 2018. "Understanding Categories of Nonfiction for Young People." *School Library Connection* 3 (5): 29–32.

Carter, Betty. 2003. "Reviewing Biography." *The Horn Book Magazine*, 79 (2): 165-174.

CBS This Morning. 2019. "Malala Yousafzai Amplifies Voices of Refugee Girls in 'We Are Displaced.'" January 7. YouTube video, 6:57. **www.youtube.com/watch?v=2afKvjMc5lw**.

Cervetti, Gina, and P. David Pearson. 2012. "Reading, Writing, and Thinking Like a Scientist." *Journal of Adolescent & Adult Literacy* 55 (7): 580–586.

César Chávez Foundation. n.d. "About César Chávez." Accessed July 25, 2019. **chavezfoundation.org/about-cesar-chavez/#1517518227969-596aaa83 -bbbe**.

———. n.d. "History." Accessed July 25, 2019. **chavezfoundation.org/history/**.

Children's Literature and Reading Special Interest Group of the International Literacy Association. n.d. "Notable Books for a Global Society." Accessed

July 25, 2019. **www.clrsig.org/notable-books-for-a-global-society-nbgs .html**.

Colonial Williamsburg. n.d. "A Day in the Life." July 25. Accessed July 25, 2019. **resourcelibrary.history.org/node/217**.

————. n.d. "In the General's Secret Service." Accessed July 25, 2019. **resourcelibrary.history.org/node/240**.

————. n.d. "No Master over Me." Accessed July 25, 2019. **resourcelibrary .history.org/node/222**.

————. n.d. "Women of the Revolution." Accessed July 25, 2019. **resourcelibrary.history.org/node/6**.

————. n.d. "Working Children." Accessed July 25, 2019. **resourcelibrary.history.org/node/83**.

Cook, Jason. 2015. "The 4 Best Chevy Marketing Campaigns." Auto Influence. **www.autoinfluence.com/four-best-chevy-marketing-campaigns/**.

Copley, John Singleton. 1763. *Mrs. James Warren (Mercy Otis).* Oil on canvas, 126.05 × 100.33 cm. Museum of Fine Arts, Boston. **collections.mfa.org/objects/32409**.

————. 1765. *Joseph Warren.* Oil on canvas, 127 × 100.96 cm. Museum of Fine Arts, Boston. **www.mfa.org/collections/object/joseph-warren-31064**.

————. 1768. *Paul Revere.* Oil on canvas, 89.22 × 72.39 cm. Museum of Fine Arts, Boston. **collections.mfa.org/objects/32401**.

Cornell Lab of Ornithology. n.d. "All About Birds." Accessed July 28, 2019. **cams.allaboutbirds.org/all-cams/**.

Cornell Lab of Ornithology. n.d. "My Media Bin: Beaks! by Sneed B. Collard III." Macaulay Library. Accessed July 28, 2019. **https://www .macaulaylibrary.org/the-internet-bird-collection-the-macaulay-library/**.

Daniels, Fred. 1929. *Anna May Wong.* Vintage Bromide Print on Red Card Mount, 13⅞ × 9½". National Portrait Gallery, United Kingdom. **www.npg .org.uk/collections/search/portrait/mw66914/Anna-May-Wong**.

Danyluk, Kaia. n.d. "Women's Service with the Revolutionary Army." Colonial Williamsburg. Accessed July 25, 2019. **www.history.org/history/teaching /enewsletter/volume7/nov08/women_revarmy.cfm**.

Delores Huerto Foundation. "DHF in Action: 15th Anniversary Video." **doloreshuerta.org/dhf-promo-video/**.

deVos, Asha. 2014. "Why You Should Care About Whale Poo." TED video, 5:46. October. **www.ted.com/talks/asha_de_vos_why_you_should_care _about_whale_poo#t-363080**.

DHF in Action: 15th Anniversary Video 2018. "Dolores Huerta Foundation." **doloreshuerta.org/dhf-promo-video/**.

Earle, Sylvia. 2009. "My Wish: Protect Our Oceans." TED video, 18:05. **www.ted.com/talks/sylvia_earle_s_ted_prize_wish_to_protect_our _oceans#t-333114**.

Ebbers, Margaretha. 2002. "Science Text Sets: Using Various Genres to Promote Literacy and Inquiry." *Language Arts* 80 (1): 40–50.

Ed Puzzle. n.d. "Author Interviews." Accessed July 25, 2019. **edpuzzle.com/.**

Ekster, Carol Gordon. 2016. "Meet Sandra Markle, Author of More Than 200 Nonfiction Books for Children." *Writer's Rumpus.* **writersrumpus. com/2016/07/08/meet-sandra-markle-author-of-more-than-200 -nonfiction-books-for-children/.**

Elemental MIT. 2016. "Ray and Maria Stata Center." YouTube video, 2:12. **www.youtube.com/watch?v=nwK4dsUdgA8.**

Elkind, Daniel. 2007. *The Power of Play: Learning What Comes Naturally.* New York: De Capo Press.

Falstaff Productions. 2014. "Tell Me Your Story—Interviewing Tips for Kids." YouTube video, 9:57. **www.youtube.com/watch?v=SWRYIAfojqk.**

Finansforbundet Norge. 2018. "Finansforbundet on Equal Pay: What Do These Kids Understand That Your Boss Doesn't?" YouTube video, 2:36. **youtu.be/snUE2jm_nFA.**

Fleming, Candace. 2015. "New Book: Giant Squid." April 28. Accessed August 2, 2019. **www.candacefleming.com/blog/2015/04/28/new-book -giant-squid/.**

Fort Ticonderoga. n.d. "One Destination, Endless Adventures." Accessed July 25, 2019. **www.fortticonderoga.org/.**

Freire, Paulo. 1970. *Pedagogy of the Oppressed.* New York: Herder and Herder.

General Henry Knox Museum. n.d. "Knox Museum." Accessed July 25, 2019. **knoxmuseum.org/.**

Girls Who Code. n.d. "Join the Girls Who Code Movement!" Accessed July 25, 2019. **girlswhocode.com/.**

Goodman, Susan. 2017. "Segregation on Trial in Children's Book 'The First Step.'" Interview by Alison Bruzek and Tonya Mosley. WBUR. **www.wbur.org/radioboston/2017/02/24/the-first-step.**

Gould, Elise, and Ann Schneider. 2018. "Poverty Persists 50 Years After the Poor People's Campaign." The Economic Poverty Institute. **www.epi.org/publication/poverty-persists-50-years-after-the-poor -peoples-campaign-black-poverty-rates-are-more-than-twice-as-high -as-white-poverty-rates/.**

Groskin, Luke. 2017. "The Giant Squid's Biggest Mystery." *Science Friday.* **www.sciencefriday.com/videos/giant-squid-vid/.**

Haudenosaunee Confederacy. n.d. "Confederacy's Creation." Accessed July 25, 2019. **www.haudenosauneeconfederacy.com/confederacys-creation/.**

———. n.d. "Welcome to the HCC." Accessed July 25, 2019. **www.haudenosauneeconfederacy.com/.**

HHMI BioInteractive. 2014a. "Galápagos Finch Evolution—HHMI BioInteractive Video." YouTube video, 16:08. **youtu.be/mcM23M-CCog.**

———. 2014b. "Natural Selection and the Rock Pocket Mouse—HMI BioInteractive Video." YouTube video, 10:32. **www.youtube.com/watch?v=sjeSEngKGrg&feature=youtu.be**.

Houghton Mifflin Harcourt. 2020. "Scientists in the Field: Where Science Meets Adeventure. Houghton Mifflin Harcourt. **www.sciencemeetsadventure.com/series-overview/**

Huerta, Dolores. 2018. "How to Overcome Apathy and Find Your Power." TED Women 2018 video, 13:28. **www.ted.com/talks/dolores_huerta _how_to_overcome_apathy_and_find_your_power**.

Infomisa. 2012. "First Lady Michelle Obama Hosts Three Sisters Garden Planting & Harvest." YouTube video, 1:39. **www.youtube.com/watch?v=69wKN1JRilc**.

Interesting Nonfiction for Kids (INK). n.d. "The Nonfiction Minute." Accessed July 25, 2019. **www.nonfictionminute.org/**.

International Civil Rights Center and Museum. n.d. "Explore the History of the American Civil Rights Movement." Accessed July 25, 2019. **www.sitinmovement.org/**.

Ippolito, Jacy, Cami Condie, Jaclyn Blanchette, and Cleti Cervoni 2018. "Learning Science and Literacy Together: Professional Learning That Supports Disciplinary Literacy Instruction for Our Youngest Learners." *Science and Children* 56 (4): 91–95.

Isaacs, Kathleen. T. 2011. "The Facts of the Matter: Children's Nonfiction, from Then to Now." *Horn Book Magazine* 87 (2): 10–18.

John, Tara. 2018. "Iceland Makes Equal Pay the Law." *Time Magazine*. January 4, 2018. **time.com/5087354/iceland-makes-equal-pay-the-law/**.

Journey North. n.d. "Journey North for Kids." Arboretum. University of Wisconsin–Madison. Accessed August 2, 2019. **journeynorth.org/KidsJourneyNorth.html**.

Kenspeckle Letter Press. n.d. "The Kenspeckle Letter Press." Accessed July 25, 2019. **kenspeckleletterpress.com/**.

Kids Discover. n.d. "Infographics." Accessed July 25, 2019. **www.kidsdiscover.com/infographics/**.

Kirkus Reviews. 2016. "Interview with Melissa Sweet." YouTube video, 3:21. **www.youtube.com/watch?v=zEiJJIBC_ww**.

Leal, Fermin. 2011. "OC Civil Rights Icon Mendez Awarded Medal of Freedom." *The Orange County Register*. February 15, 2011. **www.ocregister.com/2011/02/15/oc-civil-rights-icon-mendez-awarded -medal-of-freedom/**.

Levstik, Linda. 1993. "'I Wanted to Be There': The Impact of Narrative on Children's Historical Thinking." In *The Story of Ourselves: Teaching History Through Children's Literature*, edited by Michael Tunnell and Richard Ammon, 65-78. Portsmouth, NH: Heinemann.

Levstik, Linda, and Keith Barton. 2015. *Doing History: Investigating with Children in Elementary and Middle Schools*. 5th ed. New York: Routledge.

Lewison, Mitzi, Amy Seely Flint and Katy Van Sluys. 2002. "Taking on Critical Literacy: The Journey of Newcomers and Novices." *Language Arts* 79 (5): 382–392.

Library of Congress. n.d. "Phillis Wheatley, First African American Published Book of Poetry." America's Story from America's Library. Accessed July 25, 2019. **www.americaslibrary.gov/jb/revolut/jb_revolut_poetslav_1.html**.

———. 2017. "Justice Ruth Bader Ginsburg Visits the Young Readers Center." YouTube video, 52:39. **www.youtube.com/watch?v=OrxCs4gRJNI**.

Liu, June. 2015. "Pittsburg Woman Creates Gender Pay Gap Awareness by Asking Men to Pay More." DOGO News. **www.dogonews.com/2015/5/2 /pittsburgh-woman-creates-gender-pay-gap-awareness-by-asking-men -to-pay-more**.

Long Road to Justice. n.d. "Sarah C. Roberts vs. The City of Boston." The African-American Experience in the Massachusetts Courts. Accessed July 25, 2019. **www.longroadtojustice.org/topics/education/sarah -roberts.php**.

Mackin Educational. 2017. "Jen Bryant: Melissa Sweet Collaboration." YouTube video, 3:35. **www.youtube.com/watch?v=PXlHKyXVESg**.

Malala Fund. 2014. "Malala Yousafzai Nobel Peace Prize Speech." YouTube video, 26:44. **www.youtube.com/watch?v=MOqlotJrFVM**.

———. 2018. "Malala's Story." **www.malala.org/malalas-story**.

Marvin, David. 2014. "Lima Bean Time Lapse." YouTube video, 1:58. **www.youtube.com/watch?v=iZMjBO6A7AE**.

Massachusetts Avian Records Committee. n.d. "Official State List." Accessed August 2, 2019. **maavianrecords.com/official-state-list/**.

Massachusetts Historical Society. n.d. "Bracelet Made of Gold Beads from Necklace of Elizabeth Freeman (Mumbet)." Accessed July 25, 2019. **www.masshist.org/database/548**.

———. n.d. "The Coming of the American Revolution: 1764 to 1776." **www.masshist.org/revolution/massacre.php**. Accessed July 25, 2019.

———. n.d. "Letter from Abigail Adams to John Adams, 31 March–5 April 1776." Accessed July 25, 2019. **www.masshist.org/digitaladams/archive/ doc?id=L17760331aa**.

———. n.d. "Mumbett (Manuscript Draft), by Catharine Maria Sedgwick, 1853." Accessed July 25, 2019. **www.masshist.org/database/viewer .php?old=1&ft=End+of+Slavery&from=%2Fendofslavery%2Findex .php%3Fid%3D54&item_id=587**.

———. n.d. "Perspectives on the Boston Massacre." Accessed July 25, 2019. **www.masshist.org/features/massacre**.

MassAudubon. n.d. "Common Bird Species in Massachusetts." Accessed August 2, 2019. **www.massaudubon.org/learn/nature-wildlife/birds**.

Michals, Deborah. 2017. "Sybil Luddington." National Women's History Museum. **www.womenshistory.org/education-resources/biographies /sybil-ludington**.

Moje, Elizabeth B. 2008. "Foregrounding the Disciplines in Secondary Literacy Teaching and Learning: A Call for Change." *Journal of Adolescent & Adult Literacy* 52 (2): 96–107.

Moreau, Jordan. 2019. "Lucy Liu Speaks Out for More Diversity at Hollywood Walk of Fame." *Variety.* May 1, 2019. **variety.com/2019/film/news /lucy-liu-hollywood-walk-of-fame-second-asian-american-actress -1203202691/**.

Mount Vernon Ladies Association. n.d. "American Spies of the Revolution." George Washington's Mt. Vernon. Accessed July 25, 2019. **www.mountvernon.org/george-washington/the-revolutionary-war /spying-and-espionage/american-spies-of-the-revolution/**.

———. n.d. "George Washington's Mt. Vernon." Accessed July 25, 2019. **www.mountvernon.org/**.

M2M—Made to Measure. 2018. "Sir David Adjaye, Creator of The National Museum of African History [National Museum of African American History and Culture]." YouTube video, 6:01. **www.youtube.com/watch?v=07PoOQw2U6Q**.

mumbet.com. n.d. "Elizabeth Freeman." Accessed July 25, 2019. **elizabethfreeman.mumbet.com/**.

Museum of the American Revolution. n.d. "Timeline." Accessed July 25, 2019. **www.amrevmuseum.org/timeline/**.

The National Academies of Sciences Engineering Medicine. n.d. "Infographic: Essential Practices for K–12 Science Classrooms." Accessed July 25, 2019. **www.nap.edu/visualizations/practices-for-k-12-classrooms/**.

National Aeronautics and Space Administration (NASA). 2019. "Global Climate Change Resource Center." **climate.nasa.gov/**.

National Archives. n.d. "The Constitution of the United States: A Transcription." Accessed July 25, 2019. **www.archives.gov/founding-docs/constitution-transcript**.

National Audubon Society. n.d. "Audubon Bird Cams." Accessed July 25, 2019. **www.audubon.org/birdcams**.

National Council for the Social Studies and Children's Book Council. n.d. "Notable Social Studies Trade Books for Young People." Accessed July 25, 2019. **www.socialstudies.org/publications/notables**.

National Council for the Social Studies. 2010. *National Curriculum Standards for Social Studies*. Silver Spring, MD: National Council for the Social Studies.

——— 2013/2017. *College, Career, and Civic Life (C3) Framework for Social Studies State Standards: Guidance for Enhancing the Rigor of K–12 Civics, Economics, Geography, and History*. Silver Spring, MD: National Council for the Social Studies.

National Council of Teachers of English. n.d. "Charlotte Huck Award."
     Accessed July 25, 2019. **www2.ncte.org/awards/ncte-childrens-book
     -awards/charlotte-huck-award/**.

————. n.d. "Orbis Pictus Award." Accessed July 25, 2019.
     www2.ncte.org/awards/orbis-pictus-award-nonfiction-for-children/.

National Council of Teachers of English–International Literacy Association.
     1996/2012. "NCTE/ILA Standards for the Language Arts (1996-2019)."
     www.ncte.org/standards/ncte-ira.

National Council of Teachers of Mathematics. 2000. "Principles and Standards
     for School Mathematics." Accessed July 25, 2019.
     **www.nctm.org/Standards-and-Positions/Principles-and-Standards
     /Principles,-Standards,-and-Expectations/**.

————. 2014. *"Principles to Actions: Ensuring Mathematical Success for All."*
     Accessed March 31, 2020.
     file:///Users/maryanncappiello/Downloads/14859.pdf.

National Geographic Kids. n.d. "Animals." Accessed July 25, 2019.
     kids.nationalgeographic.com/animals/.

————. n.d. "Puffin Facts." Accessed July 25, 2019. **www.natgeokids.com/uk
     /discover/animals/birds/puffin-facts/#!/register**.

National Geographic. 2017. "See Hummingbirds Fly, Shake, Drink in Amazing
     Slow Motion." YouTube video, 2:21.
     www.youtube.com/watch?v=RtUQ_pz5wlo&feature=youtu.bem.

National Governor's Association and Council of Chief State School Officers.
     2010. The Common Core Standards for English Language Arts/Literacy.
     www.corestandards.org/ELA-Literacy/.

National Governor's Association and Council of Chief State School Officers.
     2010. The Common Core Standards for Mathematics. www.corestandards.
     org/Math/.

National Marine Sanctuary Foundation. 2018. "Whale Poop and Climate
     Change: Here's What You Need to Know."
     marinesanctuary.org/blog/whale-poop-and-climate-change/.

National Museum of African American History and Culture. n.d. "Petitioning
     for Freedom: Elizabeth Freeman." American History through an African
     American Lens. Accessed July 25, 2019. **nmaahc.tumblr.com
     /post/163991306641/petitioning-for-freedom-elizabeth-freeman**.

National Museum of American History. n.d. "Greensboro Lunch Counter."
     Accessed July 25, 2019.
     americanhistory.si.edu/exhibitions/greensboro-lunch-counter.

National Park Service. n.d. "Adams National Historic Park." Accessed July 25,
     2019. **www.nps.gov/adam/index.htm**.

————. n.d. "Boston National Historic Park." Accessed July 25, 2019.
     www.nps.gov/bost/index.htm.

————. n.d. "César Chávez National Monument." Accessed July 25, 2019.
     www.nps.gov/cech/index.htm.

National Research Council. (2012). *A Framework for K–12 Science Education: Practices, Crosscutting Concepts, and Core Ideas.* Committee on a Conceptual Framework for New K-12 Science Education Standards. Board on Science Education, Division of Behavioral and Social Sciences and Education. Washington, DC: The National Academies Press. **www.nap.edu/read/13165/chapter/1**.

National Research Council. 2012. *A Framework for K–2 Science Education: Practices, Crosscutting Concepts, and Core Ideas.* Washington, DC: National Academies Press. **doi.org/10.17226/13165**.

National Science Teachers Association and Children's Book Council. n.d. "Outstanding Science Trade Books for Students K–12." Accessed July 25, 2019. **www.nsta.org/publications/ostb/**.

naturalistoutreach. 2013. "Bird Feeding Adaptations: How Beaks Are Adapted to What Birds Eat." YouTube video, 13:01. **www.youtube.com/watch?v=lFZ8NMBDCJw**.

Nature Conservancy. n.d. "Animals We Protect." Accessed August 2, 2019. **www.nature.org/en-us/explore/animals-we-protect/**.

Nature Worldwide: Birds. n.d. "Birds of Massachusetts." World Institute for Conservation and Environment, Accessed August 2, 2019. **www.birdlist.org/checklists_of_the_birds_of_the_united_states/birds _of_massachusetts.htm**.

New Hampshire Department of Education. 2006. "New Hampshire Social Studies Curriculum Framework." **www.education.nh.gov/sites/g/files /ehbemt326/files/inline-documents/standards-socialstudies-framework .pdf?2**.

Next Generation Science Standards. 2013. "Appendix H: Understanding the Scientific Enterprise: The Nature of Science in the Next Generation Science Standards." **www.nextgenscience.org/sites/default/files/Appendix%20 H%20-%20The%20Nature%20of%20Science%20in%20the%20Next%20 Generation%20Science%20Standards%204.15.13.pdf**.

Norris, Michele. 2008. "The Woolworth Sit-In That Launched a Movement." National Public Radio. February 1, 2008. **www.npr.org/templates/story/story.php?storyId=18615556**.

Obama White House. 2012a. "Presidential Medal of Freedom Recipient: Dolores Huerta." YouTube video, 2:18. **www.youtube.com/watch?v=pDtKc4BDQFY**.

Obama White House. 2012b. "Presidential Medal of Freedom Recipient: Sylvia Mendez." YouTube video, 2:27. **www.youtube.com/watch?v=eMoAXggpj_0**.

Oliver, Mary. 2008. *Red Bird*. Boston: Beacon Press.

Onondaga Nation. n.d. "Hiawatha Belt." Accessed July 25, 2019. **www.onondaganation.org/culture/wampum/hiawatha-belt/**.

———. n.d. "Timeline." Accessed July 25, 2019. **www.onondaganation.org/history/timeline/**.

PBS. n.d. "The Facts About Dinosaurs & Feathers." Eons. Accessed August 2, 2019. **www.pbs.org/video/the-facts-about-dinosaurs-feathers-dterdr/.**

———. n.d. "Joseph Brant and Native Americans." Liberty! Chronicle of the Revolution. Accessed July 25, 2019. **www.pbs.org/ktca/liberty/popup_brant.html.**

Perry, Katy. 2010. "Firework." Genius.com. **genius.com/Katy-perry-firework-lyrics.**

Piktochart. n.d. Accessed July 25, 2019. **www.piktochart.com.**

Pocumtuck Valley Memorial Association. n.d. "Fossil Footprints: Breaking the Code." Accessed August 2, 2019. **dinotracksdiscovery.org/special/feature/.**

Poultry Hub Australia. 2013. "Chicken Embryo Development." YouTube video, 2:08. **www.youtube.com/watch?v=PedajVADLGw.**

Rainey, Emily, and Elizabeth Birr Moje. 2012. "Building Insider Knowledge: Teaching Students to Read, Write, and Think Within ELA and Across the Disciplines." *English Education* 45 (1): 71–90.

Reading Rockets. n.d. "Infographics." Pinterest. Accessed July 25, 2019. **www.pinterest.com/readingrockets/infographics/.**

———. n.d. "A Video Interview with Bryan Collier." WETA. Accessed July 27, 2019. **www.readingrockets.org/books/interviews/collier.**

———. n.d. "Video Interviews with Top Children's Authors and Illustrators." Accessed July 25, 2019. **www.readingrockets.org/books/interviews.**

Roberts, Kathryn L., Rebecca R. Norman, Nell Duke, Paul Morsink, Nicole Martin, and Jennifer A. Knight. 2013. "Diagrams, Timelines and Tables— Oh, My! Fostering Graphical Literacy." *The Reading Teacher* 67 (1): 12–23.

Sawyer, William. 2015. "The Six Nations Confederacy During the American Revolution." Fort Stanwix National Monument, National Park Service. **www.nps.gov/fost/learn/historyculture/the-six-nations-confederacy -during-the-american-revolution.htm.**

Schielack, Jane, Randall, Charles, Clements, Douglas, et al. 2006. *Curriculum Focal Points for Prekindergarten Through Grade 8 Mathematics: A Quest for Coherence.* Reston, VA: National Council of Teachers of Mathematics.

Scholastic. n.d. "Books and Authors." Accessed July 27, 2019. **www.scholastic.com/teachers/books-and-authors/#author-interviews.**

Scholastic Kids Press. n.d. "Kid Reporters' Notebook." *Scholastic News.* Accessed July 27, 2019, **kpcnotebook.scholastic.com.**

School Library Journal. n.d. "The Classroom Bookshelf." Accessed July 25, 2019. **www.theclassroombookshelf.com.**

Sedgwick, Susan Anne Livingston Ridley, 1811. *Elizabeth Freeman ("Mumbet").* 7.5 × 5.5 cm; in gilded wood frame (visible in large digital image): 13 cm × 9.7 cm. Massachusetts Historical Society. **www.masshist.org /database/viewer.php?old=1&ft=End+of+Slavery&from =%2Fendofslavery%2Findex.php%3Fid%3D54&item_id=25.**

72se. 2009. "Baby Robins—HD Video & Pictures—Eggs to Flight in 14 Days." YouTube video, 9:27. **www.youtube.com/watch?v=q64QV0rV6lo**.

Shakespeare, William. n.d. "Speech: 'All the World's a Stage.'" Poetry Foundation. Accessed July 25, 2019. **www.poetryfoundation.org/poems /56966/speech-all-the-worlds-a-stage**.

Shanahan, Cynthia, and Timothy Shanahan. 2014. "Does Disciplinary Literacy Have a Place in Elementary School?" *The Reading Teacher* 67 (8): 636–639.

Shanahan, Timothy, and Cynthia Shanahan. 2008. "Teaching Disciplinary Literacy to Adolescents: Rethinking Content-Area Literacy." *Harvard Educational Review* 78 (1): 40–59.

Sidman, Joyce. n.d. "Animals." **www.joycesidman.com/animals/**. Accessed July 25, 2019.

———. n.d. *Out & About: Cool Stuff I Find Outside* (blog). Accessed July 25, 2019. **www.joycesidman.com/animals/out--about-cool-stuff-i/**.

Sims Bishop, Rudine. 1990. "Mirrors, Windows, and Sliding Glass Doors." *Perspectives: Choosing and Using Books for the Classroom* 1 (3): 9–12.

Smithsonian. n.d. "Giant Squid." Accessed August 2, 2019. **ocean.si.edu /ocean-life/invertebrates/giant-squid**.

———. n.d. "What Motivates Us to Conduct Field Research?" Accessed August 2, 2019. **cdnapisec.kaltura.com/index.php/extwidget/preview /partner_id/347381/uiconf_id/27644131/entry_id/1_0997j3bz/embed /dynamic**.

Smolkin, Laura B., Erin M. McTigue, Carol A. Donovan, and Julianne M. Coleman. 2009. "Explanation in Science Trade Books Recommended for Use with Elementary Students." *Science Education* 93 (4): 587–610.

Spires, Hiller A., Shea N. Kerkhoff, and Abbey C. K. Graham. 2016. "Disciplinary Literacy and Inquiry: Teaching for Deeper Content Learning." *Journal of Adolescent & Adult Literacy* 60 (2): 151–161.

Stewart, Melissa. 2019. "What Is Voice?" *Celebrate Science*. **celebratescience.blogspot.com/2019/03/what-is-voice.html**.

Stewart, Melissa, and Nancy Chesley. 2014. *Perfect Pairs: Using Fiction and Nonfiction Picture Books to Teach Life Science* (3–5). Portland, ME: Stenhouse.

Story Corps. 2010. "Sylvia Mendez and Sandra Mendez Duran." March 26, 2010. **storycorps.org/stories/sylvia-mendez-and-sandra-mendez-duran/**.

TeenKidsNews. 2017. "Building the Brooklyn Bridge." YouTube video, 6:06. **www.youtube.com/watch?v=HWw4tPUzk8c**.

THISisCarpentry. 2013. "FallingWater." YouTube video. 5:45. **www.youtube.com/watch?v=EBH7vlPqX6M**.

Twin Cities PBS. 2016. "Winter Bees: Beyond the Book." March 26, 2016. **www.tpt.org/winter-bees-beyond-the-book/**.

UCLA Film and TV Archive. 2017. "Anna May Wong Visits Shanghai, China." YouTube video, 8:22. **www.youtube.com/watch?v=9mDJDt2vD7w**.

Unidentified artist. n.d. *Phillis Wheatley*. 1773. Engraving on paper, 12.8 × 10 cm. National Portrait Gallery, Smithsonian Institution. **npg.si.edu/object/npg_S_NPG.88.51?destination=node/63231%3Fedan_q%3Dwheatley.**

University of Michigan. n.d. "Online Exhibits. Balloons over Boadway." **gallery.lib.umn.edu/exhibits/show/balloons-over-broadway/book.** Accessed August 2, 2019.

University of Minnesota. n.d. "Balloons over Broadway, Melissa Sweet, and the Engineering of a Picture Book." The Children's Literature Digital Collection. Accessed July 27, 2019. **gallery.lib.umn.edu/exhibits/show/balloons-over-broadway/book.**

U.N. Refugee Agency. 2018. "UNHCR Figures at a Glance." **www.unhcr.org/en-us/figures-at-a-glance.html.**

Utah Education Network. n.d. "TRB 5.5–Acitvity 6: Bird Buffet." Utah State Board of Education and Higher Ed Utah. Accessed July 31, 2019. **www.uen.org/lessonplan/view/2715.**

Washington Crossing Historic Park. n.d. "History." Accessed July 25, 2019. **www.washingtoncrossingpark.org/history/.**

Washington Nature Mapping Program. n.d. "Bird Facts for Kids." Accessed August 2, 2019. **naturemappingfoundation.org/natmap/facts/birds-k6.html.**

Washington Post. 2018. "How to Work Out Like 'Notorious RBG.'" YouTube video, 1:32. **www.youtube.com/watch?v=aSRTx3jg4RA.**

We Need Diverse Books. n.d. "Imagine a World in Which All Children Can See Themselves in the Pages of a Book." Accessed June 25, 2019. **diversebooks.org/.**

What Kids Can Do, Inc. n.d. "How to Conduct a Strong Interview." Accessed July 27, 2019. **www.whatkidscando.org/featurestories/2007/maine_students/tip_sheets/INTERVIEWING%20TIP%20SHEET.pdf**

Widder, Edith. 2013. "How We Found the Giant Squid." TED video, 8:31. **www.ted.com/talks/edith_widder_how_we_found_the_giant_squid#t-438807.**

Wilding, Dorothy. 1930/1931. *Anna May Wong*. Gelatin silver printing out paper print, 44 × 30.5 cm (image); 65.8 × 48.3 cm (mount). Art Institute of Chicago. **www.artic.edu/artworks/137078/anna-may-wong.**

Wingmasters. n.d. "About Wingmasters." Accessed August 2, 2019. **www.wingmasters.net/aboutus.htm.**

Wisconsin Department of Public Education. n.d. "Disciplinary Literacy in Mathematics." Accessed July 25, 2019. **dpi.wi.gov/math/disciplinary-literacy.**

WNET Thirteen. n.d. "For Crown or Colony?" Accessed July 25, 2019. **www.mission-us.org/.**

Worth, Karen, Jeff Winokur, Sally Crissman, Martha Heller-Winokur, and Martha Davis. 2009. *The Essentials of Science and Literacy: A Guide for Teachers*. Newton, MA: Education Development Center and Portsmouth, NH: Heinemann.

Wright, Tanya, and Amelia Wenk Gotwals. 2017. "Supporting Disciplinary Talk from the Start of School: Teaching Students to Think and Talk Like Scientists." *Reading Teacher* 71 (2): 189–197.

Zaha Hadid Architects. n.d. **www.zaha-hadid.com/**. Accessed August 2, 2019.

Zarnowski, Myra, and Susan Turkel. 2013. "How Nonfiction Reveals the Nature of Science." *Children's Literature in Education* 44 (4): 295–310.

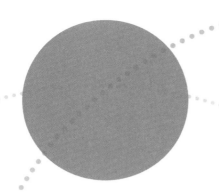

Children's Books

Abouraya, Karen Leggett. 2014/2019. *Malala Yousafzai: Warrior with Words.* Illustrated by Susan Roth. New York: Lee & Low.

Anderson, Laurie Halse. 2008. *Independent Dames: What You Never Knew About the Women and Girls of the American Revolution.* Illustrated by Matt Faulkner. New York: Simon and Schuster Books for Young Readers.

Anderson, Marcella Fisher, and Eilzabeth Weiss Vollstadt. 2004. *Young Patriots: Inspiring Stories of the American Revolution.* Honesdale, PA: Calkins Creek.

Angus, Laurie Ellen. 2018. *Paddle Perch Climb: Bird Feet Are Neat.* Nevada City, CA: Dawn Publications.

Arnold, Caroline. 2017. *Hatching Chicks in Room 6.* Watertown, MA: Charlesbridge.

Arnold, Caroline. 2012. *A Warmer World: From Polar Bears to Butterflies: How Climate Change Affects Wildlife.* Illustrated by Jamie Hogan. Watertown, MA: Charlesbridge.

Aston, Dianna. 2006. *An Egg Is Quiet.* Illustrated by Sylvia Long. Nature Books. San Francisco: Chronicle Books.

———. 2007. *A Seed Is Sleepy.* Illustrated by Sylvia Long. Nature Books. San Francisco: Chronicle Books.

Avi. 2009. *The Fighting Ground.* New York: HarperCollins.

———. 2012. *Sophia's War: A Tale of the Revolution.* New York: Beach Lane Books.

Bang, Molly. 2000. *Nobody Particular: One Woman's Fight to Save the Bays.* New York: Henry Holt.

Bang, Molly, and Penny Chisholm. 2009. *Living Sunlight: How Plants Bring the Earth to Light.* Illustrated by Molly Bang. New York: Blue Sky.

———. 2012. *Ocean Sunlight: How Tiny Plants Feed the Seas.* New York: Scholastic.

Barretta, Gene. 2012. *Timeless Thomas: How Thomas Edison Changed Our Lives.* New York: Henry Holt.

Barton, Chris. 2016. *Whoosh! Lonnie Johnson's Super-Soaking Stream of Inventions.* Illustrated by Don Tate. Watertown, MA: Charlesbridge.

Bean, Jonathan. 2013. *Building Our House.* New York: Farrar, Straus and Giroux.

Beatty, Andrea. 2007. *Iggy Peck: Architect.* Illustrated by David Roberts. New York: Abrams Books.

Becker, Helaine. 2018. *Counting on Katherine: How Katherine Johnson Saved Apollo 13.* Illustrated by Dow Phumiruk. New York: Christy Ottaviano Books.

Bergen, Michael. 2015. *The Untold Story of the Black Regiment Fighting in the Revolutionary War.* North Mankato, MN: Compass Point Books.

Berleth, Richard. 1990/2012. *Samuel's Choice.* Illustrated by James Watling. Chicago: Albert Whitman.

Bolden, Tonya. 2016, *How to Build a Museum: Smithsonian's National Museum of African American History and Culture.* New York: Viking.

Borden, Louise. 2000. *Sleds on Boston Common*: A Story from the American Revolution.* Illustrated by Robert Andrew Parker. New York: Margaret McElderry Books.

Brown, Don. 2013. *Henry and the Cannons: An Extraordinary True Story of the American Revolution.* New York: Roaring Brook.

Brown, Margaret Wise. 2016. *The Dead Bird.* Illustrated by Christian Robinson. New York: HarperCollins.

Brown, Monica. 2009. *Side by Side: The Story of Dolores Huerta and César Chávez / Lado e Lado: El Historia de Dolores Huerta y César Chávez.* Illustrated by Joe Cepeda. New York: Rayo, HarperCollins.

Bryant, Jen. 2008. *A River of Words: The Story of William Carlos Williams.* Illustrated by Melissa Sweet. Grand Rapids, MI: Eerdmans Books for Young Readers.

———. 2013. *A Splash of Red: The Life and Art of Horace Pippin.* Illustrated by Melissa Sweet. New York: Alfred Knopf.

———. 2014. *The Right Word: Roget and His Thesaurus.* Illustrated by Melissa Sweet. Grand Rapids, MI: Eerdmans Books for Young Readers.

Burgan, Michael. 2015. *The Untold Story of the Black Regiment Fighting in the Revolutionary War.* North Mankato, MN: Compass Point Books.

Burleigh, Robert. 2007. *Stealing Home: Jackie Robinson Against the Odds.* Illustrated by Mike Wimmer. New York: Simon and Schuster Books for Young Readers.

———. 2015. *Trapped! A Whale's Rescue*. Illustrated by Wendell Minor. Watertown, MA: Charlesbridge.

———. 2016. *Solving the Puzzle Under the Sea: Marie Tharp Maps the Ocean Floor*. Illustrated by Raul Colon. New York: Simon & Schuster.

Carlson, Drew. 2006. *Attack of the Turtle*. Grand Rapids, MI: Eerdmans Books for Young Readers.

Cate, Annette LeBlanc. 2013. *Look Up! Bird-Watching in Your Backyard*. Somerville, MA: Candlewick.

Chin, Jason. 2011. *Coral Reefs*. New York: Roaring Brook.

———. 2012. *Island: A Story of the Galápagos*. New York: Roaring Brook.

———. 2017. *Grand Canyon*. New York: Roaring Brook.

Cline-Ransome, Lessa. 2015. *My Story, My Dance: Robert Battle's Journey to Alvin Ailey*. Illustrated by James Ransome. New York: Paula Wiseman Books.

Collard, Sneed. 2002. *Beaks!* Illustrated by Robin Brickman. Watertown, MA: Charlesbridge.

———. 2005. *One Night in the Coral Sea*. Illustrated by Robin Brickman. Watertown, MA: Charlesbridge.

Collier, Christopher, and James Lincoln Collier. 1987. *War Comes to Willy Freeman*. New York: Yearling.

———. 2005. *My Brother Sam Is Dead*. New York: Scholastic.

Cousteau, Philippe. 2016. *Follow the Moon Home: A Tale of One Idea, Twenty Kids, and a Hundred Sea Turtles*. Illustrated by Meilo So. New York: Chronicle.

Davies, Nicola. 1997. *Big Blue Whale*. Illustrated by Nick Maland. Cambridge, MA: Candlewick.

———. 2012. *What Happens Next? Flip the Flap & Find Out*. Illustrated by Mark Boutavant. Somerville, MA: Candlewick.

DePalma, Mary Newell. 2005. *A Grand Old Tree*. New York: Arthur Levine Books.

Dougherty, Rachel. 2019. *Secret Engineer: How Emily Roebling Built the Brooklyn Bridge*. New York: Roaring Brook.

Drummond, Allan. 2011. *Energy Island: How One Community Harnessed the Wind and Changed Their World*. New York: Farrar, Straus and Giroux / Frances Foster Books.

———. 2016. *Green City: How One Community Survived a Tornado and Rebuilt for a Sustainable Future*. New York: Farrar, Straus and Giroux / Frances Foster Books.

Dunbar-Ortiz, Roxanne, Jean Mendoza, and Debbie Reese. 2019. *An Indigenous Peoples' History of the United States Young People's Edition*. Boston: Beacon Press.

Easton, Emily. 2018. *Enough! 20 Protesters Who Changed America*. Illustrated by Ziyue Chen. New York: Random House.

Elliott, David. 2009. *Finn Throws a Fit!* Illustrated by Timothy Basil Ewing. Somerville, MA: Candlewick.

Figley, Marty Rhodes. 2008. *Prisoner for Liberty*. Illustrated by Craig Orback. On My Own History. Minneapolis, MN: Millbrook.

Fleming, Candace. 2016. *Giant Squid*. Illustrated by Eric Rohmann. New York: Roaring Brook.

Freedman, Russell. 2000. *Give Me Liberty! The Story of the Declaration of Independence*. New York: Holiday House.

Frier, Raphaële. 2017. *Malala: Activist for Girls' Education*. Illustrated by Aurelia Fronty. Watertown, MA: Charlesbridge.

Gauch, Patricia Lee. 1971/2012. *Christina Katerina and the Box*. Illustrated by Doris Burns. Honesdale, PA: Boyd Mills.

Gianferrari, Maria. 2018. *Terrific Tongues*. Illustrated by Jia Liu. Honesdale, PA: Boyds Mill.

Giff, Patricia Reilly. 2010. *Storyteller*. New York: Wendy Lamb Books.

Going, K. L. 2017. *The Shape of the World: A Portrait of Frank Lloyd Wright*. Illustrated by Lauren Stringer. New York: Beach Lane Books.

Goodman, Susan. 2004. *On This Spot: An Expedition Back Through Time*. Illustrated by Lee Christiansen. New York: Greenwillow Books.

———. 2016. *The First Step: How One Girl Put Segregation on Trial*. Illustrated by E. B. Lewis. New York: Bloomsbury.

Griffin, Kitty. 2010. *The Ride: The Legend of Betsy Dowdy*. Illustrated by Marjorie Priceman. New York: Atheneum Books for Young Readers.

Guiberson, Brenda. 2016. *Feathered Dinosaurs*. Illustrated by William Low. New York: Henry Holt.

Hale, Christy. 2012. *Dreaming Up: A Celebration of Building*. New York: Lee & Low.

Harshman, Marc and Anna Egan Smucker. 2017. *Fallingwater: The Building of Frank Lloyd Wright's Masterpiece*. Illustrated by LeUyen Pham. New York: Roaring Brook.

Harvey, Jeanne Walker. 2017. *Maya Lin: Architect of Light and Lines*. Illustrated by Dow Phumurik. New York: Henry Holt.

Heppermann, Christine. 2012. *City Chickens*. Boston: Houghton Mifflin Harcourt.

Herrera, Juan Felipe. 2018. *Imagine*. Illustrated by Lauren Castillo. Somerville, MA: Candlewick.

Hudson, Cheryl Willis. 2017. *Construction Zone*. Illustrated by Richard Sobol. Somerville, MA: Candlewick.

Hutchins, Hazel, and Gail Herbert. 2008. *Mattland*. Illustrated by Dusan Petricic. Toronto, ON: Annick.

Isaacson, Philip M. 1988. *Round Buildings, Square Buildings, & Buildings That Wiggle Like a Fish*. New York: Knopf.

Jenkins, S. 1997. *What Do You Do When Something Wants to Eat You?* Boston: Houghton Mifflin Harcourt.

———. 2009. *Down Down Down: A Journey to the Bottom of the Sea*. Boston: Houghton Mifflin.

———. 2016. *Animals by the Numbers: A Book of Infographics*. Boston: Houghton Mifflin Harcourt.

Jenkins, S., and Robin Page. 2014. *Creature Features: Twenty-Five Animals Explain Why They Look the Way They Do*. Illustrated by Steve Jenkins. Boston: Houghton Mifflin Harcourt.

Judge, L. 2010. *Born to Be Giants: How Baby Dinosaurs Grew to Rule the World*. New York: Flash Point.

———. 2012. *Bird Talk: What Birds Are Saying and Why*. New York: Flash Point.

Kamkwamba, William, and Bryan Mealer. 2012. *The Boy Who Harnessed the Wind*. Illustrated by Elizabeth Zunon. New York: Dial.

Kerley, Barbara. 2012. *Those Rebels, John and Tom*. Illustrated by Edward Fotheringham. New York: Scholastic.

Kirby, Pamela F. 2009. *What Bluebirds Do*. Honesdale, PA: Boyds Mill.

Kirkpatrick, Katherine. 1999/2018. *Redcoats and Petticoats*. Illustrated by Ronald Himler. New York: Holiday House.

Krensky, Stephen. 2004. *Dangerous Crossing: The Revolutionary Voyage of John Quincy Adams*. Illustrated by Greg Harlin. New York: Dutton.

Kudlinski, Kathleen. 2005. *Boy, Were We Wrong About Dinosaurs!* Illustrated by S. D. Schindler. New York: Puffin Books.

Kügler, Tina, and Carson Kügler. 2015. *In Mary's Garden*. Boston: Houghton Mifflin.

Landau, Elaine. 2014. *The Boston Tea Party: Would You Join the Revolution?* Berkely Heights, NJ: Enslow Publishers.

Laroche, Giles. 2011. *If You Lived Here: Houses of the World*. Boston: Houghton Mifflin.

Lawler, Laurie. 2012. *Rachel Carson and Her Book That Changed the World*. Illustrated by Laurie Beingessner. New York: Holiday House.

Levy, Debbie. 2016. *I Dissent: Ruth Bader Ginsburg Makes Her Mark*. Illustrated by Elizabeth Baddeley. New York: Simon and Schuster Books for Young Readers.

Lunde, Darrin. 2007. *Hello, Bumblebee Bat*. Illustrated by Patricia Wynne. Watertown, MA: Charlesbridge.

———. 2012. *Monkey Colors*. Illustrated by Patricia Wynne. Watertown, MA: Charlesbridge.

———. 2015. *Dirty Rats?* Illustrated by Adam Gustavson. Watertown, MA: Charlesbridge.

Lyons, Kelly Starling. 2020. *Dream Builder: The Story of Architect Philip Freelon.* Illustrated by Laura Freeman. New York: Lee & Low.

Mangal, Mélina. 2018. *The Vast Wonder of the World: Biologist Ernest Everett Just.* Illustrated by Luisa Uribe. Minneapolis, MN: Millbrook.

Markel, Sandra. 2018. *The Great Penguin Rescue: Saving the African Penguins.* Minneapolis, MN: Millbrook.

Martineau, Susan. 2016. *Infographics for Kids: Putting Information in the Picture.* Illustrated by Vicky Barker. Watertown, MA: Charlesbridge.

McCarthy, Meghan. 2015. *Earmuffs for Everyone! How Chester Greenwood Became Known as the Inventor of the Earmuff.* New York: Simon and Schuster Books for Young Readers.

McDonnell, Patrick. 2011. *Me . . . Jane.* New York: Little, Brown Books for Young Readers.

McLerran, Alice. 1991. *Roxaboxen.* Illustrated by Barbara Cooney. New York: Lothrup, Lee and Shephard.

Messner, Kate. 2018. *The Brilliant Deep: Rebuilding the World's Coral Reefs: The Story of Ken Nedimyer and the Coral Restoration Foundation.* Illustrated by Matthew Forsythe. San Francisco: Chronicle Books.

Moss, Marissa. 2016. *America's Tea Parties: Not One, but Four! Boston, Charleston, New York, Philadelphia.* New York: Harry N. Abrams Books.

National Geographic Kids. 2017. *By the Numbers 3.14: 110.01 Cool Infographics Packed with Stats and Figures.* Washington, DC: National Geographic for Kids.

Newman, Patricia. 2014. *Plastic, Ahoy! Investigating the Great Pacific Garbage Patch.* Minneapolis, MN: Millbrook.

Nivola, Claire A. 2012. *Life in the Ocean: The Story of Oceanographer Sylvia Earle.* New York: Farrar, Straus and Giroux.

Noble, Trinka Hakings. 2004. *The Scarlet Stockings Spy: A Revolutionary War Tale.* Illustrated by Robert Papp. Tales of Young Americans. Ann Arbor, MI: Sleeping Bear.

Paul, Miranda. 2015. *Water Is Water.* Illustrated by Jason Chin. New York: Roaring Brook.

Peacock, Louise. 1998/2007. *Crossing the Delaware: A History in Many Voices.* Illustrated by Walter Lyon Krudop. New York: Atheneum Books for Young Readers.

Pinkney, Andrea Davis. 2010. *Sit-In: How Four Friends Stood Up by Sitting Down.* Illustrated by Brian Pinkney. New York: Little, Brown.

Pringle, Laurence. 2013. *Penguins! Strange and Wonderful.* Illustrated by Meryl Henderson. Honesdale, PA: Boyd Mills.

Rinker, Jessica. 2019. *Gloria Takes a Stand: How Gloria Steinem Listened, Wrote, and Changed the World.* Illustrated by Daria Peoples-Riley. New York: Bloomsbury.

Roberts, Cokie. 2014. *Founding Mothers: Remembering the Ladies.* Illustrated by Diane Goode. New York: HarperCollins.

Robertson, Robbie. 2015. *Hiawatha and the Peacemaker.* Illustrated by David Shannon. New York: Abrams Books for Young Readers.

Rockliff, Mara. 2015. *Gingerbread for Liberty! How a German Baker Helped Win the American Revolution.* Illustrated by Vincent X. Kirsch. Boston: Houghton Mifflin Harcourt.

Rockwell, Anne. 2002. *They Called Her Molly Pitcher.* Illustrated by Cynthia von Buhler. New York: Dragonfly Books.

Rodriguez, Rachel. 2008. *Building on Nature: The Life of Antoni Gaudi.* Illustrated by Julie Paschkis. New York: Henry Holt.

Rose, Caroline Starr. 2015. *Over in the Wetlands: A Hurricane-on-the-Bayou Story.* Illustrated by Rob Dunlavey. New York: Schwartz and Wade.

Rosen, Michael J. 2013. *Let's Build a Playground.* Photographs by Ellen Kelson and Jennifer Cecil. Somerville, MA: Candlewick.

Rosenstock, Barbara. 2018. *The Secret Kingdom: Nek Chand, a Changing India, and a Hidden World of Art.* Illustrated by Claire A. Nivola. Somerville, MA: Candlewick.

Roy, Katherine. 2014. *Neighborhood Sharks: Hunting with the Great Whites of California's Farallon Islands.* New York: Roaring Brook.

Sayre, April Pulley. 2008. *Trout Are Made of Trees.* Watertown, MA: Charlesbridge.

———. 2013a. *Here Come the Humpbacks!* Illustrated by Jaime Hogan. Watertown, MA: Charlesbridge.

———. 2013b. *Turtle, Turtle, Watch Out!* Illustrated by Annie Patterson. Watertown, MA: Charlesbridge.

———. 2015. *Raindrops Roll.* New York: Beach Lane Books.

Schanzer, Rosalyn. 2004. *George vs. George: The American Revolution as Seen from Both Sides.* Washington, DC: National Geographic.

Schnell, Laura Kahn. 2015. *High Tide for Horseshoe Crabs.* Illustrated by Alan Marks. Watertown, MA: Charlesbridge.

Scieszka, Jon. 2007. *Oh, Say, I Can't See: The Time Warp Trio.* Illustrated by Adam McCauley. New York: Puffin.

Sheinkin, Steve. 2005/2015. *King George: What Was His Problem? Everything Your Schoolbooks Didn't Tell You About the American Revolution.* New York: Square Fish.

Shetterly, Margot Lee. 2018. *Hidden Figure: The True Story of Four Black Women and the Space Race.* Illustrated by Laura Freeman. New York: HarperCollins.

Sidman, Joyce. 2005. *Song of the Water Boatman and Other Pond Poems.* Illustrated by Becky Prange. Boston: Houghton Mifflin.

———. 2010a. *Dark Emperor and Other Poems of the Night*. Illustrated by Rick Allen. Boston: Houghton Mifflin.

———. 2010b. *Ubiquitous: Celebrating Nature's Survivors*. Illustrated by Beckie Prange. Boston: Houghton Mifflin.

———. 2011. *Swirl by Swirl: Spirals in Nature*. Illustrated by Beth Krommes. Boston: Houghton Mifflin.

———. 2014. *Winter Bees and Other Poems of the Cold*. Illustrated by Rick Allen. Boston: Houghton Mifflin.

———. 2016. *Before Morning*. Illustrated by Beth Krommes. Boston: Houghton Mifflin.

———. 2017. *Round*. Illustrated by Taeeun Yoo. Boston: Houghton Mifflin.

Sisson, Stephanie Roth. 2018. *Spring After Spring: How Rachel Carson Inspired the Environmental Movement*. New York: Roaring Brook.

Snyder, Laurel. 2016. *Swan: The Life and Dance of Anna Pavlova*. Illustrated by Julie Morstad. San Francisco: Chronicle Books.

Staib, Walter and Jennifer Fox. 2010. *A Feast of Freedom: Tasty Tidbits from City Tavern*. Illustrated by Fernando Juarez. Philadelphia, PA: Running Press Kids.

Stewart, Melissa. 2009/2015. *A Place for Birds*. Illustrated by Higgins Bond. Atlanta: Peachtree.

———. 2014a. *Feathers: Not Just for Flying*. Illustrated by Sarah Brannen. Watertown, MA: Charlesbridge.

———. 2017. *Can an Aardvark Bark?* Illustrated by Steve Jenkins. New York: Beach Lane Books.

———. 2018. *A Seed Is the Start*. Washington, DC: National Geographic.

———. 2019. *Seashells: More Than a Home*. Illustrated by Sarah Brannen. Watertown, MA: Charlesbridge.

St. George, Judith. 2014. *The Journey of the One and Only Declaration of Independence*. Illustrated by Will Hillenbrand. New York: Puffin Books.

Sweet, Melissa. 2011. *Balloons over Broadway: The True Story of the Puppeteer of the Macy's Thanksgiving Day Parade*. Boston, MA: Houghton Mifflin.

———. 2016. *Some Writer! The Story of E. B. White*. Boston: Houghton Mifflin Harcourt.

Tate, Don. 2015. *Poet: The Remarkable Story of George Moses Horton*. Atlanta, GA: Peachtree.

Tavares, Matt. 2015. *Growing Up Pedro: How the Martinez Brothers Made It from the Dominican Republic All the Way to the Major Leagues*. Somerville, MA: Candlewick.

Tonatiuh, Duncan. 2014. *Separate Is Never Equal: Sylvia Mendez and Her Family's Fight for Desegregation*. New York: Abrams Books for Young Readers.

———. 2015. *Funny Bones: Posada and His Day of the Dead Calaveras.* New York: Abrams.

Turner, Ann Warren. 1992/1997. *Katie's Trunk.* Illustrated by Ronald Himler. New York: Simon and Schuster Books for Young Readers.

Van Dusen, Chris. 2012. *If I Built a House.* New York: Dial Books.

Williams, Lily. 2017. *If Sharks Disappeared.* New York: Roaring Brook.

Winter, Jeanette. 2014. *Malala: A Brave Girl from Pakistan/Iqbal: A Brave Boy from Pakistan.* New York: Beach Lane Books.

———. 2017. *The World Is Not a Rectangle: A Portrait of Architect Zaha Hadid.* New York: Beach Lane Books.

Winters, Kay. 2008/2015. *Colonial Voices: Hear Them Speak.* Illustrated by Larry Day. New York: Dutton Children's Books.

Woelfe, Gretchen. 2016. *Answering the Cry for Freedom: Stories of African Americans and the American Revolution.* Illustrated by R. Gregory Christie. Honesdale, PA: Calkins Creek.

———. 2012. *Write On, Mercy! The Secret Life of Mercy Otis Warren.* Illustrated by Alexandra Wallner. Honesdale, PA: Calkins Creek.

———. 2014. *Mumbet's Declaration of Independence.* Illustrated by Alix Delinos. Minneapolis, MN: Carolrhoda Books.

Woodruff, Elvira. 2012. *George Washington's Socks.* Time Travel Adventures. New York: Scholastic.

Yaccarino, Dan. 2009. *The Fantastic Undersea Life of Jacques Cousteau.* New York: Knopf.

Yoo, Paula. 2009. *Shining Star: The Anna May Wong Story.* Illustrated by Lin Wang. New York: Lee and Low.

Young, Ned. 2011. *Zoomer's Summer Snowstorm.* New York: Harper.

Yousafzai, Malala. 2017. *Malala's Magic Pencil.* Illustrated by Kerascoët. New York: Little, Brown.

Figure Credits

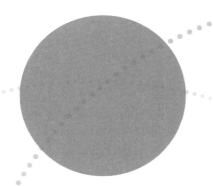

Index